Entrepreneurship in Latin America

Entrepreneurship in Latin America

A STEP UP THE SOCIAL LADDER?

Edited by

Eduardo Lora and Francesca Castellani

A COPUBLICATION OF THE INTER-AMERICAN
DEVELOPMENT BANK AND THE WORLD BANK

Latin American Development Forum Series

This series was created in 2003 to promote debate, disseminate information and analysis, and convey the excitement and complexity of the most topical issues in economic and social development in Latin America and the Caribbean. It is sponsored by the Inter-American Development Bank, the United Nations Economic Commission for Latin America and the Caribbean, and the World Bank. The manuscripts chosen for publication represent the highest quality in each institution's research and activity output and have been selected for their relevance to the academic community, policy makers, researchers, and interested readers.

Advisory Committee Members

Titles in the Latin American Development Forum Series

About the Authors

Editors
Eduardo Lora
Independent Consultant, former Chief Economist of the Inter-American
Development Bank
e-mail: eduardo.a.lora@gmail.com

Francesca Castellani
Lead Economist, Andean Countries Department, Inter-American Development Bank
e-mail: francescac@iadb.org

Chapters 1 and 2
Andrés Solimano
Independent Consultant
e-mail: asolimano@gmail.com

Chapter 3
Hugo D. Kantis
Director, Entrepreneurial Development Programme (PRODEM)
Institute of Industry, Universidad Nacional de General Sarmiento, Buenos
Aires, Argentina
e-mail: hkantis@ungs.edu.ar

Juan S. Federico
Researcher and Lecturer, Entrepreneurial Development Programme
(PRODEM), Institute of Industry, Universidad Nacional de General
Sarmiento, Buenos Aires, Argentina
e-mail: jfederic@ungs.edu.ar

Luis A. Trajtenberg
Assistant Professor of Statistics and Econometrics II, Facultad de Ciencias
Económicas, Universidad de Buenos Aires, Buenos Aires, Argentina
e-mail: trajtenberg@economicas.uba.ar

Chapter 4
Viviana Vélez-Grajales
Inter-American Development Bank
e-mail: vivianav@iadb.org

Roberto Vélez-Grajales
Centro de Estudios Espinosa Yglesias, México DF, 01040
e-mail: rvelezg@ceey.org.mx

Chapter 5
José Anchorena
Coordinator of Economic Development Section, Fundación Pensar,
Buenos Aires, Argentina
e-mail: janchorena@fundacionpensar.org

Lucas Ronconi
Researcher, Center for Social Research and Action (CIAS), Buenos Aires,
Argentina
e-mail: ronconilucas@gmail.com

Chapter 6
Xavier Ordeñana
Professor, ESPAE Graduate School of Management, Escuela Superior Politécnica del Litoral, Guayaquil, Ecuador
e-mail: xordenan@espol.edu.ec

Elizabeth Arteaga
Professor, ESPAE Graduate School of Management, Escuela Superior Politécnica del Litoral, Guayaquil, Ecuador
e-mail: marteaga@espol.edu.ec

Contents

TABLES

Foreword

Decades of policies to support micro and small enterprises as a means of boosting incomes and promoting social mobility in Latin America have raised more questions than answers: Do Latin American entrepreneurs ascend in the income rankings faster than non-entrepreneurs of their own generation? Do current generations experience more barriers to social mobility than previous generations? Do entrepreneurs from different social origins face different prospects for mobility? Should public policy promote entrepreneurial activity in order to increase social mobility and further the possibilities of advancement for the lower classes?

Entrepreneurship is often seen as a vehicle for upward social mobility, especially for the middle class. Countries strive to support a vigorous middle class under the assumption that middle-class values and attitudes are often conducive to investing and innovating. However, the alleged entrepreneurial spirit of the middle classes is debatable and in apparent contradiction to the fact that more entrepreneurs come from the upper classes.

Similarly, although public policies often encourage entrepreneurship as a means of creating employment and promoting growth, the effectiveness of such policies is far from proven. This is especially true in developing countries, where entrepreneurship may be the only recourse for many workers facing labor markets characterized by high informality. In these countries, some of the observed entrepreneurship may be a response to taxes on formal employment and implicit subsidies to informal activity. A proliferation of (mostly small) firms may be interpreted as a sign of "strong entrepreneurship," but may only reflect deep distortions that misallocate resources and induce productivity losses.

Entrepreneurship in Latin America: A Step Up the Social Ladder? addresses these questions by combining the literature on entrepreneurship and new developments in the analysis of the middle class and social mobility. Several country studies portray a kind of entrepreneurship that bears little resemblance to the Schumpeterian hero who contributes to growth and development. The book paints a picture of a small and heterogeneous group that, though more mobile than employees, faces higher income volatility.

This analysis provides interesting insights into the limits of policies to promote entrepreneurship as a vehicle for social mobility across heterogeneous segments of society. Promoting entrepreneurship may be a way to foster job creation and innovation for social mobility, but it may also induce into entrepreneurial occupations many people who could be employed more productively as salaried workers in formal firms.

The dilemma in designing policies to promote social mobility and reduce inequality is whether to focus on policies that benefit specific sociodemographic groups or on policies that facilitate mobility in general. The book argues for a level playing field for lower- and middle-class entrepreneurs, but defends the need to combine more general policies to facilitate firm creation and growth, such as reducing the costs of doing business, improving the functioning of labor and credit markets, and strengthening social capital.

This book will be very useful to policy makers committed to encouraging social mobility and will provide a realistic assessment of how far that objective can be reached by promoting entrepreneurship.

Santiago Levy
Vice President, Sectors and Knowledge
Inter-American Development Bank
August 2013

Acknowledgments

This book is the result of a project carried out by the Inter-American Development Bank's (IDB) Latin American and the Caribbean Research Network. The project was led by Eduardo Lora and Francesca Castellani, with advice and guidance from Santiago Levy, Juan José Listerri, Luis Felipe López-Calva, and Andrés Solimano. The following research teams participated in the project:

- Argentina: José Anchorena and Lucas Ronconi, with Eloy Aguirre and Marianela Rodríguez as research assistants and Miguel Braun as external adviser
- Bolivia: Werner Hernani Limarino, Ahmed Eid, and Paul Villarroel
- Colombia: Marcela Meléndez and Paula Mejía
- Ecuador: Xavier Ordeñana, Elizabeth Arteaga, and Ramón Villa
- México: Viviana Vélez-Grajales and Roberto Vélez-Grajales
- Uruguay: Néstor Gandelman, Daniel Bukstein, and Virginia Robano
- Latin America as a region: Hugo D. Kantis, Juan S. Federico, and Luis A. Trajtenberg.

This book contains abridged versions of a selection of the papers produced by the research teams. Further papers will be published in a special issue of the *Latin American Journal of Economics*. During the research process, the teams benefited from comments and suggestions by Hugo Ñopo, Julian Messina, Jamele Rigolini, the Studies Committee of the IDB, and two anonymous referees.

Rita Funaro and Santiago Pombo provided very valuable editorial guidance. Nancy Morrison carefully edited earlier drafts of the chapters. Book design, editing, and production were coordinated by the World Bank's Publishing and Knowledge Division, under the supervision of Patricia Katayama and Janice Tuten.

For administrative and logistical support, the authors acknowledge Patricia Arauz, María Consuelo Yépez, Raquel Gómez, Kai Hertz, Elton Mancilla, and Mariela Semidey.

Finally, the authors and the IDB express their gratitude and appreciation to the Korea Poverty Reduction Fund and the Fund for Special Operations of the IDB, which made this research effort possible.

Abbreviations

EAP	economically active population
EDS	Social Development Survey
EPH	Permanent Household Survey
GEM	Global Entrepreneurship Monitor
IDB	Inter-American Development Bank
IESS	Social Security Institute
INEC	National Institute of Statistics and Census (Ecuador)
MSMS-2006	Mexican Social Mobility Survey 2006
PPP	purchasing power parity
SME	small and medium enterprise

All amounts are presented in U.S. dollars unless otherwise indicated.

Part I

Overview

1

Overview and Policy Implications

Andrés Solimano

Entrepreneurship is a critical process in a dynamic capitalist economy. It generates new productive capacities, processes, and goods; promotes innovation; and fosters employment creation, growth, and development. At the same time, distorted patterns of entrepreneurship can lead to resource misallocation and low productivity.

Entrepreneurship is an important and fascinating topic. It cuts across many disciplines, including psychology, the theory of production, labor economics, talent economics, risk theory, and public policy. The prototypical view depicts entrepreneurs as ambitious, competitive, creative, independent-minded individuals with the courage to undertake new endeavors in uncertain contexts: the ideal of competitive capitalism. Business school literature focuses on complex practical themes, such as the objectives and skills of the entrepreneur, the core strengths of the firm, the devising of strategic and business plans, and the discovery of opportunities, market niches, and financing possibilities.

From a public policy perspective, it is desirable that entrepreneurs come not only from rich elites but also from middle-class and low-income groups, creating broader opportunities to realize the hidden productive potential of individuals at all levels of society. The promotion of entrepreneurship is envisaged as a way to foster upward social mobility and boost economic dynamism and productive transformation.

However, entrepreneurial traits—such as a propensity to envision opportunities, mobilize resources, take risks, and innovate—are not widely distributed in the general population. Entrepreneurs as a group represent a small proportion of the economically active population, although the impact of successful entrepreneurship can be quite large.

Historically, the middle class was a main source of entrepreneurship in the development of capitalism in England and other countries. Landed aristocracies in decline gave way to an up-and-coming segment of the entrepreneurial middle class centered in urban areas. In contemporary times, major breakthroughs in technological innovations with large market potential (such as the development of software and emblematic products such as Google and Facebook) have been carried out by young, educated individuals operating independently in small-scale firms. The extent to which this largely spontaneous process can be replicated in different places and contexts remains an open question.

At the same time, these success stories coexist with a very different kind of entrepreneurship that is widespread in Latin America and other parts of the developing world. "Necessity entrepreneurs" launch their own business not by choice, but by necessity: the need to earn a living when other options, such as wage employment, are lacking. They often operate in the informal sector. Their ventures have low levels of technology and earn a rate of return equivalent to that of a relatively modest salaried job, but entrepreneurs face more risks than employees in the formal sector. The distance between the idealized bold, innovative, and daunting entrepreneur described by economist and political scientist Joseph Schumpeter[1] and the numerous modest entrepreneurs of the developing world is striking. In practice, entrepreneurship is a very heterogeneous segment of the economy, and entrepreneurs are a heterogeneous segment of the population. This makes the support of entrepreneurship and entrepreneurs a potentially elusive target of public policy.

Public policies, if properly designed, should aim to exploit synergies between educational capabilities, family background in households with an entrepreneurial tradition, and the quest for independence and a drive to undertake productive projects. Many policy makers around the world are also driven by the goal of promoting a growing middle class, which is viewed as a source of political moderation, social stability, and, as this book will show, entrepreneurial capacities and the associated upward social mobility. For these reasons, public policies in Latin America and elsewhere that seek to promote entrepreneurship should aim to engage the middle class and the lower parts of the income distribution.

Overview of the Book

This book looks at the potential but also the limits of policies to promote entrepreneurship as a main vehicle for social mobility across broad social segments of society as well as steps to remove the resource constraints that hamper entrepreneurship in areas such as credit markets and education. This volume assesses the relevant literature on entrepreneurship and connects it with new developments in the analysis of the middle class and social mobility.

Chapter 2 undertakes a review of the economic literature on entrepreneurship and relates it to the economic and sociological literature on middle class and social mobility. Andrés Solimano examines some main theories of entrepreneurship and evaluates their relevance and validity for promoting growth, development, and social mobility. The underlying focus is the Latin American and Caribbean region, although some of the issues can be of more general validity for both advanced and developing countries.

Chapter 3 describes Latin American middle-class entrepreneurs and their firms. Hugo Kantis, Juan Federico, and Luis Trajtenberg draw from surveys designed to study the entrepreneurial process of dynamic new ventures in selected Latin American countries (Argentina, Brazil, Chile, Ecuador, El Salvador, Mexico, and Peru) as well as selected countries from other regions (East Asia and Mediterranean Europe). Although the samples are small and not representative of the entire population of entrepreneurs, the surveys provide many insights into the circumstances and conditions affecting middle-class entrepreneurship.

From the outset, Latin American middle-class entrepreneurs have fewer resources and skills than upper-class entrepreneurs, who tend to have had more exposure to business experience at an early stage, from both their parents and families and their university education. Likewise, in comparison with middle-class entrepreneurs from other regions, Latin American middle-class entrepreneurs are less exposed to the business world and to entrepreneurial role models. As a result of their lack of exposure, they tend to rely on a support network that is poorly qualified for entrepreneurial activities. Moreover, start-up financing is more difficult to obtain in Latin America. This adds to the lack of dynamism exhibited by firms created by middle-class entrepreneurs in Latin America compared to those in other regions.

The role played by entrepreneurship in fostering intergenerational social and economic mobility is the topic of chapter 4, by Viviana Vélez-Grajales and Roberto Vélez-Grajales. They concentrate on Mexico, drawing on the Mexican Social Mobility Survey 2006. Although it is not a longitudinal survey, it provides information about the social origins and living conditions of the parents of the respondents. On this basis, the study constructs wealth measures to assess social and economic mobility across generations and wealth persistence over time.

The authors conduct three main exercises. First, they analyze whether entrepreneurs experienced greater upward social mobility than the self-employed or employees. Second, they use discrete-choice econometric (probit) models to identify whether certain characteristics are the main determinants of the decision to become an entrepreneur. Third, they estimate the effect of entrepreneurial activity on income, using the propensity score matching method.

The results support the hypothesis that entrepreneurs have more options for upward social mobility than employees and the self-employed.

However, this result is conditional on the socioeconomic characteristics of the parents. It is more difficult for entrepreneurs from lower-class families to move up the socioeconomic ladder than for entrepreneurs from middle- or upper-class families. In addition, the probability of becoming an entrepreneur increases when the respondent's father was also an entrepreneur (there is a strong role model effect). Father's occupation turns out to be a more important explanatory factor than initial wealth or education. Thus a family-transmission effect of occupational *values* (to become an entrepreneur) seems to be operating. Finally, the authors find that the mean effect of entrepreneurial activity on income is positive and larger for entrepreneurs with parents from the extremes of the income spectrum: either the lower or the upper class.

The role of values in shaping the choice of becoming an entrepreneur is further pursued in chapter 5, by José Anchorena and Lucas Ronconi. The chapter presents a rich collection of facts and statistical analysis about entrepreneurship in Argentina. As in Mexico, the probability of becoming an entrepreneur is substantially higher for individuals raised in families headed by entrepreneurs: more specifically, the probability is 15.8 percentage points higher if the parents were owners of a firm, while it is only between 1.5 and 6.3 percentage points higher if the parents were rich.

Since this result suggests that family values are more important than parental wealth in the choice of entrepreneurship, the authors analyze the extent to which Argentine society supports entrepreneurial values. For that purpose, they use the World Values Survey, a data set with more than 50,000 interviews in more than 50 countries. A main question investigates "qualities that children can be encouraged to learn at home." Respondents can choose up to 5 of 10 alternatives: independence, hard work, feeling of responsibility, imagination, tolerance and respect for other people, thrift (saving money and things), determination and perseverance, religious faith, unselfishness, and obedience. The authors compare the set of values prevalent in Argentina with those in other countries in Latin America (Brazil, Chile, Colombia, Mexico, Peru, and Uruguay) and resource-rich nations such as Australia and New Zealand. They find that Argentine society has values better aligned with entrepreneurship than the rest of Latin America. According to the authors, Argentine society promotes seven values supportive of entrepreneurship: higher responsibility, higher tolerance or respect, higher independence, lower obedience, lower religious faith, lower thriftiness, and higher imagination. However, while Argentine society may promote entrepreneurial values, it does so less than some successful economies that are abundant in natural resources, such as Australia and New Zealand.

Anchorena and Ronconi note that the share of entrepreneurs in the economically active population in Argentina decreased from a peak of 13 percent between 1989 and 1992 period to a historic low of about

8 percent in 2011. They hypothesize that this may be partly due to public employment policies that have attracted potential entrepreneurs to bureaucratic positions in government, especially during the 2000s. To test this hypothesis, they assess the statistical relationship between public employment and entrepreneurship across 32 urban areas between 2003 and 2010. They conclude that the increase in public employment (0.9 percent of the economically active population) is responsible for a reduction of approximately 6 percent in the initial stock of entrepreneurs, implying a large crowding-out effect. Public employment crowds out entrepreneurs who are somewhere in the middle of the "quality" spectrum—that is, not the most or the least dynamic entrepreneurs, but people who would have started a small and informal firm and eventually would have hired some workers, were it not for public employment.

While family background and values strongly influence the decision to be an entrepreneur, support networks are essential for the survival and growth of very young entrepreneurial projects. In chapter 6, Xavier Ordeñana and Elizabeth Arteaga explore the role that social capital plays in the dynamism of firms in Ecuador. They use data from their own survey of entrepreneurs, combined with secondary data from several official sources, as well as from opinion surveys conducted by private organizations.

While the problems facing upper- and middle-class entrepreneurs are remarkably similar, the resources accessed to solve them are not. Although Ecuadorian entrepreneurs in general are supported by relatively weak networks, middle-class entrepreneurs resort to external support more than upper-class entrepreneurs (60 and 49 percent, respectively) and rely substantially more than their upper-class peers on a variety of resources, including friends and family, suppliers and customers, other entrepreneurs, business associations, and universities. Upper-class entrepreneurs make more use of two sources: work colleagues and consultants. But most of the resources used by entrepreneurs seem to make little difference in the outcomes of their business. Only those resources associated with a close network of support (friends, family, and colleagues) increase the probability that a nascent firm will become dynamic.

Public Policy Implications

The research contained in this book has important implications for public policies that seek to promote entrepreneurship in society. A set of reasonably well-designed public policies should answer the difficult question of what exactly should be promoted. Is it productive entrepreneurship, personal economic autonomy, business creation and consolidation, economywide growth, innovation, employment generation, or a combination of all these factors?

Making Trade-offs

Two critical characteristics of entrepreneurial activity documented in this book matter when formulating public policies to promote entrepreneurship. The first is the relatively small numbers of entrepreneurs in the economically active population. (Of course, the impact of this minority activity can be high.) The second is the heterogeneity of entrepreneurial activity.

As mentioned, entrepreneurial traits—such as a propensity to envision opportunities, mobilize resources, take risks, and innovate—are not widely distributed in the population at-large. Therefore, pro-entrepreneurial policies will not be mass policies, in spite of their apparent objective of creating a majority of entrepreneurs in the population and extending the reach of "popular capitalism" to the middle and lower classes. The wide range of entrepreneurship, including a small group of large-scale entrepreneurs with access to credit, technology, and market and innovative capacities and a much larger group of small and medium entrepreneurs and micro "necessity entrepreneurs" with much less access to these capabilities, makes the targeted segment—the entrepreneur—potentially *diffuse, elusive, and very heterogeneous.*

These considerations highlight the various trade-offs implicit in the objectives of policies that aim to promote entrepreneurship. For example, entrepreneurial policies that seek to promote economic autonomy, employment, and income generation may collide with entrepreneurial policies that aim to promote objectives such as innovative capabilities, new products, new technologies, and economywide economic growth. The first type of policies seek to support micro, small, and medium entrepreneurship in activities that have low technological sophistication but a capacity to generate employment and to provide the means of economic survival for those who are out of the reach of social protection policies. The second set of policies may support technological entrepreneurs and larger-scale entrepreneurship.

Should public policy tilt toward middle- and lower-class entrepreneurship, making the social origin of the entrepreneur a valid criterion for entrepreneurial policy? Some argue that promoting middle-class entrepreneurial policy can ultimately be a misguided policy. A similar argument could be extended to policies oriented to promote lower-class entrepreneurship.

The arguments against directly promoting lower- and middle-class entrepreneurship can be evaluated on at least two accounts. First, fostering entrepreneurship in the middle- and lower-income segments of society may be a compensatory policy that helps to *level the playing field* of general entrepreneurship in view of the fact that entrepreneurs who do not come from high-income families often start from disadvantageous conditions with respect to resources such as education, parental support, role models, and financing. Policies must ensure that an entrepreneur's functioning and capabilities (in Amartya Sen's sense)[2] are turned into actual realizations by providing supportive factors such as training and financing.

Second, public policy can help to *democratize entrepreneurship* when markets are dominated by a few big players that impede the entry and competition of small and middle-size participants through de facto barriers, such as their superior access to funding, economies of scale, better technologies, and greater capacities to lobby policy makers.

Establishing Clear Guidelines and Operational Criteria for Sound Policy

Once an agreement is reached on the need to have some entrepreneurial policy that cuts across individuals from different social classes and ethnic backgrounds—and does not cater only to entrenched, upper-class entrepreneurial elites—it is important to develop clear guidelines and operational criteria to design and evaluate the type of entrepreneurship that is desired. Reasonable criteria for such entrepreneurial policy can include the contribution of entrepreneurship to firm creation, productivity, innovation, employment generation, lower- and middle-class incomes, resource mobilization, and export orientation.

Building on Role Models

The studies on Argentina, Ecuador, and Mexico included in this book suggest that policies should take into account and exploit the importance of role models for encouraging entrepreneurship. These role models often come from parents, but they also may come from outside the family. Dynamic entrepreneurs like Bill Gates and Steve Jobs, to name just two, are role models for new generations of entrepreneurs.

Lowering the Costs of Doing Business

In recent years, the concepts of the "cost and ease of doing business" have been advanced and empirically assessed to consider obstacles to entrepreneurship and business creation and consolidation. This line of work highlights the importance of investment climate and regulations as a key set of considerations for investment and entrepreneurship. Since 2003, the World Bank Group has been publishing an annual report called *Doing Business* that surveys a vast array of countries spanning a wide range of income levels per capita and stages of development. In 2011 the report included 182 countries (World Bank 2010). The report gauges measures such as time, number, and costs devoted to complying with regulations and focuses on variables such as the requirements for starting a business, dealing with construction permits, employing workers, registering property, getting credit, protecting investors, paying taxes, trading across borders, enforcing contracts, closing a business, and getting electricity.

In general, the rankings on ease of doing business are closely correlated with a country's income per capita. Typically, these rankings are led by high-income Organisation for Economic Co-operation and Development (OECD) nations and trailed by South Asian countries, followed by Sub-Saharan African economies. The countries in the Latin American and Caribbean region are often in the lower middle of the ranking. The report also regularly updates progress made by countries in reducing red tape and simplifying regulations. These reforms take place in very different countries, without a clear pattern related to level of development.

The studies in this book confirm that red tape and bureaucracy are certainly external obstacles to entrepreneurship—although they are not the full story. Reforms in some Latin American countries to make it easier to create a firm are a step in the right direction. Reducing the time and cost of legally incorporating a firm will favor the creation of new enterprises. In several Latin American countries, the cost of closing a firm and going out of business is often high due to the stringent bureaucratic procedures to stop a firm from operating. Policy makers must keep in mind that when the costs of exit are high, the entry of firms is also penalized. Impeding the process of creating and closing a firm can be harmful to entrepreneurship. Bankruptcy procedures should be reviewed. The high pecuniary and legal costs of bankruptcy procedures that prevail in several countries in the region tend to impede the reallocation of resources after a business has failed. In addition, the social stigma of bankruptcy seems higher in the Latin American culture than in Anglo-Saxon cultures. Programs aimed at easing the registration and formalization of small firms may not just facilitate entrepreneurship but also raise the effectiveness of economic and social programs in general.[3]

Building Entrepreneurial Capacities

The studies in this book, as well as the literature surveyed in chapter 2, show that an important obstacle to entrepreneurship is a *shortage of capacities* among many entrepreneurs and managers to manage human resources, technology, and cash flows properly. These obstacles are particularly acute for middle- and lower-class entrepreneurs. Although, as chapter 6 on Ecuador shows, middle-class entrepreneurs may have better access to a variety of forms of social capital than their upper-class entrepreneurs, the effectiveness of that support is far from guaranteed. This finding suggests the need to level the playing field by designing entrepreneurial policies oriented to help entrepreneurs to strengthen their firm's internal capacity to manage the enterprise. Furthermore, it may call for further efforts to make postsecondary education not only more accessible but also more relevant.

The role of education and training in nurturing entrepreneurship is an important but largely unresolved topic. Developing the skills needed to be an entrepreneur through the education system may help to compensate for disadvantages associated with social origin at the beginning of the entrepreneurial career. However, in many developing countries, access to the education system is strongly correlated with the socioeconomic level of the student. Without reform, the education system will tend to perpetuate—rather than correct—existing inequalities of income and wealth and is unlikely to contribute to democratizing entrepreneurship.

If university-level training in entrepreneurship is pursued, then it is important to engage public universities in this effort, since middle- and low-income students are more likely to attend public universities than private universities. Universities in Europe and North America have been increasingly promoting courses and master's programs oriented to nurture and provide tools for effective entrepreneurship. These programs seek to differentiate themselves from the standard master's in business administration degrees that are oriented to produce managers and not necessarily entrepreneurs. This trend has started to spread to Latin America, with a proliferation of short courses and diplomas catered to fostering *el emprendimiento* (entrepreneurship) as the new mantra for growth and development. It is important to ensure that training and education efforts are in line with the vocation and interests of the students and that appropriate systems for detecting and nurturing entrepreneurial traits are developed.

Beyond the formal education system, small business assistance programs and active labor market programs (which may or may not be run by government entities) often include training components aimed at developing the skills of potential entrepreneurs who may have previous labor market experience but insufficient formal education. Unfortunately, there is a dearth of knowledge on how to design effective training programs in this context, given the diversity of experiences and the lack of experimental design for evaluating them.[4]

Improving Financing

Beyond education and training, it is important to consider carefully what empirical studies indicate are the main constraints and obstacles facing entrepreneurs, particularly those with a middle-class and lower-class family background. The lack of financing is an almost perennial obstacle that faces entrepreneurs who do not come from an upper-class background as well as the children of the affluent who do not automatically inherit the wealth and contacts of their parents. Many funding schemes offered by public banks and second-tier commercial banks are far from a resounding success in Latin America and other parts of the world. Nonetheless, some positive examples exist, and lessons from success and failure should be considered to improve financing options. Public policy can focus on securing external financing for the firm and connecting demand and supply in the credit market. Policies to monitor the cost of credit in markets and address the lack of financial education that many poor and middle-income entrepreneurs face are essential in markets plagued by asymmetrical information and unethical lending practices.

Strengthening Management within Firms

Studies also show that deficits in attracting and managing human resources, securing clients, managing new technologies, and improving accounting and financial management are all internal factors that impede entrepreneurship.

Improving Networks

Studies also identify the growing importance played by networks and family, friends, and community institutions in overcoming these obstacles and paving the way for sound and vibrant entrepreneurship at all social levels. Promoting social capital and facilitating communication and networking can have a significant payoff.

Topics for Further Research

Since the study of entrepreneurship cuts across different fields of knowledge, expanding the interdisciplinary vistas of the topic can be rewarding. Inviting dialogue and joint research among business experts, economists, psychologists, venture capitalists, talent specialists, and experts in the labor market and industrial relations could yield important insights.

Basic issues such as the definition and measurement of entrepreneurship and the middle class need work. The use of proxies such as measures of ownership, self-employment, size of the firm, and business creation to gauge entrepreneurship demonstrates that the topic is still in an early phase from an empirical viewpoint.[5] In turn, the lack of longitudinal studies in Latin America for tracking the family and occupational history of individuals over long periods of time limits the study of entrepreneurship in Latin America and other developing regions. The studies in this book feature empirical methods that overcome this lack of longitudinal data.

More research is needed in areas such as the values of the entrepreneur. The classic depiction of a frugal individual willing to postpone consumption and endure sacrifices to make his or her vision of a business a reality may remain valid, but the role of sophisticated capital markets and family inheritances changes the picture somewhat. Another area for more analysis is to compare the role of generalization and the capacity to multitask with the role of specialization and technical knowledge.

The theme of how to manage risk and embark on productive ventures in uncertain contexts remains a critical topic. More work is needed in understanding and measuring the intergenerational transmission of values at the family level, given the importance of parental and family roles in the propensity for entrepreneurship. It is also important to study the importance of role models *outside the family* in shaping entrepreneurship.

Understanding the gender component of entrepreneurship is an important emerging subject. Entrepreneurship is strongly biased toward males in Latin America. The influence of family factors, exclusion patterns, and female participation rates in the labor force in shaping the role of women in entrepreneurial activities needs to be better understood.

More work is needed on occupational dynamics and their impact on social mobility. A sequence of employee first and entrepreneurship later often prevails, with a switch from employee status to entrepreneurial status sometime between the ages of the late 30s and early 40s. More needs to be known about how robust this age threshold is to changes in occupation over time and in different places. The influence of age on the ability to take risks is an interesting but largely neglected topic. A similar question can be asked about the influence of class and ethnic background on the tolerance for risk taking and entrepreneurship.

The growing importance of information technology in business management and the importance of networks for gathering a client base and recruiting human resources are new areas of investigation.

The influence of cities, location, and international mobility of talent on entrepreneurship is a critical topic. Most entrepreneurial activity takes place in cities, rather than in isolated places, but there are important differences in entrepreneurial concentrations across cities of relatively similar size. The concepts of "ecosystems," "bottom-up innovation," and "clustering" in the literature all indicate the importance of favorable contexts, interdependence, location, decentralization, and spontaneity in the entrepreneurial function. The role of the consumer base, access to human resources, availability of inputs, and supply of entrepreneurial capacities are all dimensions in the growth of cities that point to a dynamic, mutually causal interaction between cities and entrepreneurship.

The international mobility of talent is a critical feature of globalization, and part of this pool of talent engages in entrepreneurial activities (see Solimano 2008). International differences in regulatory policies, ease of doing business, immigration regimes, availability of credit and venture capital, and growth prospects are all factors that affect the international allocation of entrepreneurship among nations. The role of the Latin American region in this new landscape is an important topic for further research.

Notes

1. Schumpeter ([1911, 1934] 1989, [1949] 2000). For more on his views, see chapter 2 of this volume.

2. Sen (1985). Sen's capability approach focuses on what individuals are able to do. The emphasis is not only on how human beings function but also on their ability—that is, the practical choice—to function in important ways if they so wish. The approach emphasizes functional capabilities, including the ability to engage in economic transactions.

3. An anonymous referee pointed out that, in Brazil, the Brasileiro de Apoio às Micro e Pequenas Empresas (SEBRAE) initiative called Emprendedor Individual (Individual Entrepreneur), which started in 2009, has formalized more than 2.5 million microentrepreneurs in three years.

4. These programs are found in the United States and many European countries as well as in the developing world. Partly as a result of data limitations and the lack of experimental design in program evaluations, few studies for the United States are able to identify any causal relation between small business assistance programs and business creation or other outcomes (Sanders 2002; Gu, Karoly, and Zissimopoulos 2008). A revision by the World Bank of 13 evaluations of microenterprise and self-employment assistance programs (most of which included a training component) concludes, "These programs can provide effective support for the small minority of unemployed workers who are interested in starting their own business. However ... some evaluations show negative or insignificant effects ... Much more evaluation needs to be taken to understand the impacts of [these] programs ... particularly in the case of transition and developing countries" (Betcherman, Olivas, and Dar 2004). More specific evidence for Romania indicates that self-employment and small business assistance programs help to improve participants' economic outcomes (Rodríguez-Planas 2010; Rodríguez-Planas and Jacob 2010). Although these programs seem to foster upward mobility, they also "cream off" the most qualified candidates, implying that their ability to level the playing field is somewhat limited.

5. See discussion in chapter 2, especially box 2.1.

References

Betcherman, G., K. Olivas, and A. Dar. 2004. "Impacts of Active Labor Programs: New Evidence from Evaluations with Particular Attention to Developing and Transition Countries." Social Protection Discussion Paper Series 0402, World Bank, Washington, DC.

Gu, Q., L. A. Karoly, and J. Zissimopoulos. 2008. "Small Business Assistance Programs in the United States: An Analysis of What They Are, How Well They Perform, and How We Can Learn More about Them." RAND Corporation, Santa Monica, CA. http://www.rand.org/pubs/working_papers/WR603.

Rodríguez-Planas, N. 2010. "Channels through which Public Employment Services and Small Business Assistance Programmes Work." *Oxford Bulletin of Economics and Statistics* 72 (4): 458–85.

Rodríguez-Planas, N., and B. Jacob. 2010. "Evaluating Active Labor Market Programs in Romania." *Empirical Economics* 38 (1): 65–84.

Sanders, C. K. 2002. "The Impact of Microenterprise Assistance Programs: A Comparative Study of Program Participants, Nonparticipants, and Other Low-Wage Workers." *Social Service Review* 76 (2): 321–40.

Sen, A. K. 1985. *Commodities and Capabilities*. Oxford, U.K.: Oxford University Press.

Schumpeter, J. (1911, 1934) 1989. *The Theory of Economic Development: An Inquiry into Profits, Capital, Credit, Interest Rates, and the Business Cycle.* Repr. of 1934 trans., New Brunswick, NJ: Transaction Publishers.

———. (1949) 2000. "Economic Theory and Entrepreneurial History." In *Essays: On Entrepreneurs, Innovations, Business Cycles, and the Evolution of Capitalism,* edited by R. Clemence. Repr., New Brunswick, NJ: Transactions Publishers.

Solimano, A., ed. 2008. *The International Mobility of Talent: Types, Causes, and Development Impact.* Oxford, U.K.: Oxford University Press.

World Bank. 2010. *Doing Business 2011: Making a Difference for Entrepreneurs.* Washington, DC: World Bank.

2

Entrepreneurship, the Middle Class, and Social Mobility: An Overview of Literature

Andrés Solimano

Studies on entrepreneurship, the middle class, and social mobility often run in quite separate directions. Entrepreneurship is seen as a dynamic process of business creation and destruction and is therefore linked to the process of economic growth. However, entrepreneurship has not always been given a central role in economic analysis that is dominated by theories of the production process. Instead, the main role has been given to the mechanical accumulation of capital and labor, with little attention to the fundamental entrepreneurial process of organizing production, envisioning opportunities, mobilizing factors of production, and linking them with credit and product markets—all in a context of uncertainty and risk.

The literature on the middle class has often remained in the realm of sociological approaches more concerned with issues of social identity and class differentiation. Links with entrepreneurship and economic growth have been largely neglected.

Social mobility is also a critical and dynamic process for promoting equality of opportunity, reducing inequality, and advancing progress up the economic ladder from one generation to the next. Yet the literature on social mobility is scant. Integrating these various strands of thought is needed not only to improve analysis, but also to improve public policy. New avenues of thought are required to identify novel economic and social mechanisms to spur economic dynamism and social equity. Economists are rediscovering some alleged virtues of the middle class as a source of entrepreneurship, a particular set of values, consumer power, and socio-political stability. These propositions need proper empirical verification, using a variety of methods such as econometric testing, historical evidence, and country and micro case studies.

More needs to be known about the nature and characteristics of entrepreneurs and the determinants of the choice of becoming an entrepreneur, the extent to which entrepreneurship advances social mobility, and the influences of family background, education and values, risk taking, and occupational choice in shaping entrepreneurship. This chapter reviews the main issues and accompanying literature on the subject of the middle class, entrepreneurship, and social mobility, with an eye toward their relevance for public policy in the Latin American region.

Entrepreneurship

The word "entrepreneur" comes from the French verb "to undertake" and was first used by Richard Cantillon in the eighteenth century. Cantillon was an early writer on the functions of the entrepreneur as an agent who deals with risk in business and production. In the nineteenth century, British philosopher and political economist John Stuart Mill and French economist and businessman Jean Baptiste Say, influenced by Cantillon, elaborated on the role of the entrepreneur as an organizer of new business, bearing risk and exerting control of the production process. German philosopher and social revolutionary Karl Marx developed a theory of the "capitalist" (in some sense, the equivalent of the entrepreneur), stressing the role of capitalists as a new class that revolutionizes the modes of production—and social relations along the way. Marx highlighted the function of the capitalist factory system in combining technology and the use of wage labor to attain profits, which could be reinvested in the search for more profits. The discussion that follows briefly examines how different schools of thought and thinkers have viewed entrepreneurs and their main role in the economic process.

Neoclassical Theory of Production: Is There a Role for the Entrepreneur?

The theory of the entrepreneur is a complex subject in economic theory. In neoclassical economics, production and growth follow from a production function (whose origin is rarely discussed) that offers managers, entrepreneurs, and administrators a blueprint of economically efficient combinations of factors of production such as labor, capital, and technology to produce goods and services. The production function, however, is ultimately a "black box." The question of who leads, monitors, and carries out the process of organizing production, hiring labor, and combining it with capital according to a blueprint of technologies is absent or hidden. The role of the entrepreneur as an organizer and coordinator of the production process and a link with goods and credit markets is not present in the production function framework. (That is, a variable E—say, for entrepreneur—is not a factor of production). The preferences, skills, attitudes, and capabilities of such an organizer of production, the entrepreneur, is absent from the model.

The Entrepreneur According to Joseph Schumpeter and Frank Knight

The main theoretician of the entrepreneur in the twentieth century was the Austrian American economist and political scientist Joseph Schumpeter. The American economist Frank Knight also offered important insights on the subject. Schumpeter developed a theory of the entrepreneur based on a mix of direct observation, psychological theory, and economic analysis. In his theory, the entrepreneur has a talent for combining capital and labor and for entertaining a vision of opportunities and the prospects for profits (see Schumpeter [1911, 1934] 1989). The critical role of the entrepreneur is making innovations such as introducing a new good or a new line of production or opening a market in a process of "creative destruction" in which new technologies and ways of doing business replace the old ones. Schumpeter emphasized the peculiarities that make the entrepreneur different from the manager, the pure inventor, and the owner of capital: the capacity to undertake new decisions in the unchartered waters of new activities, under conditions of uncertainty and risk. A "developing" economy, in Schumpeter's terms, is one that jumps from one "circular flow" (equilibrium) to another driven by innovations. An economy may be growing but is not developing if it stays in the same (stationary) circular flow using the same technology and organization: recall that Schumpeter's classic 1911 book was called *The Theory of Economic Development.*

Frank Knight, in turn, influenced both by the Austrian School of Economics of Menger, Von Mises, Bohm-Bawerk, and Hayek and by neoclassical theory, linked entrepreneurship and profits with risk and uncertainty. He stressed the role of the entrepreneur and the manager as being to organize production when the productivity of workers is unknown and other contingencies relevant in production cannot be ascribed precise probabilities, chiefly because of the presence of "uncertainty." For Knight, profit was the remuneration of risk taking, a different category than the return on capital invested in the firm. Some interpretations of Knight also emphasize that the entrepreneur needs the residual property right (as owner) to exercise the function of "specializing in judgment, common sense, and intuition as vehicles to carry productive decisions in a world of uncertainty" (Langlois and Cosgel 1993, 460).

Keynes's Volatile Investors

The British economist John Maynard Keynes was interested in the psychology of the "investor"—both in financial assets and in physical production—as well as the context under which the investor undertakes investment decisions. Keynes did not share Schumpeter's almost romantic view of the entrepreneur as the "hero of capitalism," who, against all odds, carries forward his vision of innovation and productive creativity. Keynes did share with Knight (and Schumpeter) an awareness of the complications that the effects of intrinsic uncertainty introduce to rational economic calculation.[1] However, he depicted the investor-capitalist of the real world more as a "casino player": a bit of a gambler, rather than a hardworking Puritan who would delay gratification (sacrifice consumption) in favor of capital accumulation. Keynes coined the expression "animal spirits" to denote human behavior driven by something more than enlightened values and a rational calculation of pecuniary costs and benefits. The original passage by Keynes (1936, 161–62) reads as follows:

> Even apart from the instability due to speculation, there is the instability due to the characteristic of human nature that a large proportion of our positive activities depend on spontaneous optimism rather than mathematical expectations, whether moral or hedonistic or economic. Most, probably, of our decisions to do something positive, the full consequences of which will be drawn out over many days to come, can only be taken as the result of animal spirits—a spontaneous urge to action rather than inaction, and not as the outcome of a weighted average of quantitative benefits multiplied by quantitative probabilities. Thus, if animal spirits are dimmed and spontaneous optimism falters, leaving us to depend on nothing but a mathematical expectation, enterprise will fade and die.

This quote conveys two important features often ascribed to entrepreneurs: an urge to action rather than inaction and the role of optimism. Keynes also stressed the point that investors are affected by herd behavior, interdependent expectations, and changes of mood and perceptions that lead to waves of optimism, euphoria, and manias, followed by periods of pessimism and depression—all of which generates sharp business and financial cycles.

The Choice to Be an Entrepreneur

There is consensus that the psychology of the entrepreneur is different from that of the employee. The wage earner is supposed to be more risk averse than the entrepreneur and has a lower quest for independence than the entrepreneur and the self-employed. To achieve long-run economic success, it is not clear that the entrepreneur is a superior choice. A well-educated, adept employee who can make a career in a corporation (or move from one corporation to another) can reach a senior managerial position that can be well remunerated and rewarding from a professional viewpoint. In contrast, entrepreneurship is risky and not at all guaranteed to succeed. In addition, pursuing an entrepreneurial career may have a component of irreversibility that prevents entrepreneurs from returning to the position of an employee; eventually, entrepreneurial paths may erode certain capacities, such as developing reporting capacities and exercising tolerance and patience for collective decision making, that are required for successfully holding an employee position.[2]

As discussed below, empirical evidence indicates that for many individuals the choice of entrepreneurship comes after being an employee for a while—the reverse seems to occur less frequently.[3] Choice-theoretic models derive rules of occupational choice depending on risk preference and other parameters, including wage-to-profit ratios. Some authors have tried to make endogenous the formation of preferences such as the propensity to save, the preference for leisure and work, and the tolerance for and even love of risk taking. The mechanism for preference formation stems from the efforts of parents to instill their own values in their children.[4] In fact, the probability of becoming an entrepreneur is higher in families in which parents are (or have been) entrepreneurs than in households without an entrepreneurial background.

The relationship between endowments of human capital and entrepreneurship is also an interesting subject and not always obvious. Entrepreneurs are not necessarily people with a high stock of formal education (who hold a Ph.D. or a master's degree), such as the scientist, the expert, or the intellectual, who is usually identified with "human capital." Empirical studies confirm this assertion. Along these lines, Lazear (2004) puts forward the "balanced skills hypothesis" of the entrepreneur and tests it empirically. The basic notion is that entrepreneurs possess a varied skill set in areas such as management, interpersonal interaction, and a capacity to deal with financial and technical problems, while employees and professionals are "specialists." Using longitudinal data of top universities in the United States comprising study and employment stories of the same individuals over time, Lazear finds that those who choose a greater variety of subjects in graduate school and also have a more varied occupational experience have a higher propensity to become entrepreneurs than individuals who choose more specialized educational strategies and employment experiences. See box 2.1.

Entrepreneurship and Family Background

The previous discussion underlines the role of family background, risk attitudes, education levels, and preferences for understanding

Box 2.1 Measuring Entrepreneurship

There are three main ways of measuring entrepreneurship:

- *Self-employment with hired workers*. Self-employment simply measures the share of people who lead their own firm. The statistics of the economically active population typically distinguish between owners and managers, employees, and self-employed.
- *Business creation*. This measure focuses on *new* business creation. The World Bank Group Entrepreneurship Snapshots (WBGES), in particular, focuses on new business creation in the formal sector. It measures the number of newly registered firms in a given year as a share of the total number of firms registered. Registered firms are legal entities that can incur debts with the banking system, pay taxes, and undertake legal transactions with other firms and the state.
- *The stage of business development*. This approach sees entrepreneurship as a dynamic process and focuses on the *stages* of the process of business creation, development, and consolidation. The Global Entrepreneurship Monitor (GEM) uses this measure, focusing on early-stage entrepreneurial activity regardless of formal registration. The approach distinguishes between *nascent entrepreneurship* and *baby entrepreneurship*; the latter is counted as the proportion of the adult population that has been operating a business for less than 42 months.

Each of these approaches has some drawbacks. On the one hand, the WBGES may *underestimate* actual entrepreneurial activity by excluding informal sector entrepreneurship. On the other hand, the GEM method may *overestimate* new business creation, since nascent firms may not materialize and may vanish from the market.

In this book, the chapters adopt different definitions according to a country's characteristics as shown in table B2.1.1.[a]

Table B2.1.1 Definitions Employed in this Book

Type of worker	Term used in a chapter (if different)
Independent	
Employer	Entrepreneur (chapter 4)
Employer-entrepreneur	Entrepreneur (chapter 5)
Self-employed	
Self-employed entrepreneur	Entrepreneur (chapter 5)
Pure self-employed	
Employee	

a. The author thanks an anonymous referee for suggesting this table.

the formation and development of entrepreneurship. Dynastic models tend to see persistence across generations of fathers (and mothers) and sons (and daughters) regarding patience, time preference, demand for leisure, and attitude toward work. According to these models, the parents' propensity to be entrepreneurial tends to be inherited, to some degree, by their children, who also seek to be entrepreneurs.[5] An additional hypothesis is that the children of managers of big corporations are less likely to become entrepreneurs than the children of the owners of small firms (see Glaeser, Rosenthal, and Strange 2009). This interesting twist underscores the importance of small-scale firms in promoting entrepreneurship.

An empirical study by Wadhwa et al. (2009) sheds some light on these issues. The report, based on a survey of 549 company founders mainly in the technology sector in the United States (computer and electronics, defense, health care, and services sector), finds that a majority of founders of new companies (71 percent) are of middle-class background,[6] with a very small percentage (less than 1 percent) coming from extremely wealthy or extremely poor backgrounds. In addition, the average age for starting a business is 40. Most company founders have high levels of education (over 95 percent have a bachelor's degree and 47 percent have a more advanced degree). Their academic performance puts them among the top 30 percent in high school and college (with better academic performance in high school). Company founders (entrepreneurs) generally do not initiate a start-up right after graduating from college. They generally have previous work experience as an employee (around six years), suggesting that the choice between being an employee or becoming an entrepreneur may be *sequential* in time. Finally, slightly more than half of them are the first to initiate a business in their family, and their motivation to become an entrepreneur reflects a combination of aspirations of building wealth, commercializing an idea, being their own boss, and, when relevant, continuing a family tradition of entrepreneurship.

International Mobility of Entrepreneurs

From an international perspective, entrepreneurs can transfer their innovative and wealth-creating capacities from one country to another. Historically, the immigration of people with entrepreneurial capacities and a favorable attitude toward risk taking contributed to business creation, resource mobilization, colonization, and innovation—all factors that supported economic growth in countries of destination. In the U.S. and European economies of the nineteenth and early twentieth centuries, successful entrepreneurs (and bankers)—such as Mellon, Vanderbilt, Carnegie, Rockefeller, and, more prominently, the famous banking dynasty of the Rothschilds, with operations in London, Paris, Zurich, and other financial centers—were foreign born or first descendants of immigrants. In Latin America, Argentina was the main recipient of migrants with entrepreneurial skills in the late nineteenth century and early decades of the twentieth century. This country relied both on net immigration (entrepreneurs and working class), primarily from Spain and Italy, and on capital, from England and Germany, for its economic development, using both to mobilize its vast natural resources. In turn, the Chinese diaspora has been an important source of entrepreneurs in South and East Asia, as have Palestine and the Syrian Arab Republic in South America. More recently, in the late twentieth and early twenty-first centuries, entrepreneurial emigrants from China; India; Israel; and Taiwan, China, have provided human resources to support the creation of high-technology industries in hardware and software in Silicon Valley in the United States and to connect them with technological industries in their home countries. These foreign-born entrepreneurs, many of whom came to study in the United States and Europe before becoming entrepreneurs, have played a critical role, both in the receiving and in the home country, in transferring entrepreneurial talent, market connections, and new products and technologies among distant economies. Their location and mobility have helped to develop technological industries in developing nations that have traditionally been importers of high-tech goods (see Saxenian 2006; Solimano 2008).

Heterogeneity, Firm Size, Credit Constraints, and Entrepreneurship

Entrepreneurs in Latin America and other developing regions often operate under highly differentiated productive structures. This heterogeneity is reflected in significant differences between microenterprises, small and medium enterprises (SMEs), and large firms in terms of capital intensity, employment generation, technology development, credit access, and export orientation. The SMEs are often viewed as important sources of employment creation, but not necessarily of technological development. This view can be challenged by the experience of the United States. The U.S. Small Business Administration reports that small firms innovate more than large firms and have a higher percentage of patents per employee than big companies; in turn, younger firms are more likely to have more patents per employee than older firms (Wadhwa et al. 2009).

Entrepreneurs are highly heterogeneous. The entrepreneurial profile of Bill Gates or Michael Bloomberg is certainly different from that of an owner of a hot dog stand in the United States or a small shop in a developing country. Large-scale entrepreneurs with capacities to mobilize capital and technology can have a different impact on economic activity than small entrepreneurs. The urban economist Edward Glaeser (2007) makes the simple but important point that the number of firms in an industry or a city is an important consideration for assessing levels of entrepreneurship (and capacity for employment growth as well). If a given level of employment is distributed among a larger number of firms, then the number of firm leaders or entrepreneurs per worker must be higher. This suggests that countries with relatively larger SME sectors must have a higher degree of entrepreneurship.

An interesting empirical result in the regressions reported in Glaeser (2007) is the negative relationship between the average size of firms and employment growth. This result is statistically significant for a sample of 533 firms in the United States. It is common to think of an inverse relation between firm size and employment levels, but the regressions also identify the relation in terms of employment growth. The study, and other empirical work, indicates that entrepreneurship and employment growth seem to go hand in hand.

An important difference between large and small companies is the nature of the restrictions they face. The financial markets generally operate with asymmetric information between credit suppliers and loan applicants as to their repayment capacity and the economic viability of companies. This point was raised years ago in a seminal paper by Stiglitz and Weiss (1981), which showed that increasing the cost of credit (raising interest rates) could be an inefficient mechanism for sorting out good and bad debtors.

The balance sheet and financial information of smaller companies are usually less developed and systematized than those of larger companies. This lack of information inhibits banks from making loans to smaller companies and encourages them to concentrate on a portfolio of larger companies. Another factor along these lines is the size of credit operations. If banks want to serve small and medium companies, they must reduce the size of their loans: they must divide the fixed costs of collecting information and analyzing clients among numerous smaller operations. This makes it less profitable for banks to extend credit to smaller companies.

The result is often a chronic lack of access to working capital and investment funding for SMEs. Small entrepreneurs must face this hurdle, which tends to discourage entrepreneurial activity. In addition, they often face other handicaps, including disadvantages in accessing inputs, delays in receiving payment from providers of inputs and buyers of final products, lower technological development, and more time spent dealing with the bureaucracy to obtain permits and licenses. To top it off, their managerial capacities are often limited.

The Social Origins of the Entrepreneur and the Middle Class

Business and economic historians have highlighted the middle-class origins of the entrepreneur in the historical context of nineteenth-century capitalism in England. The emerging middle class or "bourgeoisie" was seen as different from the landed aristocracy who lived off the rent on land holdings. The new entrepreneurial class was interested in making profits in industrial production organized around the capitalist factory, using wage laborers rather than craftsmen (as before the Industrial Revolution). The social origin of the entrepreneur in nascent capitalism came more from the middle class than from the aristocracy or landed elite.

The tradition of tracing the social class origin of the entrepreneur has been largely lost in economic analysis.[7] Nonetheless, interest seems to be growing in reappraising the social background of entrepreneurs, using broader definitions of the middle and lower classes in the context of developing countries and emerging economies, including the Latin American region.

In Latin America, "necessity entrepreneurship" is widespread. People who cannot find a job as an employee or worker in the formal sector of the economy choose to engage in independent "entrepreneurial" activities as a strategy of economic survival rather than as a rational choice among alternative occupations. These people often come from the lower segments of the middle class; many others are poor. They often operate in a context of informality. This issue is discussed further later in this and the next chapter.

With regard to social class, entrepreneurs may come from the economic elites, from the middle class, and from the lower class and the poor. This underscores the heterogeneity in their scale of operations, family background, education levels, wealth, values, and attitudes. A critical question is the extent to which class background affects the decision—or the necessity—to become an entrepreneur. In turn, defining a social class is not an easy matter. Karl Marx, for example, defined social classes in terms of the relation of people to the "modes of production," a concept that entailed social relations, technology, and patterns of ownership of the means of production (feudalism, capitalism, and socialism are all economic systems and modes of production).[8]

Max Weber, writing in early twentieth century, shared Marx's notion that social classes were important and determined largely by their role in production and the ownership of productive assets. However, Weber created a more complex concept of social class, in which prestige, status, occupation, and mobility played an important role. For Weber, social class was the main determinant of individuals' "life chances": their capacity to enjoy a good, secure, prestigious, and enjoyable lifestyle or, in contrast, a life of hardship, insecurity, and anonymity.

Modern analysis of stratification and social class (see Gilbert 2008) is eclectic and uses the insights of Marx, Weber, and others. Stratification and class analysis tends to use a multivariable approach in which income, occupation, education level, status and prestige, values, worldview, and lifestyle are used to define social classes.

The Middle Class: The Economic Perspective

For a long time, economists had forgotten and even dismissed class analysis. However, the last decade witnessed a resurgence of interest in the subject and renewed vitality in analysis of the middle class. The Massachusetts Institute of Technology (MIT) economist Lester Thurow, in the mid-1970s, did somewhat pioneering work on the middle class in the context of the U.S. economy. At that time, the U.S. economy was hit by a combination of higher inflation and supply shocks (stagflation) that squeezed the prospects of a rising middle class accustomed to steady prosperity in the three decades following the end of World War II. Thurow stressed the importance for capitalism and democracy of having a strong middle class. He cautioned that the rise of lower-paying jobs in the United States was a sign of economic polarization and that the eventual shrinking of the middle class would have adverse consequences for social cohesion. These trends were reinforced in subsequent decades by higher inequality, stagnant median wages, and middle-class indebtedness. Thurow used an income metric and defined middle class as persons between 75 and 125 percent of median income.

In the early 2000s, Thurow's arguments were taken up in the context of international development by Birdsall, Graham, and Pettinato (2000) and by Easterly (2001). Later in the decade, Solimano (2009), using a sample of 130 countries, looked at cross-country correlations between the relative size of the middle class and variables such as income per capita, inequality (measured by the Gini coefficient), size of the state, share of SMEs, and an index of democracy.[9]

Easterly (2001), basing his conclusions on panel regressions, argues for a "middle class consensus" showing that a higher share of income for the middle class (and lower ethnic polarization) are empirically associated with higher income, higher growth, more education, and other favorable development outcomes. According to Easterly, countries with a middle-class consensus are "fortunate societies" because they have "higher levels of human and infrastructure capital accumulation" (Easterly 2001, 24). Such countries also "have a higher level of income and growth.... And because they have more human capital and infrastructure accumulation, they have better national economic policies, more democracy, less political instability, more 'modern' sector structure, and more urbanization" (Easterly 2001, 29).

A caveat here is the need not to jump from correlation to causality. While it is a well-established empirical fact that advanced economies with higher per capita incomes and good levels of social cohesion also have a large middle class, it does not necessarily follow that the middle class *causes* these positive outcomes (see Solimano 2009).

Entrepreneurial and Other Roles of the Middle Class in the Development Process

The new interest in the middle class is closely linked to the contribution that the middle class can make to the development process, public policy, and the stability of democracy. At least three roles of the middle class are evident. The first highlights entrepreneurial capacities.

The Middle Class as a Source of Various Types of Entrepreneurs (Supply Side)

As mentioned, the identification of the middle class as a source of entrepreneurial activities has an historical root. Before the Industrial Revolution in England, the dominant landed aristocracy was considered as a low-saving, low-investing segment of the population who preferred leisure to hard work, risk taking, and entrepreneurship (see the summary of these views in Doepke and Zilibotti 2008).

A somewhat similar theme, in the American context of the late nineteenth century, was developed by Thorsten Veblen in *The Theory of the Leisure Class* (1899). Veblen stressed the propensity of economic elites to prefer conspicuous consumption and leisure over hard work and savings. In that sense, the leisure class was *not* an entrepreneurial class. Max Weber ([1905] 2001) noted the influence of an emerging capitalist class influenced by a Protestant ethic more oriented to saving (a lower time preference), hard work, and a willingness to take risks. This new entrepreneurial middle class, in his view, tolerated delayed gratification in order to save and accumulate capital, earn profits, and ascend in the social hierarchy. This new set of values—the "spirit of capitalism"—would be embedded in the patterns of behavior of this new bourgeoisie. In modern times, with developed capital markets and available credit, in principle, entrepreneurs would not need to be strong savers to finance their productive ventures with their own resources. However, the presumed efficiency of modern capital markets to offer credit to all who need it must be qualified. Small and medium entrepreneurs often face much tighter credit constraints than large firms and well-connected, large-scale entrepreneurs. The rise of the venture capital industry has somewhat filled this gap for start-ups, a niche that commercial banks are reluctant to enter.[10]

The identification of the middle class with (idealized?) entrepreneurial values of thriftiness, hard work, and delayed gratification must be qualified,[11] as the "middle class" is a heterogeneous segment of the population that includes individuals with different values *within* the same class. For example, the middle class contains several occupational categories, such as entrepreneurs, self-employed, and employees. Members of each category have different attitudes and preferences toward risk.[12] In addition, within the entrepreneurial segment of the middle class, two kinds of entrepreneurs coexist: "opportunity entrepreneurs" and "necessity entrepreneurs."

An empirical study of 13 low- to middle-income countries provides evidence of the pervasiveness of necessity entrepreneurs in the developing world (Banerjee and Duflo 2008). The typical middle-class entrepreneur in the sample has one employee (at most three employees, in some cases). Their stores, or "firms," have minimal productive assets such as machines and equipment. Their business activities occur at very low levels of technological intensity. In interpreting these findings, it should be noted that the sample is dominated by low-income countries with large informal sectors. Moreover, the definition of middle-class individuals, which is in the low range (those earning between $2 and $10 a day), is highly likely to include people in poverty and therefore captures mostly necessity entrepreneurs.

The Middle Class as a Source of Consumer Power (Demand Side)

The argument here is that a strong middle class with growing purchasing power can be a source of steady increases in aggregate demand for goods and services of companies and also help the country to avoid recessionary trends and keep the economy at or near full capacity (Solimano and Gutierrez 2008). The marginal propensity of the middle class to consume may be higher than the propensity of the rich (although lower than that of the poor). Moreover, the middle class can be an important source of demand for education, health services, housing, durable goods, entertainment, and other goods and services.[13]

The notion of the middle class as an economically robust and solid social segment must be qualified, however. Middle-class people and families often rely on debt to finance the acquisition of housing, durables goods, university education, and so on; therefore, middle-class expenditure is vulnerable to real and financial shocks that may force middle-class consumers to cut consumption in the wake of adverse shocks. Typically, middle-class families depend on jobs as their main source of income. A recession or a financial crisis is bound to affect them significantly.

The Middle Class as a Stabilizing Segment in Society (Political Economy Argument)

The argument here is that a large and consolidated middle class brings a moderate political center and that this reinforces economic and political stability. In contrast, unequal societies that are economically polarized with strong elites, a weak and frustrated middle class, and a disenfranchised group of poor people may be attracted by authoritarianism and populism, which are inimical trends for a stable democracy. High inequality tends to be correlated with social conflict, authoritarian cycles, populism, and recurrent economic crises in Latin America (see Smith 2005; Solimano 2006). Easterly (2001) shows that, for a large sample of developing countries, a higher share of income going to the middle class (along with lower ethnic polarization) is empirically associated with higher income, higher growth, more education, and other favorable outcomes.

Econometric evidence may not be enough to settle the issue, however. The behavior of the middle class during political crises in Latin America and Europe in the first half of the twentieth century suggests a more nuanced relation between the middle class and democracy. Authoritarian experiences in Latin America, such as the military coups of the 1960s, 1970s, and 1980s, do not render convincing support for the hypothesis that the middle class is always and everywhere a staunch guardian of democracy. The authoritarian regimes that governed Argentina, Brazil, Chile, and Uruguay at different times in those decades had different degrees of support from the middle classes, apparently pleased that military rule was "restoring order" in societies affected by mass movements pushing to redistribute economic and political power from the elites. Further back in history, the regimes of Mussolini in Italy and Hitler in Germany in the 1920s and 1930s were popular among wide circles of the Italian and German middle classes frightened by the economic insecurity, unemployment, and rise of left-wing political movements that affected Italy and the Weimer Republic after the Great War.[14]

Alternative Definitions of the Middle Class

Researchers have used a range of definitions and measurements in discussions about what constitutes a middle class in any one country, whether in advanced capitalist economies or in the developing world. The literature concurs that defining and measuring a "middle class" are tasks subject to caveats and ambiguities. Economists tend to prefer an income-based (or consumption-based) definition of the middle class. Sociologists also use definitions of occupations and asset ownership, values, attitudes toward risk, and aspirations to achieve upward social mobility or conformity to a certain status quo.[15]

Definitions Based on Income and Consumption

Relative definitions—based on the middle range of national income distributions—make the lower and upper boundaries country specific (that is, they associate the middle class with median income). Thurow (1987) defines middle class as the group with incomes lying between 75 and 125 percent of the median income, as do Birdsall, Graham, and Pettinato (2000) for developing countries. Davies and Huston (1992) use the 50–150 percent thresholds, as do Castellani and Parent (2011) and OECD (2011). Easterly (2001) defines the middle class as those households in the second, third, and fourth quintiles (twentieth to eightieth deciles). Solimano (2009) adopts a definition of the middle class encompassing the third to ninth deciles, distinguishing between a lower-middle class (third to sixth deciles) and an upper-middle class (seventh to ninth deciles).[16]

   Absolute definitions of middle class assume fixed (that is, absolute) income ranges adjusted for purchasing power parity (PPP)—that is, correcting for differences in purchasing power across countries. Among absolute measures, Milanovic and Yitzhaki (2002) take average incomes of Brazil and Italy as the respective floor and ceiling. This translates into roughly $12–$50 per person a day (PPP in 2000 dollars). Banerjee and Duflo (2008) apply the concept to several developing countries and use consumption ranges between $2 and $10 a day (roughly between $800 and $3,600 a year). Ravallion (2009) adopts income ranges of between $2 and $13 a day at 2005 PPP prices, as $2 a day is a commonly accepted definition of the poverty line in developing countries; people above this line are "middle class" in the sense that they have moved out of poverty. Kharas and Gertz (2010) focus on expenditure in the range of $10–$100 a day, as do Cardenas, Kharas, and Henao (2011). Birdsall (2010) uses a mixed definition of income from $10 a day up to the ninetieth percentile. More recently, Ferreira et al. (2013) propose daily income between $10 and $50 (PPP in 2005 dollars), following López-Calva and Ortíz-Juárez (2011). Birdsall (2013) also uses this definition.

Beyond actual income or expenditure, there are *subjective definitions* of the middle class. In a subjective definition, people are asked for their perceived position on a wealth scale (ranging from 1 to 10). Respondents are then classified into three subjective social classes: poor, middle class, and rich, using the relative size of the objective classes as a reference (Lora and Fajardo forthcoming). Empirical estimates of the middle class in Latin America (16 countries) using objective and subjective definitions and the 2007 World Gallup Survey produce a variety of values.[17]

As one might expect, the size of the middle class varies according to the definition (relative or absolute) employed. In the case of Latin America, literature provides estimates for countries as well as for the entire region. Cardenas, Kharas, and Henao (2011) estimate the Latin American middle class at 36 percent (daily expenditures between $10 and $100 per person in PPP terms). Castellani and Parent (2011), using national household data, find that the Latin American middle class ranges between 35 and 50 percent, when employing a definition of 50–150 percent of median income, and between 55 and 75 percent, when employing a definition of $2–$20 PPP per day.[18] Lora and Fajardo (forthcoming), using the 2007 Gallup World Poll and the definition of 50–150 percent of median income, find that the size ranges between 40 and 60 percent of the population (between $2–$10 PPP a day and $2–$13 PPP a day). In the countries studied by Birdsall (2013), the middle class accounts for 15 to 35 percent of the population ($10 to $100 a person in PPP terms). According to Ferreira et al. (2013), using household surveys and the $10–$50 PPP a day definition, the size of the middle class in Latin America and the Caribbean reached 152 million or 30 percent of the continent's population.

Definitions Based on Occupation and Source of Income

One body of literature—exemplified by Dennis Gilbert, a sociologist widely regarded as the expert on class structure in the United States—associates classes with job positions (occupations) in the economic system and sources of income (income-bearing property, job earnings, and government transfers). In *The American Class Structure in an Age of Growing Inequality*, Gilbert (2008) defines middle class as the "majority" class. His taxonomy of the six social classes is as follows: (a) a *capitalist class,* in which people obtain their income from profits and the return on productive and financial assets; (b) an *upper-middle class* of college-trained professionals and managers; (c) a *middle class,* whose members have significant skills and perform varied tasks, under loose supervision (lower managers, semiprofessionals, nonretail sales workers, craftsmen); (d) a *working class,* consisting of less skilled workers than the middle class who work at routinized and supervised manual and clerical jobs; (e) a *poor working class* of people employed at low-skill jobs, often at marginal firms (laborers, service workers, and low-paid operatives); and (f) an *underclass* of unemployed and part-time workers who depend on government transfers. Gilbert then aggregates these six classes into a three-class scheme: (a) a *privileged class* (composed of capitalists and the upper-middle class), (b) a *majority class* (composed of the middle and working class), and (c) a *lower class* (formed by the working poor and the underclass).[19]

The three-class classification of Gilbert is not very different from the rich, middle class, and poor classification often used in income- and consumption-based definitions of social classes. Gilbert's majority class comprises 60 percent of the population. Gilbert's approach puts more emphasis on the *qualitative characteristics of jobs* and *sources of income* than on total incomes.

The Values of the Middle Class and the Values of the Entrepreneur

A social class is not just a statistical abstraction concocted by economists or sociologists. In the real world, its members hold certain values, attitudes, and aspirations and play a certain political and economic role in society.

The popular notion of "middle-class values" points to a social segment that attaches great importance to economic and political stability, safety, a solid job, moderate political views, and a capacity to progress economically, educate their children, and own a house. The values of the entrepreneur are subject to some dispute. Max Weber stressed a capacity for delayed gratification, thriftiness, and hard work, connected to the Protestant ethic. Schumpeter emphasized the resilience of the entrepreneur and his or her innovative capacities. Keynes viewed the investor (entrepreneur) as dealing chiefly with the intricacies of uncertainty and having features of a "gambler." Business schools nowadays stress various features, such as resilience, innovative capacity, and vision. Implicitly, they draw their views of the entrepreneur from a thinker on the subject rather than from practice-based knowledge. Empirical evidence reviewed in the next section provides new insights on the subject.

Various theories have been formulated about the origin of values and culture and their causal relations with the economic system. Neoclassical economics considers values, tastes, and culture as exogenous variables that are generally constant or, at best, change very slowly over time. Max Weber ([1905] 2001) highlighted the importance of religion, especially the Protestant work ethic, which rewards saving, working, and accumulating wealth and so facilitates the spread of capitalism. Capitalism needs a value structure that will support capital accumulation, technological change, and accelerated social mobility. These values are different from those prevailing in the feudal order based on the divine origin of authority and tradition. In Max Weber's view, the implicit causality goes from values (affected by religious preferences) to the economic system. However, this is not the only line of causation. Mutual interaction is also possible between values and culture and the material base of society.

Karl Marx ([1848] 1979)—in his effort to contest Hegelian idealistic philosophy that prevailed in the early to middle nineteenth century—stressed the role of the economic structure, modes of production, and the concomitant supportive social relations in shaping ideas, beliefs, values, and ideology in society.[20] Thus Marx postulated a different line of causality (although his analysis did not mention this term) than Max Weber.[21]

The Italian theorist and political activist Antonio Gramsci developed the concept of "cultural hegemony" (see Forgacs 1988). This concept refers to the prevalence and acceptance in the population of the beliefs, values, and ideas of the dominant social classes. Once these values and perceptions are shared by the population at-large (various social classes), they become "common sense" for society. In turn, this common sense helps to maintain the legitimacy of the economic and social system. Ideas and culture could be even more important for maintaining and cementing social orders than traditional forms of political power based on coercion. A variant of this thesis was developed by the MIT professor and father of modern linguistics Noam Chomsky, who coined the concept of the "manufacturing of consent" as the action of the media and education to legitimize certain values (chief among them the profit motive) in a capitalist society. According to Chomsky, mass media are effective and powerful ideological institutions that carry out a system-supportive propaganda function by relying on market forces, internalized assumptions, and self-censorship, without overt coercion (Chomsky and Herman 1988, 306).

An important question in the literature on culture, values, and social structures is the extent to which they are *class dependent*. If values are "class dependent," the values of the middle class may not necessarily coincide with the values of the rich or the values of the poor.[22] An additional question concerns the extent to which the values of the middle class overlap with the values of the entrepreneur. Of course, one first needs to know what the values of these two segments are. Weber's cultural story of the "spirit of capitalism" is, certainly, class dependent: the old elite (landed aristocracy and the "old rich") had different values from the new middle class regarding delayed gratification, leisure, the work ethic, and thrift.

Another possibility, in line with theories of cultural hegemony, is that the values of the "dominant social class"[23] become shared values in the rest of society through the construction of a *common sense* shared by wide segments of society. The concept of "cultural homogeneity" (along the lines of Gramsci) would be equivalent to the hypothesis that the middle class (or the poor) lack particularism in values, a recent idea advanced in the literature.

Empirical Verification

Recently, several attempts have been made to use large international panel data sets to assess the values of the middle class and test their degree of particularism (or the lack of it).[24] These studies use, respectively, the World Values Survey (around 80 countries and several years) and Ecosocial, a value survey applied to seven Latin American countries. The results obtained in these studies are based on (subjective) survey responses. People are classified into different social strata or classes according to various criteria such as (subjective) self-perception and (objective) income and expenditure measures. These studies look at the type of values held by middle-class individuals and the degree to which these values are shared (or not) by the rich and the poor. If the values of the middle class differ from the values of the rich and poor, then one can talk about "middle-class particularism." The World Value Survey identifies "values" that are correlated with variables such as economic growth and accountability and includes questions about market competition, gender equality, upward mobility, trust in others, trust in institutions, social tolerance, nationalism, political activism, and adaptation of technology.

An Asian Development Bank study by Amoranto, Chun, and Deolalikar (2010) shows significant regional variations in values. In addition, respondents from member-countries of the Organisation of Economic Co-operation and Development (OECD) are found to be more liberal in some values than respondents from developing countries. In addition, this study shows that the middle class has a higher degree of political activism than the rich or the poor.

A Center for Global Development study by López-Calva, Rigolini, and Torche (2012) finds no support for the hypothesis of "middle-class particularism"—that is, no statistically systematic differences are detected in values between the middle class and the upper and lower classes. Middle-class values seem to be dictated by moderation and lie between those of the poor and the rich. López-Calva, Rigolini, and Torche (2012) also find evidence of large cross-country and regional differences in responses about values, in line with the findings of Amoranto, Chun, and Deolalikar (2010). This may reflect underlying cultural attitudes that may have a strong country, historical, and religious bias. Their paper also shows that income is a reasonably good predictor of social and political orientation.

This new empirical work on class and values advances a complex and difficult topic, but the results should be taken as tentative and suggestive, not definitive. What are considered as "values" in these studies could also reflect "opinions" of individuals. These opinions on different topics tend to have more short-term variation than values that are more "structural" and change only slowly over time. In addition, the presence of mutual causation between social class and values should not be ruled out.

Growth, Inequality, and the Middle Class

Recent economic literature has highlighted the positive effects of economic growth on the formation of an ample middle class. The rise of a new middle class in China and India, as well as in Latin America and even Sub-Saharan Africa—areas that have experienced respectable growth in recent years (or decades)—is shown as evidence of the positive effect of growth on the middle class, as growth pulls people out of poverty. However, economic growth is not all that is needed to have a strong and well-consolidated middle class. The level of inequality also matters. In an empirical cross-section study of 130 countries, Solimano (2009) shows a strong negative association between the (income) Gini coefficient and the relative size of the middle class. The effect of economic growth on expanding the size of the middle class could be at least partly offset by inequality. The rise of inequality in China and India conspires against a stable middle class.

A statistically growing middle class—measured by income or expenditure—does not imply, per se, that the middle class has significant influence on the process of policy making in society or that it is finan-cially sound enough to deal with a variety of contingencies such as health, financial, and employment shocks and natural disasters (López-Calva and Ortíz-Juárez 2011).

A broader concept is that of *empowerment*. This concept refers to the capacity of individuals to exercise their economic, social, and political rights, have voice and vote in the democratic process, and exert a reason-able degree of influence in the public policy process. A growing middle class composed of individuals who exert consumer power is not necessar-ily equivalent to a middle class composed of individuals who assert their citizenship and hold authorities accountable.

The Effects of Vulnerability on the Middle Class

A framework for identifying and measuring potential sources of vulnerability and fragility of the middle class (and other social classes) has been prepared at Yale University (supported by the Rockefeller Foundation).[25] The Economic Security Index (ESI) focuses on three dimensions: (a) the *labor market* (loss of employment and fall in wages); (b) *financial markets* (over-indebtedness and the tightening of credit); and (c) *health shocks* such as catastrophic illnesses, injuries, disabilities, and death. The index seeks to ascertain the impact on individuals and households of a variety of unsettling events, such as recessions, unemployment, tight credit, high debt, and low financial protection for dealing with adverse health contingencies.

Economic insecurity affects all social classes, but its impact is higher on the poor and the middle class than on the upper class, since these two large segments of the population are less protected from adverse shocks. The ESI shows that, in the last quarter of century, the degree of overall economic insecurity (across all social classes) has increased in the United States. Moreover, the Great Recession of 2008–09 further exacerbated it.[26] As discussed, "the squeeze on the middle class" was already ongoing in the 1980s, 1990s, and 2000s. Moreover, the fall in private household savings since the 1990s and the rise of household debt are evidence of financial vulnerability of the middle class.

In a recent empirical analysis of the vulnerability of the middle class in Latin America, López-Calva and Ortiz-Juárez (2011) focus on Chile, Mexico, and Peru. The study identifies a relative threshold of 60 percent of the income distribution and proposes defining the middle class as persons having $10 to $50 PPP a day in 2005 dollars. This is a much more reasonable threshold for defining the middle class than those offered in other studies, which are not suitable for studying the behavior of this segment in upper-middle-income countries (low thresholds tend to include many households living in poverty). The study also makes the relevant point that not all people who are *above* the poverty line are middle class. Those in the vicinity of the poverty line are very vulnerable to fall into poverty and should not be considered as middle class, according to this study. The authors document an increase in the absolute number of households in the middle class between 1992 and 2000 in Chile, Mexico, and Peru and show a lower probability of falling into poverty in the late 2000s compared to the late 1990s.[27]

Social Mobility

Social mobility indicates the efficiency of the economic system to reward individuals who work hard and succeed in their productive or intellectual endeavors. In addition, social mobility is relevant for income distribution and for social integration. Milton Friedman, a strong believer in the capacity of competitive capitalism to reward ingenuity and effort properly, distinguished between temporary, short-run differences in incomes and long-run differences in income status in his famous book *Capitalism and Freedom* (Friedman 1962, 170–71). He compared a "dynamic society," in which individuals and families move up (and down) the income ladder, with a "static society," with great rigidities and lower mobility. The dynamic society with high social mobility would be less socially unequal in a longer-term sense. Free-enterprise capitalism would be such a dynamic society, according to Friedman.

Entrepreneurship is an important component of capitalism. Successful entrepreneurship can foster upward social mobility, which takes place when the entrepreneur succeeds and makes good, sustained profits. Conversely, this mobility can be downward if the entrepreneur fails and descends into debt or goes bankrupt.

However, entrepreneurship is only one mechanism for social mobility. In general, an individual can choose from among four such mechanisms: entrepreneurship, work as an employee, education, and independent activities and self-employment.

The choice between these vehicles of mobility depends on several considerations. Some of them are discussed in this chapter and the next one (see also box 2.2). These choices are not necessarily substitutes for one another: they may well be sequential. Education is often a prerequisite for broader occupational choices, including entrepreneurship. The empirical evidence suggests that people often choose first to be employees and, after acquiring enough experience and knowledge, decide to become entrepreneurs or to be independently self-employed. However, this is not always the case.

Box 2.2 Entrepreneurship and Social Mobility: Empirical Possibilities

Most of the country studies used in this project analyze both short-term (intragenerational) mobility and medium- to long-term (intergenerational) mobility. For that purpose, they use at least one of the following empirical methods to gauge mobility.

Taking a *time-dependence approach*, econometric studies of mobility make a distinction between *unconditional* and *conditional* mobility (or convergence). Typically in a simple regression framework of unconditional convergence in which current income, $y(t)$, is regressed against lagged income, $y(t-1)$, and a random term, the coefficient of lagged income lies in the interval $[0-1]$. In the case of full income convergence, say, $y(t) = y(t-1)$ (lack of social mobility), the coefficient of $y(t-1)$ would be equal to 1. A coefficient of 0 would mean a lack of persistence in incomes

(continued next page)

Box 2.2 Entrepreneurship and Social Mobility:
Empirical Possibilities (*continued*)

and thus a high degree of income mobility: past incomes would have no
effect in predicting current incomes. Conditional convergence adds to the
regression a set of determinants of current income (age, human capital,
asset ownership, productivity, and so on). So income convergence is conditional on the variables determining income.

Positional mobility analyzes the degree to which an individual's position in the income distribution in the past determines his or her position in the present; this is a natural complement to an analysis of time
dependence. In this approach, *origin-destination transition matrixes* typically are constructed (estimated) to analyze the transition between social
classes or income levels across individuals.

In the absence of such longitudinal studies, which is the case in the
Latin American region, two empirical methodologies can be used to
assess mobility.

The *pseudo-panel approach*, originally developed in Deaton (1985),
applies the convergence methodology by constructing pseudo-panels
using a series of repeated cross-sections. A pseudo-panel, an indirect
method (when longitudinal data are not available), yields synthetic observations obtained from averaging the observations of groups of individuals
(usually called cohorts) with similar time-invariant characteristics in a
sequence of repeated cross-sectional data sets.

The *Social Mobility Index (SMI) approach,* initially developed by Behrman, Birdsall, and Székely (1999), provides a way of measuring social
mobility in the absence of data following the same individuals through
time. Surveys using the SMI approach ask respondents to self-assess the
wealth and income of their parents as an indirect or subjective measure of
the intergenerational transmission of educational attainment. For a family
with children, the SMI calculates an indicator of future opportunities for
them. The basic notion in this methodology is that if family background
(parents' education and income) is important in determining opportunities for children, then social differences tend to be perpetuated over time.
Then social mobility can be enhanced, and the education system can function as an equalizing device allowing for greater social mobility.

Super-star entrepreneurs such as Bill Gates (Microsoft), Sergei Brin and
Larry Page (Google), Steve Jobs (Apple), and Mark Zuckerberg (Facebook)
all decided at some point to suspend or abandon their studies and turn to
entrepreneurial endeavors, with great success. Of course, many dropouts
from college do not succeed. Many studies of entrepreneurship and its
merits suffer from some degree of selection bias, as they do not include the
stories of failure.

Analyses of social mobility make a further distinction between short-term mobility and long-term mobility. A related distinction is between intragenerational and intergenerational mobility.

Intergenerational mobility refers to the correlation in economic and financial outcomes between parents and children.[28] It is an important measure of the degree of equality of opportunity (or lack of it). A society with a high degree of intergenerational mobility is one in which the correlation between the economic fortunes of parents and children is low. Conversely, intergenerational mobility is low when that correlation is high. This correlation refers to economic and financial considerations. Inherited genetic attributes, the transmission of values, and socialization are all important factors in society, and families play a critical role in them.

Variables identified to measure intergenerational mobility are the level of occupation, income, or wealth of the son compared to the occupation, income, or wealth of the father.[29] In general, transition matrixes (of income, occupation, or education) tend to show that the father's occupation (income and wealth) is a good predictor of the son's occupation (income and wealth), but this prediction often has a range of variation. There can be upward mobility (sons doing better than fathers), downward mobility (sons doing worse than fathers), or no mobility.

A mobile society is one in which the tendency is toward upward mobility over time. Empirically, this is not simple to measure unless longitudinal data on various measures of economic performance are available for the same individuals and cohorts over time.[30] Some studies have found a greater influence of parental economic conditions on children's outcomes in the United States and the United Kingdom (two industrial countries with relatively higher income Ginis) than in the more egalitarian Sweden (see Torche 2009).

The degree of intergenerational mobility in the Latin American countries varies from country to country. For Chile, the evidence shows increased intergenerational mobility in the middle and lower classes, but closed patterns of mobility in the top decile (Torche 2009). This is consistent with a high concentration of income and wealth at the top, but a more even distribution of income for the bottom 90 percentiles. Studies for Brazil find that family background plays an important role in explaining overall earnings inequality (Bourguignon, Ferreira, and Menendez 2007). In Mexico, a changing occupational structure has led to greater opportunities for social mobility in the last four decades or so, but family background continues to play an important role in the economic possibilities of children. In general, the evidence for Latin America, drawn mainly from cross-sectional surveys, including retrospective information about social origins and economic characteristics of parents, points in the direction of strong mechanisms of transmission of inequality of wealth and status across generations, but not necessarily reproduction of poverty (see Torche 2009).

The transition from an agrarian to an industrial society reduced the relative importance of low-wage jobs in agriculture and increased the share of higher-paid jobs in the industrial sector. This led to social mobility from rural to urban areas, leading to improved productivity and higher earnings. However, this mobility also entailed some costs and dislocations (stress, less time devoted to family life, and hardship associated with urban life in crowded cities). Social mobility is not always equivalent to improved welfare.

The industrial society gave way to a post-industrial society, also called the "knowledge economy," the "service economy," or simply the "new economy." This transition entailed profound changes in the occupation structure (decline in the share of manufacturing jobs and increase in the share of service and tertiary occupations).[31] It also affected the nature of the middle class and the patterns of entrepreneurship (both opportunity and necessity entrepreneurship) and created new dynamics of upward and downward social mobility. The financial sector, technological entrepreneurs, and big corporations are the big winners in the new economy. A new middle- and upper-middle class has been created around these sectors, as technological entrepreneurs come from the middle class and a plethora of managers, professionals, and financial and technological experts linked to the newly dynamic industries has developed.

The knowledge economy puts a premium on individuals with high education levels, special skills, and marketable knowledge. Still, many jobs in the new economy are far from the glamorous high-prestige jobs of well-paid lawyers, financial experts, engineers, technical experts, and others. In contrast, many new jobs are in the services sector, such as retail trade, food services, cleaning, and so on, with relatively modest remuneration.

There seems to be a tendency toward internal differentiation in the middle class. Successful opportunity entrepreneurs, professionals, experts, and managers have tended to move up in the income, occupation, and wealth ladders. For them, social mobility works, and they become the upper strata of the middle class (or the lower strata of the wealthy class). Mid-level managers, office workers, clerical workers, and salespersons are also members of the middle class, but their economic fortunes are considerably lower.

A relevant question concerns the extent to which choosing to be an entrepreneur improves the chances for upward social mobility compared with choosing to be an employee. The distribution of payoffs for an entrepreneur may have a larger mean, but also greater variance. In contrast, the mean income (salary) of the employee may be lower, but the variance is also lower. For necessity entrepreneurs, mean income is very similar to the salary of a worker with comparable educational background and skills, but the variability of incomes tends to be higher.

The best strategy to improve the prospects of upward social mobility will depend on an individual's preferences for risk as well as the market for those careers he or she faces, in addition to good luck and other random factors. If an individual enters a big corporation (but not necessarily an SME), stays there for a sufficient time, and performs well, his or her chances of upward mobility within the firm may be higher than if he or she chooses a more volatile occupation path involving entrepreneurial activities.

Recent evidence from several Latin American countries reveals that, while only a very small proportion of the population can be regarded as entrepreneurs, entrepreneurship is a vehicle for increased social mobility. Hernani-Limarino, Eid, and Villarroel (2012), using various approaches such as estimating the parameters of time-dependence equations, positional transition matrixes, and steady-state class distributions as equalizers of long-run incomes, find that the degree of social mobility depends on the type of entrepreneurs. For them, opportunity entrepreneurs (defined as those who use hired labor in production) experience higher mobility than both self-employed workers and paid employees (formal and informal).[32] In addition, they find that employers are significantly more likely to move upward in both labor and overall income distributions and much more likely to end up in the upper-income class relative to other types of self-employed workers and even relative to paid employees.[33]

According to Mejía and Meléndez (forthcoming),[34] entrepreneurship in Colombia is scarce and socially segmented: it is more frequent in the upper class than in the middle or lower classes. In turn, middle-class entrepreneurs are, on average, better off than middle-class employees with similar characteristics. Nevertheless, there are significant differences between middle-class and upper-class entrepreneurs regarding schooling attainment, the size of the businesses they run, and their outcomes. While entrepreneurs appear to have more intergenerational income mobility (lower income persistence) than the average worker, the study fails to find "middle-class particularism" in entrepreneurship. In other words, the mobility of middle-class entrepreneurs is not systematically higher than the mobility of lower- and upper-class entrepreneurs. Therefore, social mobility in Colombia seems to be associated with entrepreneurship in general, irrespective of the social origin of the entrepreneur.

Gandelman and Robano (forthcoming) point to the decline in intergenerational social mobility between 1982 and 2010 as a proximate cause of increased social segmentation and inequality in Uruguay. Looking at intergenerational mobility measured as the relationship between the parents' schooling and income and the children's schooling, they find a strong persistence in the education levels of different generations reducing the degree of social mobility, particularly for disadvantaged individuals in society. Family background variables play a small role in determining schooling outcomes for families of entrepreneurs and for middle-income families. According to Gandelman and Robano, the public school system in Uruguay successfully provides primary education for everybody and, to a lesser extent, the first years of secondary school. Nevertheless, there are important differences in the quality of education for children of opportunity entrepreneurs and the middle class. Finally, the study argues that entrepreneurship is indeed a channel for higher intergenerational social mobility.[35]

Conclusion

This review of issues and the literature highlights the importance but also the complexity of entrepreneurship, the middle class, and social mobility. Entrepreneurship is an intricate topic. Heterogeneity of entrepreneurs is extensive, and competing theories about the nature and motivations of the entrepreneur are difficult to reconcile. The historical record, casual evidence, and empirical research indicate that the middle class has been a source of entrepreneurship (of various kinds) in the nascent capitalism of the eighteenth and nineteenth centuries and in the last wave of technological entrepreneurship of the late twentieth and early twenty-first century. The nature of entrepreneurship has varied through time and space, and its determinants involve a complex interaction of family background, quest for independence, education, desire to accumulate wealth, need for economic survival, ingenuity, and risk-taking capacities. Heterogeneity is evident when comparing entrepreneurship in developing countries, which is dominated largely by necessity entrepreneurs, with entrepreneurship in advanced economies, which is dominated by technological entrepreneurs of middle-class background. In Latin America, opportunity entrepreneurs can play a valuable role in promoting growth and creating employment. Still, necessity entrepreneurship in the developing world is largely a mechanism that enables lower-middle-class households and the poor to cope with informality, scarce jobs in middle- and lower-end occupations, and public sector regulations and taxation.

The international mobility of entrepreneurs is a growing trend that has the potential to increase the presence of developing countries in the technological sector and to transfer contacts, market information, skills, and knowledge. This is an emerging subject, although one that is, comparatively, little studied so far.

In the case of Latin America, recent studies show that a very small proportion of the population can be regarded as entrepreneurs, taking into account different definitions. Entrepreneurs generally represent less than 10 percent of the economically active population, ranging from 3.5 percent in Colombia (Mejía and Meléndez forthcoming) to 5 percent in Uruguay (Gandelman and Robano forthcoming) and 8 percent in Argentina (chapter 5) and Mexico (chapter 4).[36] For Bolivia and Ecuador, entrepreneurial activity is concentrated in microenterprises, and necessity entrepreneurship is often the dominant type of entrepreneurship (Hernani-Limarino, Eid, and Villarroel 2012 and chapter 6 of this volume).

Middle-class entrepreneurs tend to be male and middle-aged and to have completed secondary and often tertiary education. They also tend to come from families in which a parent is or was an entrepreneur, highlighting the importance of role models in this activity. In fact, the occupational choice of the father or mother is more important in the decision to become an entrepreneur than the parents' wealth, income, or education, although these variables tend to be correlated. Middle-class entrepreneurship tends to be dominant, in part because this is the majority class in society. However, as a percentage of each social class, entrepreneurship tends to be higher in the upper class, followed by the middle and lower class. Entrepreneurs concentrate in the segment of microenterprises; productive units with less than five employees predominate. Social mobility is greater for entrepreneurs than for employees and the self-employed, but it is not always upward. Average incomes are also higher for entrepreneurs than for employees and self-employed, but the variance in incomes is greater. Opportunity entrepreneurship tends to be procyclical: it increases in boom periods and falls in recessions, downturns, and crisis situations. The values of the entrepreneur are a topic of some controversy. Positive qualities such as hard work, responsibility, imagination, and tolerance are common to success in any activity, not only in entrepreneurship.

Analysis of the middle class is a complex subject. At an analytical level, the concept and definition of "middle class" is still not a settled issue. Understanding the relationship between the middle class and entrepreneurship requires further research. The middle class is certainly a source of consumer power in a growing economy, but its apparent tendency to rely on debt to finance durable consumption, pay education fees, and acquire housing makes it vulnerable to financial shocks, recessions, unemployment, and health events. The potential contribution of the middle class to the stability of democracy is a theme in the literature on the middle class. Claims of a pro-democracy middle class seem to be broadly supported by recent surveys of values. However, contemporary and historical experiences of Latin America in the 1970s and 1980s and Europe in the 1920s and 1930s show that the middle classes may support authoritarian regimes.

Upward social mobility is a desired feature for economic progress in any dynamic society and is viewed as an antidote to entrenched inequality of social origin and institutional rigidities. However, the mechanisms for middle-class mobility vary widely. Mobility can be achieved in various ways, such as engaging in entrepreneurial activities or choosing to be an employee (the "intrapreneurial" option) or to be self-employed.

The public policy implications of the literature reviewed raise a range of issues, including the potential, but also the limits, to promoting entrepreneurship as a large-scale policy; the perennial theme of how to ease obstacles to and restrictions on the latent entrepreneurial potential of individuals facing constraints in access to credit, education, technology, and markets; and the ability of policies to promote small- and medium-scale entrepreneurship that creates new jobs, enhances social mobility, and generates income in face of the power and influence of big corporations, conglomerates, and economic elites that pressure governments to limit competition, making it difficult for new actors to enter the market.

Notes

1. See Knight's classic book, *Risk, Uncertainty, and Profit* (1921).
2. I thank Jorge Rosenblut for making this point.
3. Some individuals start as entrepreneurs at the beginning of their economically active life, like the new wave of technology entrepreneurs, including Steve Jobs, Bill Gates, and Mark Zuckerberg.
4. See Doepke and Zilibotti (2008) and the references on the cultural transmission of values contained in that work.
5. Determining the degree of persistence in entrepreneurship through different cohorts and generations is an empirical task.
6. Wadhwa et al. (2009) define "middle class" according to the six-class definition of Gilbert (2008).
7. The most influential figures in the analysis of social classes were Karl Marx (1818–83) and Max Weber (1864–1920). However, important contributions to the analysis of society, elites, and classes were also made by Vilfredo Pareto (1848–1923), Gaetano Mosca (1858–1941), and Thorsten Veblen (1857–1929). The "Italian School" (with Vilfredo Pareto and Gaetano Mosca as the main exponents) held a merit-oriented view of elites, their dynamics, and their interactions with other social classes, although it did not specifically link elites with entrepreneurial activity (see Mosca 1939; Pareto [1901] 1991). Veblen, in turn, focused on the business elite and the importance of symbolic (conspicuous) consumption and a culture of leisure for signaling prosperity and abundance in America's Gilded Age.
8. Social classes also develop views of the world or ideologies about their place in society and the economic process. Marx, who wrote in the middle of the nineteenth century at the peak of the Industrial Revolution, stressed two classes: the bourgeoisie (capitalists), who own the means of production and control wealth, shape institutions, and control political power, and proletarians, who own their own labor power and are disenfranchised. In this view, the dynamics of social change and the transformation of society came from class conflict and were viewed as an engine of long-term change. According to Marx, capitalism would lead to increasing polarization and social differentiation. He dismissed the idea of a "permanent middle class" and portrayed the "petit bourgeoisie"—our equivalent of the middle class—as essentially averse to social change due to their interest in protecting their assets and social position in society, even though they are not in the highest echelons of the social hierarchy.
9. The study finds a nonlinear relation between income per capita and size of the middle class and inequality and a strong inverse relation between inequality and size of the middle class. The rest of the variables show a milder relation with the middle class, according to the available data.
10. See the Latin American Private Equity and Venture Capital Association (LAVC) for scores on the availability of capital in Latin America. http://lavca.org/.
11. The implicit theory is that different social classes have distinct values and cultural traits (the class-value specificity hypothesis).
12. Middle-class individuals who are employees tend to prefer a steady and more stable flow of income (salary) than to face potentially more profitable but also more risky income- profit profiles associated with entrepreneurial activities. As a result, middle-class individuals who are employees often work in the public sector as clerical workers, mid-level staff, and executives of ministries and public agencies. A similar logic could be extended to middle-class individuals who are employees of firms and corporations in the private sector.
13. Banerjee and Duflo (2008) find that as the share devoted to food falls and income rises, middle-class people spend more on entertainment, education, health care, and home improvement.

14. See Hobsbawm (2002) and Frieden (2006) for good historical accounts of those periods in Europe.

15. While income-based definitions might enjoy higher analytical rigor than subjective concepts, they are also debatable. Absolute thresholds might be arbitrary when applied to heterogeneous development levels and may fall short of accounting for country-specific features. Conversely, relative definitions might provide less homogeneous boundaries, as they are country tailored.

16. This distinction could be useful for understanding the dynamics of the middle class: the lower-middle class may become poor in the event of an adverse shock, while the upper-middle class may become rich under certain favorable economic conditions.

17. For Latin America, using absolute definitions, between 58 and 66 percent of the population is identified as middle class. Using relative definitions, around 60 percent of the population is middle class. Estimates based on a percentage of the median income yield a middle class of 42 percent. With mixed measures, the size of the middle class drops to 22 percent. It is apparent that the size of the middle class is very sensitive to the empirical definition used.

18. They also consider $2–$10 a day and $2–$13 a day for countries like Peru and Colombia. See Castellani, Parent, and Zenteno (2013).

19. Gilbert (2008) calculates typical annual household income levels for the United States as follows: $2 million for the capitalist class and $150,000 for the upper-middle class (the privileged class, the top 15 percent of the population); $70,000 for the middle class and $40,000 for the working class (the middle 60 percent of the population); $25,000 for the working poor and $15,000 for the underclass (the lower class, the bottom 25 percent of the population).

20. For a philosophically oriented treatment of the issue, see Wolff (2003). For an economist's perspective, see Foley (2006).

21. In his study of capitalism, Marx highlighted the "commoditization" of human work under conditions of wage labor and the creation of a market for labor power in which the typical worker has little or no control whatsoever of the production process—very different from the craft of the skilled artisan under previous, precapitalist economic formations. Karl Marx also emphasized the alienation of work in the factory system (see Hobsbawm 2011).

22. The concept of "rich" has varied over time (from landed aristocracy to new bourgeoisie to leisure class).

23. The concept includes the ruling elites, which are different from the entrepreneurial class.

24. These empirical studies include Amoranto, Chun, and Deolalikan (2010) at the Asian Development Bank and López-Calva, Rigolini, and Torche (2012) at the Center for Global Development.

25. See http://www.economicsecurityindex.org.

26. According to ESI calculations, one in five Americans experienced a decline of more than 25 percent of household income between 2008 and 2010, without having the financial resources to cope with this decline.

27. See also OECD (2011) for a discussion.

28. In the sociological tradition, the degree of social mobility is linked to the productive and occupational structure of the society as well as the educational background, social connections, and social class of the individual.

29. Torche (2009) provides a very useful overview of empirical studies of intergenerational mobility for Latin America and other developing countries.

30. Empirical studies have developed a variety of indexes of social mobility based on rank ordering, time-independence, positional movement, share movement, and nondirectional and directional income movement (see Fields 2010). Most of these measures tend to study social mobility using current (single-year) income as a measure comparing an initial and final year. As Fields (2010) shows, the equalization

of long-term income is a very different concept from the equalization of single-year income. Fields develops a class of axiomatic statistical measures to study equalization (or the lack of it) of long-term income compared to a base year. When these measures are applied to the United States, he finds a tendency to equalization of long-term income for men in the 1970s, but not in the 1980s and 1990s. He observes that tendency in France since the 1960s. A similar interest in studying mobility in connection with long-run income distribution is shared by inequality experts such as Atkinson, Bourguignon, and Morrison (1992) and Shorrocks (1978).

31. In the United States, the transition from an agrarian to an industrial society took place between about 1870 (after the Civil War) and the 1930s. The transition to a post-industrial society started in the 1970s. The 1990s and 2000s were considered high points of the knowledge economy, new economy, or finance-dominated economy.

32. Formal workers are those who contribute to social security.

33. The segment of entrepreneurs (employers) is small in Bolivia (as well as in other countries) as a proportion of the working population. Therefore, their higher potential for social mobility may not trickle down to larger segments of the population, such as independent self-employed workers and paid employees, who constitute the majority of the economically active population.

34. The study uses microeconomic data about individuals and their parents' education collected by household surveys at the national level for 1997, 2003, 2008, and 2010.

35. This finding might be connected with the migration process to Uruguay. There are abundant examples of migrants who were scarcely educated but had tremendous creative drive that helped them to progress, ascend socially, and provide better living conditions for their descendants.

36. In Argentina, the percentage of entrepreneurs in the economically active population increased between 1974 and 1980, from around 10 percent to 13 percent, followed by a decade of relative stability in entrepreneurial activity, ending in an (unexpected) high peak in the hyperinflation years of 1989–92. This increase in entrepreneurial activity is surprising (unless it is dominated by necessity entrepreneurship). As is well known, the second half of the 1970s and early 1980s in Argentina was a period of high inflation, failed stabilization, erratic policies, and autocratic rule, all (or most) elements that are expected to penalize (productive) entrepreneurship. From then on, the measure of entrepreneurship has declined, from almost 13 percent to near 8 percent in 2011. This trend started in the early 1990s, a period of high inflation followed by stabilization, the convertibility plan, and pro-market policies. That drift continued in the 2000s with more heterodox economic policies. Bukstein and Gandelman (forthcoming) report a similar finding in Uruguay.

References

Amoranto G., N. Chun, and A. Deolalikar. 2010. "Who Are the Middle Class and What Values Do They Hold? Evidence from the World Values Survey." Working Paper 229, Asian Development Bank, Manila.

Atkinson, A. B., F. Bourguignon, and C. Morrison. 1992. *Empirical Studies of Earnings Mobility*. Newark, NJ: Harwood Publishers.

Banerjee, A. V., and E. Duflo. 2008. "What Is Middle Class about the Middle Class around the World?" *Journal of Economic Perspectives* 22 (2, Spring): 3–28.

Behrman, J., N. Birdsall, and M. Székely. 1999. "Intergenerational Mobility in South America: Deeper Markets and Better Schools Make a Difference."

In *New Markets, New Opportunities? Economic and Social Mobility in a Changing World*, edited by Nancy Birdsall and Caroll Graham. Washington, DC: Brookings Institution Press and Carnegie Endowment for International Peace.

Birdsall, N. 2010. "The (Indispensable) Middle Class in Developing Countries, or the Rich and the Rest Not the Poor and the Rest." Working Paper 207, Center for Global Development, Washington, DC.

———. 2013. "A Note on the Middle Class in Latin America." In *Inequality in Asia and the Pacific*, edited by C. Rhee, J. Zhuang, and R. Kanbur. Manila: Asian Development Bank.

Birdsall, N., C. Graham, and S. Pettinato. 2000. "Stuck in the Tunnel: Is Globalization Muddling the Middle Class?" Working Paper 14, Center on Social and Economic Dynamics, Brookings Institution, Washington, DC.

Bourguignon, F., F. H. G. Ferreira, and M. Menendez. 2007. "Inequality of Opportunity in Brazil." *Review of Income and Wealth* 53 (4): 585–618.

Bukstein, D., and N. Gandelman. Forthcoming. "Intragenerational Social Mobility and Entrepreneurship in Uruguay." *Latin American Journal of Economics*.

Cardenas, M., H. Kharas, and C. Henao. 2011. "Latin America's Global Middle Class." Research Paper, Brookings Institution, Washington, DC.

Castellani, F., and G. Parent. 2011. "Being 'Middle Class' in Latin America." Working Paper 305, Organisation for Economic Co-operation and Development Centre, Paris.

Castellani, F., G. Parent, and J. Zenteno. 2013. "Latin America's Middle Class: Economic Characteristics and Consumer Behavior." Unpublished paper, Inter-American Development Bank, Washington, DC.

Chomsky, N., and E. S. Herman. 1988. *The Political Economy of the Mass Media.* New York: Pantheon Books.

Davies, J. C., and J. H. Huston. 1992. "The Shrinking Middle-Income Class: A Multivariate Analysis." *Eastern Economic Journal* 18 (3): 277–85.

Deaton, A. 1985. "Panel Data from Time Series of Cross-Sections." *Journal of Econometrics* 30 (1–2): 109–26.

Doepke, M., and F. Zilibotti. 2008. "Occupational Choice and the Spirit of Capitalism." *Quarterly Journal of Economics* 123 (2): 747–93.

Easterly, William. 2001. "The Middle-Class Consensus and Economic Development." *Journal of Economic Growth* 6 (4): 317–35.

Ferreira, Francisco H. G., Julian Messina, Jamele Rigolini, Luis-Felipe López-Calva, Maria Ana Lugo, and Renos Vakis. 2013. *Economic Mobility and the Rise of the Latin American Middle Class.* Washington, DC: World Bank.

Fields, G. 2010. "Does Income Mobility Equalize Longer-Term Incomes? New Measures of an Old Concept." *Journal of Economic Inequality* 8 (4): 409–87.

Foley, D. 2006. *Adam's Fallacy: A Guide to Economic Theology.* Cambridge, MA: Belknap Press of Harvard University.

Forgacs, D. 1988. *An Antonio Gramsci Reader: Selected Writings, 1916–1935.* London: Lawrence and Wishart.

Frieden, J. 2006. *Global Capitalism: Its Fall and Rise in the Twentieth Century.* New York: W. W. Norton.

Friedman, M. 1962. *Capitalism and Freedom.* Chicago: University of Chicago Press.

Gandelman, N., and V. Robano. Forthcoming. "Intergenerational Mobility, Middle Sectors, and Entrepreneurship in Uruguay." *Latin American Journal of Economics*.

Gilbert, D. 2008. *The American Class Structure in an Age of Growing Inequality*, 7th ed. Los Angeles: Pine Forge Press.

Glaeser, E. 2007. "Entrepreneurship and the City." NBER Working Paper 13551, National Bureau of Economic Research, Cambridge, MA.

Glaeser, E., S. Rosenthal, and W. C. Strange. 2009. "Urban Economics and Entrepreneurship." NBER Working Paper 15536, National Bureau of Economic Research, Cambridge, MA.

Hernani-Limarino, W. L., A. Eid, and P. Villarroel. 2012. "Entrepreneurship and Economic Mobility: A Case Study of Bolivia." Unpublished paper, Inter-American Development Bank, Washington, DC.

Hobsbawm, E. 2002. *Interesting Times: A Twentieth Century Life*. London: Allen Lane, an Imprint of Penguin Books.

———. 2011. *How to Change the World: Tales of Marx and Marxism*. London: Little, Brown.

Keynes, M. 1936. *The General Theory of Employment, Interest, and Money*. Cambridge, U.K.: Macmillan Cambridge University Press for the Royal Economic Society.

Kharas, H., and G. Gertz. 2010. "The Global Middle Class: A Cross-Over from East to West." In *China's Emergent Middle Class: Beyond Economic Transformation*, edited by C. Li. Washington, DC: Brookings Institution Press.

Knight, F. 1921. *Risk, Uncertainty, and Profit*. Hart, Schaffner, and Marx Prize Essays 31. Boston: Houghton Mifflin.

Langlois, R., and M. Cosgel. 1993. "Frank Knight on Risk, Uncertainty, and the Firm: A New Interpretation." *Economic Inquiry* 31 (July): 456–65.

Lazear, E. 2004. "Balanced Skills and Entrepreneurship." *American Economic Review* 94 (2, May): 208–11.

López-Calva, L. F., and E. Ortíz-Juárez. 2011. "A Vulnerability Approach to the Definition of the Middle Class." Policy Research Working Paper 5902, World Bank, Washington, DC.

López-Calva, L., J. Rigolini, and F. Torche. 2012. "Is There Such a Thing as Middle Class Values? Class Differences, Values, and Political Orientations in Latin America." Working Paper 286, Center for Global Development, Washington, DC.

Lora, E., and J. Fajardo. Forthcoming. "Latin American Middle Classes: The Distance between Perception and Reality." *Economía*.

Marx, K. (1848) 1979. *The Communist Manifesto*. Repr., London: Penguin Books.

Mejía, P., and M. Meléndez. Forthcoming. "Middle-Class Entrepreneurs and the Prospects of Social Mobility through Entrepreneurship in Colombia." *Latin American Journal of Economics*.

Milanovic, B., and S. Yitzhaki. 2002. "Decomposing World Income Distribution: Does the World Have a Middle Class?" *Review of Income and Wealth* 48 (2): 155–78.

Mosca, G. 1939. *The Ruling Class: Elementi di Scienza Politica*. New York: McGraw-Hill.

OECD (Organisation for Economic Co-operation and Development). 2011. *Latin American Economic Outlook 2011: How Middle Class Is Latin America?* Paris: OECD Publishing.

Pareto, V. (1901) 1991. *The Rise and Fall of Elites: An Application of Theoretical Sociology.* Trans., New Brunswick, NJ: Transaction Publishers.

Ravallion, M. 2009. "The Developing World's Bulging (but Vulnerable) Middle Class." *World Development* 38 (4): 445–54.

Saxenian, A. 2006. *The New Argonauts: Regional Advantage in a Global Economy.* Cambridge, MA: Harvard University Press.

Schumpeter, J. (1911, 1934) 1989. *The Theory of Economic Development: An Inquiry into Profits, Capital, Credit, Interest Rates, and the Business Cycle.* Repr. of 1934 trans., New Brunswick, NJ: Transaction Publishers.

Shorrocks, A. F. 1978. "Income Inequality and Income Mobility." *Journal of Economic Theory* 19 (2): 376–93.

Smith, P. 2005. *Democracy in Latin America: Political Change in Comparative Perspective.* Oxford, U.K.: Oxford University Press.

Solimano, A. 2009. "Stylized Facts on the Middle Class and the Development Process." In *Stuck in the Middle: Is Fiscal Policy Failing the Middle Class?* edited by A. Estache and D. Leipziger. Washington, DC: Brookings Institution Press.

———, ed. 2006. *Vanishing Growth in Latin America: The Late Twentieth Century Experience.* Cheltenham, U.K.: Edward Elgar Publishers.

———, ed. 2008. *The International Mobility of Talent: Types, Causes, and Development Impact.* Oxford, U.K.: Oxford University Press.

Solimano, A., and M. Gutierrez. 2008. "Savings, Investment, and Capital Accumulation." In *International Handbook of Development Economics,* vol. 1, edited by A. K. Dutt and J. Ross. Cheltenham, U.K.: Edward Elgar Publishers.

Stiglitz, J., and A. Weiss. 1981. "Credit Rationing in Markets with Imperfect Information." *American Economic Review* 71 (3, June): 393–410.

Thurow, L. 1987. "A Surge in Inequality." *Scientific American* 256 (5): 30–37.

Torche, F. 2009. "Sociological and Economic Approaches to the Intergenerational Transmission of Inequality in Latin America." Working Paper, United Nations Development Programme, New York.

Veblen, T. 1899. *The Theory of the Leisure Class.* New York: Macmillan.

Wadhwa, V., R. Aggarwal, K. Holly, and A. Salkever. 2009. *The Anatomy of an Entrepreneur: Family Background and Motivation.* Kansas City, MO: Ewing Marion Kauffman Foundation.

Weber, M. (1905) 2001. *The Protestant Ethic and the Spirit of Capitalism.* Repr., New York: Routledge.

Wolff, J. 2003. *Why Read Marx Today?* Oxford, U.K.: Oxford University Press.

Part II

International Comparisons and Country Studies

3

Middle-Class Entrepreneurs and Their Firms: A Regional View and International Comparison

Hugo D. Kantis, Juan S. Federico, and Luis A. Trajtenberg

In the last decade, interest has grown in the role of the middle class as an engine of growth and social stability in Latin America. The proportion of middle-class households in Latin America has grown steadily since the late 1990s (Franco, Hopenhayn, and Leon 2011). Moreover, there are solid grounds to affirm that a stronger and more stable middle class will contribute to higher incomes, higher growth, and more education (Banerjee and Duflo 2008; Birdsall, Graham, and Pettinato 2000; Easterly 2001, 2002; Torche and López-Calva forthcoming).

Within this context, the Research Department at the Inter-American Development Bank (IDB) organized a project to study the relationship between entrepreneurship and social mobility, in particular, the role of the middle class (Lora and Castellani 2011). A paper written as part of that project explores this relationship using household surveys (Kantis, Federico, and Trajtenberg 2011). It suggests that entrepreneurship, especially middle-class entrepreneurship, could be a vehicle for social mobility, given the importance of capabilities and resources that are present in higher proportions in the middle class than in the lower classes.

However, the results are less conclusive than expected. One possible reason may be that entrepreneurs are defined generically and grouped with business owners in general. Household survey data do not allow for a more detailed differentiation inside this generic occupational category.

Therefore, the study is not able to differentiate between different types of entrepreneurs: namely, those owning a microenterprise or a vibrant small business and those managing a high-growth young firm.

Today, it is widely recognized that most businesses in Latin America are micro and small enterprises. In addition, the business landscape is dominated by "necessity entrepreneurs": individuals motivated by financial need to set up a new business (Kelley, Bosma, and Amoros 2010). This kind of entrepreneurship is not always associated with dynamism and wealth creation (Schoar 2010). As shown by Kantis, Federico, and Trajtenberg (2011), most micro and small enterprises show low growth potential and thus have little impact at the macro level on innovation, diversification, dynamism, and structural change. In aggregate terms, however, they do have a great impact on employment.

Furthermore, as Kantis, Moori Koening, and Angelelli (2005) indicate, middle-class entrepreneurs create the vast majority of dynamic new firms in Latin America. Dynamic new firms contribute decisively to employment creation as well as economic diversification.[1] Thus it is important to understand the entrepreneurial process they have followed and the variables affecting it in order to design policy interventions aimed at increasing the number of middle-class entrepreneurs and creating a favorable climate for their businesses to grow.

Based on a data set obtained by combining data from two research projects—*Entrepreneurship in Emerging Economies* (Kantis, Ishida, and Komori 2002) and *Developing Entrepreneurship: Experience in Latin America and Worldwide* (Kantis, Moori Koening, and Angelelli 2005)—this study sheds light on the main characteristics of Latin American middle-class entrepreneurs, their firms, and their venture creation process.

Entrepreneurship and the Entrepreneurial Process in Latin America: Some Concepts and Evidence

Compared to other regions, Latin America still has several cultural, social, and economic factors that adversely affect the entrepreneurial context (Kantis, Moori Koening, and Angelelli 2005). One is the limited number of growth-oriented and innovative ventures. Most newly established businesses are microenterprises with expectations of lower growth and hence little impact at the macro level (Kelley, Bosma, and Amoros 2010). As Kantis and colleagues (Kantis, Ishida, and Komori 2002; Kantis, Moori Koening, and Angelelli 2005) show, the entrepreneurial process considers business creation as a continuum of events and stages influenced by multiple cultural, social, and economic variables, such as factor market conditions and industry structure. A systemic approach is needed to understand this process.

Broadly defined, the entrepreneurial process starts with the *gestation stage,* when the entrepreneurial vocation, the motivation to be an entrepreneur, and the main entrepreneurial capabilities are acquired, the business idea is identified, and the project is designed. Since this implies a process of building competencies, it is important to explore the role of the family, prior work experience, and educational system as learning contexts (see, for example, Gimeno et al. 1997; Colombo and Grilli 2005).

The second stage is the *launching* or *start-up stage,* which includes the final evaluation of the project, as well as steps to access and organize the resources needed to start the business. At this stage, the focus is on the sources that entrepreneurs use to access information and other resources required to launch the venture. Since access to financing tends to be an obstacle for entrepreneurs, the role of networks can be important.

The launching stage is followed by the *early development stage.* This stage is characterized by market entry and efforts to address the operational problems faced by new firms in interacting with customers and suppliers (Garnsey 1998; Veciana 2005).

This recognition of the stages of the entrepreneurial process suggests that research about entrepreneurship should concentrate not only on the individual behavior of entrepreneurs, but also on the economic and social structure (including social fragmentation and importance of the middle class) that could influence the development of "human entrepreneurial capital" in a society.

Despite significant heterogeneity among Latin American countries, several common features affect the demand for and supply of entrepreneurship in this region. In general, the risk propensity of the population is rather low (Hofstede, Hofstede, and Minkov 2010).[2] Human capital and the general educational level are also low, which constrains the supply of entrepreneurs (UNDP 2010).[3] In addition, Latin American societies tend to be highly fragmented. With the exception of a few countries, the middle class has emerged only in the last decade. In addition, the culture tends to be hierarchical, affecting the number and quality of contacts that are relatively accessible to individuals (the so-called social capital platform) and that either facilitate or inhibit networking. This feature imposes significant restrictions on access to business networks and resources.[4] All of these characteristics constrain the development of dynamic entrepreneurship in the region (Kantis, Moori Koening, and Angelelli 2005).

Moreover, the structure and strategies of Latin American firms are not conducive to entrepreneurship. Many firms are reluctant to take on risk and to innovate. Investment in research and development (R&D) by firms is lower in Latin America than in more advanced economies (UNESCO 2010). As a whole, the Latin American business sector is less likely to encourage the creation of new, innovative firms or the emergence of corporate ventures (Kantis and Drucaroff 2009). In the same vein, according to the *Global Competitiveness Report,* the Latin American business sector is perceived as less sophisticated and less innovative than the European and East Asian business sectors. This also affects the demand for innovative entrepreneurial firms (WEF 2010).[5]

Despite the strong economic growth that most Latin American countries have experienced in recent years, consumption patterns may also inhibit the emergence of innovative and dynamic new ventures. Consumers in Latin America are perceived to be more oriented to price than to quality than consumers in more developed countries, which may result in less sophisticated buyers (WEF 2010).

In addition, cultural, social, and other structural factors increase transaction costs in Latin American economies. For instance, red tape and inefficiencies in certain factor markets, such as labor, information, and finance, impose barriers to entrepreneurs willing to start and run a new venture. Today, despite efforts to reduce the costs of transacting, most Latin American countries remain at the bottom of the ranking on ease of doing business (World Bank 2010).

Access to financial resources constitutes a significant barrier in most Latin American countries. The business environment for private equity and venture capital is still underdeveloped, according to the Latin American Private Equity and Venture Capital Association (LAVCA 2010).

Finally, organizations that provide assistance and training to entrepreneurs tend to be financially and technically weak. They do not provide systemic support (Kantis 2010) and do not reach a critical mass of entrepreneurs. The number of entrepreneurs trained and projects undertaken is too small to generate a noticeable impact. Moreover, the services provided to entrepreneurs and their projects are often poor quality.

In summary, structural factors in Latin American countries are not conducive to dynamic entrepreneurship that contributes to economic growth, industry diversification, or income mobility. Previous research has confirmed the importance of the middle class for the creation of dynamic new firms, but very little is known about their characteristics, their entrepreneurial processes, or how they differ from firms created by individuals from other social classes. Those issues, among others, constitute the main research questions that guided this study.

Data Set and Sample Description

The statistical information for this study was obtained by combining data sets from two research projects: *Entrepreneurship in Emerging Economies* (Kantis, Ishida, and Komori 2002) and *Developing Entrepreneurship: Experience in Latin America and Worldwide* (Kantis, Moori Koening, and Angelelli 2005). The new data set includes information about entrepreneurs' origins, firm characteristics, and the venture creation process in seven Latin American countries (Argentina, Brazil, Chile, Ecuador,

El Salvador, Mexico, and Peru) and four comparator economies from other regions: two from East Asia (the Republic of Korea and Taiwan, China) and two from Mediterranean Europe (Italy and Spain). For methodological details, see the annex.

After controlling for missing and invalid observations, 1,074 entrepreneurs were included in the regional database. Just over half (54.5 percent) belong to the middle class, 27 percent belong to the lower class, and 18.5 percent belong to the upper class.[6] The definitions of social class are based on interviewees' self-perceptions about the social origins of their household.[7] As Pressman (2007) notes, people tend to over- or underestimate their position; therefore, these definitions must be interpreted with caution. To minimize this problem, social origin was grouped by joining adjacent categories into three groups: (a) upper class and upper-middle class (upper class); (b) middle class; and (c) lower-middle class and lower class (lower class).

Since the database used in this study was designed to study the entrepreneurial process of dynamic new ventures, some limitations arose, especially when using it for analysis at the country level. These problems were related to the limited number of observations of upper-class entrepreneurs in some countries. For example, in Argentina and Mexico, this number was almost the minimum required for conducting the statistical tests (z-test) applied in this research. Therefore, in these cases, the results should be interpreted with caution. In Brazil and El Salvador, the number of observations of upper-class entrepreneurs was not large enough to perform any statistical tests. Therefore, the results for these countries are not reported in the country-level analysis. The composition of the sample is described in table 3.1.

Another characteristic of this database is that it is biased toward dynamic new ventures, defined as young firms (between 3 and 10 years old) with more than 15 employees when the survey was done. Almost 60 percent of the sample consists of dynamic new firms. Therefore, some caution should be used when analyzing the results, since the firms included in this study are not representative of the general entrepreneurial population, which consists mainly of microenterprises and necessity-based businesses; rather they are representative of relatively dynamic firms.

As table 3.2 illustrates, the middle class plays an important role as an incubator of dynamic new ventures in Latin America. This role is even greater in European countries such as Italy and, to a lesser extent, Spain.

Characteristics of Middle-Class Entrepreneurs

This section describes middle-class entrepreneurs in Latin America by looking at their age and family characteristics, educational and work experience, entrepreneurial vocation and motivation, and learning contexts.[8]

Table 3.1 Composition of the Sample, by Social Class, 2004

	Upper class		Middle class		Lower class		Total	
Economy	N	%	N	%	N	%	N	%
Argentina	25	16	97	62	35	22	157	100
Brazil	11	7	77	48	72	45	160	100
Chile	49	24	107	53	47	23	203	100
Ecuador	44	23	109	58	34	18	187	100
El Salvador	10	12	40	47	35	41	85	100
Mexico	27	19	81	57	33	23	141	100
Peru	33	23	74	52	34	24	141	100
Latin America	199	18	585	54	290	27	1,074	100
Korea, Rep.	52	26	80	40	70	34	202	100
Taiwan, China	20	9	47	23	144	68	211	100
Italy	14	10	103	70	30	20	147	100
Spain	19	13	82	57	42	30	143	100

Source: Based on the IDB database.
Note: N = number.

Table 3.2 Dynamic New Firms, by Social Class of the Founder, International Comparison, 2004

	Upper class		Middle class		Lower class		Total	
Economy	N	%	N	%	N	%	N	%
Argentina	17	16.5	63	61.2	23	22.3	103	100
Brazil	7	6.2	53	46.9	53	46.9	113	100
Chile	25	22.5	61	55.0	25	22.5	111	100
Ecuador	22	24.7	49	55.1	18	20.2	89	100
El Salvador	7	19.7	19	48.7	13	33.3	39	100
Mexico	25	23.8	54	51.4	26	24.8	105	100
Peru	22	25.3	41	47.1	24	27.6	87	100
Latin America	125	19.3	340	52.6	182	28.1	647	100
Korea, Rep.	42	26.9	64	41.0	50	32.1	156	100
Taiwan, China	20	11.3	37	20.6	122	68.1	179	100
Italy	11	11.2	72	73.4	15	15.4	98	100
Spain	13	12.9	58	57.4	30	29.7	101	100

Source: Based on the IDB database.
Note: N = number.

Age and Family

In general, Latin American entrepreneurs launch their first ventures when they are around 30 years old (31.3 years old, on average), but they begin exploring the idea of being an entrepreneur a few years earlier (when they are 27 years old, on average). However, entrepreneurs from the wealthiest social class tend to start their entrepreneurial process at an earlier age. On average, they create their first venture when they are 29 years old, and they begin to consider doing so when they are 25 years old.

This result could be related to the earlier exposure of more affluent families to the business experience.[9] Half of all middle-class entrepreneurs in Latin America come from families where the father used to work as an employee or independently (he was self-employed or an independent professional); see table 3.3.

One-third of the entrepreneurs (32.8 percent) have fathers who themselves were entrepreneurs or were executives or managers. However, this proportion is significantly higher in the upper class (63 percent) than in the middle class (33 percent). In other words, the families of middle-class entrepreneurs are less exposed to the business world than the more affluent ones. This feature is even more pronounced in the lower social class, where only 13 percent of the sample entrepreneurs have a father who was an entrepreneur or an executive.[10]

Education and Work Experience

Most middle-class entrepreneurs are well educated. Two out of three (67 percent) are university graduates or have graduate or professional

Table 3.3 Occupation of the Founder's Father, by Social Class, Latin American Sample, 2004
(percent)

Father's occupation	Upper class	Middle class	Lower class
Entrepreneur	49**	26	13**
Executive or manager	14**	6	0**
Subtotal	63**	33	13**
Self-employed or independent	20	25	26
Employee	15**	31	38**
Other	2**	11	22**
Total	100	100	100

Source: Based on the IDB database.
Note: The reference category is always the middle class, which means that differences are calculated for the upper class and lower class with respect to the middle class.
Significance level: ** = 5 percent.

education. But this proportion is smaller than in the more affluent class, where 78 percent have a university degree or more education. Conversely, entrepreneurs from the lower social class are less educated (45 percent).[11]

Before they created their current venture, middle-class entrepreneurs worked as employees (57 percent), mostly in small and medium enterprises (SMEs; 31 percent); see table 3.4. Having prior experience as an entrepreneur is less common among middle-class entrepreneurs than among the wealthiest class (43 percent and 50 percent, respectively).[12] This is not the case among European middle-class entrepreneurs, who have more prior business experience.

Entrepreneurial Vocation and Motivation

In Latin American countries, most middle-class entrepreneurs acquire the desire to become entrepreneurs (business motivation) on the job (50 percent), followed by the family environment (38 percent); see table 3.5. The influence of the family is significantly lower among middle-class than among upper-class entrepreneurs (38 percent and 48 percent, respectively). However, the contribution of work experience is significantly greater for middle-class entrepreneurs. The role of the university in shaping the desire to be an entrepreneur is also much less significant in middle-class than in upper-class entrepreneurs (14 percent and 19 percent, respectively). In summary, family context and the university are more important for the upper class than for the middle class.

The role of the university and the family context in the acquisition of an entrepreneurial vocation is even smaller in the poorest classes (8 percent and 29 percent, respectively). This coincides with the fact that

Table 3.4 Previous Occupation of Entrepreneurs, Interregional Comparison, 2004
(*percent*)

Previous occupation	Latin America	Korea, Rep.	Taiwan, China	Spain	Italy
Employee in an SME	31	47**	25	30	23
Employee in a large firm	26	20	55**	17	7**
Subtotal	57	67*	81**	47*	30**
Entrepreneur	34	28	6**	49**	55**
Other	9	5	13	4	15**
Total	100	100	100	100	100

Source: Based on the IDB database.
Note: Only data from middle-class entrepreneurs are reported. SME = small and medium enterprise.
Significance level: * = 10 percent, ** = 5 percent.

Table 3.5 Context Where Entrepreneurs Acquired the Desire to Become an Entrepreneur, by Social Class, Latin American Sample, 2004
(*percent*)

Context	Upper class	Middle class	Lower class
University	19	14	8**
Previous work experience	43	50	53
Family	48**	38	29**

Source: Based on the IDB database.
Note: The reference category is always the middle class, which means that differences are calculated for the upper class and lower class with respect to the middle class. Data add up to more than 100 percent because respondents could cite multiple answers.
Significance level: ** = 5 percent.

the lowest proportion of university graduates is found among the least affluent segments. Likewise, fewer lower-class families have experience with the business world.[13]

Entrepreneurs were asked about their main motivations for starting a business, using a set of options that appear in the literature (Kantis, Moori Koening, and Angelelli 2005). Middle-class entrepreneurs mentioned not just one factor but a set of motives, including positive economic factors as well as noneconomic ones. The top five motives for middle-class entrepreneurs in Latin America are self-realization (87 percent), the desire to apply their knowledge (81 percent), the desire to improve their income (76 percent), the desire to be independent (60 percent), and the desire to contribute to society (59 percent). Although these motives are important for entrepreneurs from all social classes, some differences are evident in the regional database. For instance, following in the family tradition appears more frequently as a motive among the wealthiest than among middle-class entrepreneurs (13 percent and 18 percent, respectively).[14] Similarly, family role models are more important for wealthy entrepreneurs than for middle-class entrepreneurs.[15] Negative reasons, such as unemployment or the impossibility of continuing one's studies, are not common motives for starting a business in general, although they are more frequent among lower-class entrepreneurs.[16]

The importance of having positive role models in motivating new entrepreneurial vocations is significantly higher in Korea and Taiwan, China, than in Latin America. Such role models go beyond the family to include the positive influence of friends and acquaintances from the same city. The mass media also plays an important role in creating and disseminating entrepreneurial role models (see table 3.6).

Table 3.6 Role Models of Entrepreneurs, Interregional
Comparison, 2004
(*percent*)

Role model	Latin America	Korea, Rep.	Taiwan, China	Spain	Italy
Family	17	47**	17	10	17
Friends	9	40**	38**	11	13
Acquaintances from the same city	9	57**	21**	11	13
The media	8	42**	60**	13	12

Source: Based on the IDB database.
Note: Only data from middle-class entrepreneurs are reported. Data add up to more than 100 percent because respondents could cite multiple answers.
Significance level: ** = 5 percent.

Main Learning Contexts

In most countries, the family context is more relevant for upper-class than for middle-class entrepreneurs, particularly with respect to the acquisition of negotiation skills. This contribution is consistently less important for lower-class entrepreneurs, especially for the acquisition of problem-solving and social skills.[17] Beyond the specific form it assumes in each country, the contribution of work experience to the acquisition of entrepreneurial skills tends to be greater among middle-class entrepreneurs than among the wealthiest entrepreneurs in the database. As table 3.7 shows, this is particularly true with respect to social skills, risk tolerance, negotiation, teamwork, creativity, marketing, hard work, and planning.[18]

Finally, universities play a larger role for the more affluent segments than for the middle class, particularly in acquiring managerial capabilities such as marketing, administration, planning, and even technical knowledge. This result could be related to the prevalence of entrepreneurship courses in private universities, where the presence of upper-class students is higher.[19]

In summary, middle-class entrepreneurs tend to be young employees from small and large firms and to be university graduates. However, they tend to start their entrepreneurial process later and are less exposed to prior business experience than upper-class entrepreneurs, who consistently tend to accumulate more entrepreneurial experience before launching their own business.

The influence of entrepreneurial role models in Latin America is more important for the upper class than for the middle class. This contrasts with East Asian countries, where the influence of entrepreneurial role models is strong for the middle class as well.

Differences in learning context are also apparent. While middle-class entrepreneurs who were formerly employees or professionals tend to acquire their business motivation and most of their entrepreneurial skills

Table 3.7 Main Learning Context of Entrepreneurs, by Social Class, Latin American Sample, 2004 (percent)

Learning context	Work experience			Family			University		
	Upper class	Middle class	Lower class	Upper class	Middle class	Lower class	Upper class	Middle class	Lower class
Problem solving	68	72	68	32	35	26**	33	32	24**
Social skills	47**	58	60	37	40	31**	31	25	18**
Risk tolerance	54**	63	62	36	30	31	9*	14	9**
Negotiation	68	75	72	30**	20	18	9	12	10*
Team work	59**	67	69	20	17	13	35	31	19**
Creativity	44	51	52	28	24	25	31	29	20**
Technical knowledge	51	56	57	7	6	7	58**	46	32**
Marketing	50**	58	54	5	4	4	39**	24	17**
Administration	57**	66	63	18	13	9*	36*	29	20**
Hard work	54**	66	61	47	40	43	14	13	7**
Planning	52**	69	59**	18	15	14	37	30	25**
Communication	54**	66	56**	23	24	24	24	22	14**
Motivation	61**	70	62**	25	24	18*	19*	13	12

Source: Based on the IDB database.
Note: The reference category is always the middle class, which means that differences are calculated for the upper class and lower class with respect to the middle class. Data add up to more than 100 percent because respondents could cite multiple answers.
Significance level: * = 10 percent, ** = 5 percent.

on the job, the more affluent segments have an advantage because of their higher exposure to and links with the business world provided by their families. In addition, universities play a greater role as learning platforms among upper-class entrepreneurs than among middle- and lower-class entrepreneurs. This finding suggests that universities could play a significant role in fostering entrepreneurial motivation and developing entrepreneurial skills, given that two out of three middle-class entrepreneurs are university graduates.

The Entrepreneurial Process and Firm Characteristics

The gap in time from the moment the business idea is conceived until the first venture is created is longer in Latin American countries (4.4 years in Latin America on average) than in the comparators (1.5 years in Korea; 2.4 years in Taiwan, China; and 3.4 years in Italy and Spain). This fact points to possible differences in personal skills and accumulated contacts, but also to the existence of important economic, regulatory, and motivational contrasts between the two contexts. Those differences could be affecting the gap between motivation and firm creation. As argued in previous studies, this could reveal the existence of more "entrepreneur-friendly" environments in those countries than in Latin America. Some key factors—such as culture (for instance, role models), industry structure, networks, and financing—encourage entrepreneurship in those regions (Kantis, Moori Koening, and Angelelli 2005). This section analyzes some of the factors affecting this process and their implications.

From Business Idea to Start-up

Middle-class entrepreneurs tend to develop their business ideas by using the information they have acquired on previous jobs (75 percent) or through networking (76 percent). Although networking is an important source of information to identify and validate business ideas in all social classes, upper-class entrepreneurs tend to have more contacts than middle-class entrepreneurs with other SME owners (49 percent and 42 percent, respectively) and with professionals (44 percent and 39 percent, respectively); see table 3.8. Entrepreneurs from the lowest social classes tend to interact mostly with other employees. These results suggest that social origins affect the quality of the networks accessed by entrepreneurs.[20]

Beyond the particularities observed in each country, the higher the social origins of the entrepreneur, the more frequent is the use of professional tools to evaluate the decision to start a business. As table 3.9 illustrates, this fact is evident in the development of business plans, cash-flow analysis, and the estimation of payback periods, sales and operational costs, and personal opportunity costs.

Table 3.8 Networks Accessed by Entrepreneurs, by Social Class, Latin American Sample, 2004 (*percent*)

Network accessed	Upper class	Middle class	Lower class
Executive from a large firm	42	33	31
SME owner	49**	42	41
Professional	44**	39	29**
Bank officer	2**	2	1
Member of a public institution	4	5	2**
Employee	17	24	38**

Source: Based on the IDB database.
Note: The reference category is always the middle class, which means that differences are calculated for the upper class and lower class with respect to the middle class. Data add up to more than 100 percent because respondents could cite multiple answers. SME = small and medium enterprise.
Significance level: ** = 5 percent.

Table 3.9 Evaluation Process and Criteria Used by Entrepreneurs, by Social Class, Latin American Sample, 2004 (*percent*)

Evaluation criteria	Upper class	Middle class	Lower class
Business plan development	66**	51	39**
Cash-flow analysis	62**	50	36**
Internal rate of return estimation	46	41	27**
Payback period estimation	61**	50	36**
Sales and costs estimation	87**	75	68**
Opportunity cost estimation	71**	60	52**

Source: Based on the IDB database.
Note: The reference category is always the middle class, which means that differences are calculated for the upper class and lower class with respect to the middle class. Data add up to more than 100 percent because respondents could cite multiple answers.
Significance level: ** = 5 percent.

Sources of Finance

Regardless of social origin, most entrepreneurs in Latin America (around 80 percent) finance their start-up mainly with personal savings (see table 3.10). However, distinct social segments have distinct capacity to generate savings. Moreover, differences in the availability of finance tend

Table 3.10 Sources of Finance Accessed by Entrepreneurs, by Social Class, Latin American Sample, 2004 (*percent*)

Source of finance	Upper class	Middle class	Lower class
Personal savings	83	79	79
Family and friends	28	25	21
Private external sources	39**	30	25
Private banks	32*	26	23
Venture capital	9	7	4*
Public support	1	7	4
Bootstrapping	48	53	58

Source: Based on the IDB database.

Note: The reference category is always the middle class, which means that differences are calculated between the upper class and lower class with respect to the middle class. Data add up to more than 100 percent, and components of an item add up to more than the total of the item, because respondents could cite multiple answers.

Significance level: * = 10 percent, ** = 5 percent.

to be accentuated by differences in the degree of access to external sources of funds.

Moreover, in Latin America, access to private external sources of financing, such as bank loans and private investors, is more common among more affluent entrepreneurs (39 percent) than among middle-class entrepreneurs (30 percent) or lower-class entrepreneurs (25 percent). To compensate for this situation, lower-class entrepreneurs tend to use bootstrapping measures, such as purchasing secondhand equipment and obtaining cash advances from clients. Public support is rarely used by any social class.

Middle-class entrepreneurs in other regions are less constrained with respect to financing a start-up than their counterparts in Latin America (see table 3.11). Although personal savings continue to be the main source of financing in all regions, the degree of access to external financing is lower in Latin America, providing a weaker platform for start-ups. In Italy, Spain, and Korea, middle-class entrepreneurs use private banks significantly more than they do in either Latin America or Taiwan, China. In East Asia, principally in Taiwan, China, they use risk capital (both formal and informal) more frequently than in other areas. Public financial support also tends to be higher outside of Latin America.

The relative lack of access to external funds adversely affects new firms in Latin America. Both middle-class and lower-class entrepreneurs may have to adjust their original projects to make them feasible. This implies starting

Table 3.11 Sources of Finance Accessed by Entrepreneurs, Interregional Comparison, 2004
(*percent*)

Source	Latin America	Korea, Rep.	Taiwan, China	Spain	Italy
Personal savings	79	62**	68**	84	79
Family and friends	25	25	66**	11**	4**
Private banks	26	42**	25	44**	51**
Venture capital	7	12**	25**	5	4
Public financial support	7	15**	4	11**	17**
Bootstrapping	53	30**	40**	56	23**

Source: Based on the IDB database.
Note: Only data from middle-class entrepreneurs are reported. Data add up to more than 100 percent because respondents could cite multiple answers.
Significance level: ** = 5 percent.

smaller (65 percent), or with a lower level of technology (59 percent), or later than desirable to be competitive (41 percent). They also make greater efforts to obtain support from suppliers or new partners (60 percent).

The consequences of not having access to external financing also vary among regions. European entrepreneurs tend to be less affected by the lack of external funding. One out of four Italian entrepreneurs affirmed that they did not face significant negative consequences on start-up, while just 21 percent had to start smaller or later than expected (versus 62 percent in Latin America). Conversely, entrepreneurs tend to rely more often on third parties to overcome financial shortfalls, especially new partners, in East Asia than in Latin America (57 percent and 9 percent, respectively).

To sum up, financing is a clear area where specific policies could help to level the playing field among entrepreneurs from different social classes. Middle-class entrepreneurs in Latin America face disadvantages compared with more affluent entrepreneurs and with middle-class counterparts in other regions.

Features of Middle-Class Entrepreneurs' Firms

Most middle-class firms in Latin America are located in large cities (66 percent). However, relatively more middle-class firms are located in local areas dominated by SMEs than new firms founded by upper-class entrepreneurs (34 percent and 22 percent, respectively).[21] The existence of entrepreneurial networks and "proximity relationships" in these local areas tends to reduce transaction costs and other barriers to entry for new firms. This feature introduces a regional dimension into the consideration of policies to foster middle-class entrepreneurship in Latin America. This phenomenon is also evident in Italy, where many entrepreneurs (61 percent) are located in areas dominated by SMEs.

The presence of entrepreneurial teams, rather than solo entrepreneurs, in Latin America is significantly more prominent in firms founded by middle-class entrepreneurs than in firms founded by lower-class entrepreneurs (75 percent and 68 percent, respectively). This trend is even more pronounced among middle-class entrepreneurs from other regions. In Spain; Italy; and Taiwan, China, all of the firms surveyed were created by teams.

Middle-class firms in Latin America tend to build their competitive advantage on product differentiation (56 percent). Lower prices and innovation are much less frequent strategies (27 percent and 38 percent, respectively). But the most relevant contrast appears in the comparison with firms from other regions. In Taiwan, China and Spain, firms created by middle-class entrepreneurs tend to be more innovative (70 percent and 54 percent, respectively).

Two-thirds (66 percent) of the firms created by middle-class entrepreneurs in Latin America tend to operate in conventional manufacturing industries such as metalworking, furniture, food, and textiles. Middle-class entrepreneurs are more involved in creating knowledge-based companies than lower-class entrepreneurs (34 percent and 23 percent, respectively).[22] But their role in creating such firms is less prominent than in other economies, such as Taiwan, China (where 68 percent of the firms created by middle-class entrepreneurs are knowledge-based firms). In other words, although middle-class entrepreneurs contribute to the creation of knowledge-based firms, they do so less in Latin America than in other regions of the world.

Most of the young firms surveyed—regardless of social origin or region—tend to sell their production to other firms. This situation is even more frequent in East Asia and Mediterranean Europe (91 percent in both regions versus 80 percent in Latin America). Outsourcing is a less exploited source of business opportunities in Latin America than elsewhere (50 percent in East Asia, 40 percent in Mediterranean Europe, and 24 percent in Latin America). This could reflect the fact that industrial structure is more fragmented and linkages between large and small firms are weaker in Latin America than in East Asia and Europe. In other words, the business environment in Latin America is less advantageous for emerging firms, which pay a price for being new as well as small.

Young Latin American firms tend to sell their production almost entirely in their domestic markets (around 80 percent).[23] The export coefficient—among firms that export—tends to be larger for the highest social class.[24] The percentage of young firms that sell part of their output to foreign markets is significantly higher in other regions.[25]

Initial Investment and Firm Size

Middle-class entrepreneurs in Latin America tend to start with smaller initial investments than their more affluent counterparts. Almost 85 percent of them begin with less than $100,000 (compared to 75.7 percent of upper-class entrepreneurs). As expected, this percentage is even higher (92.9 percent) among lower-class entrepreneurs.[26] Lower-class entrepreneurs are more likely to face financial constraints and to downsize their projects before start-up. Investing large amounts of resources is less frequent among middle-class entrepreneurs in Latin America than in East Asia and Europe. In those regions, 1 in 5 entrepreneurs invests more than $500,000 to launch a venture (as against just 1 in 20 in Latin America).[27]

Employment data confirm some differences among Latin American firms. Firms created by upper-class entrepreneurs tend to employ around 15 people, while middle-class firms initially employ fewer than 10 people.[28] Nevertheless, the initial downsizing of middle-class firms does not imply that entrepreneurs relinquish their ambitions. In fact, early in the life of their company, they abandon the world of microenterprises to become SMEs. On average, three years after establishing the firm, they are employing 16 workers (see table 3.12). Nonetheless, three years after start-up, firms created by middle-class entrepreneurs remain smaller than those founded by upper-class entrepreneurs (16 versus 26 employees, on average).

This contrast is even more pronounced in comparison to firms in Korea and Taiwan, China (which employ 32 and 37 employees in the third year, respectively); see table 3.13. This difference is even greater if indirect employment created through subcontracting—a common feature of the productive structure of these countries—is taken into account.

Table 3.12 Mean Employment Size of Firms during the First Few Years of Operation, by Social Class, Latin American Sample, 2004
(number of employees)

Year of operation	Upper class	Middle class	Lower class
First year	14.5**	9.1	8.0
Third year	26.2**	16.6	15.2

Source: Based on the IDB database.

Note: The reference category is always the middle class, which means that differences are calculated for the upper class and lower class with respect to the middle class.

Significance level: ** = 5 percent.

Table 3.13 Mean Employment Size of Firms during the First Few Years of Operation, Interregional Comparison, 2004 (*number of employees*)

Year of operation	Latin America	Korea, Rep.	Taiwan, China	Spain	Italy
First year	9.1	22.7**	10.8	8.2	9.2
Third year	16.6	31.7**	36.8**	13.8	16.1

Source: Based on the IDB database.
Note: Only data from middle-class entrepreneurs are reported.
Significance level: ** = 5 percent.

Obstacles to Survival and Growth

Once the firm is created, the three main problems faced by middle-class entrepreneurs in Latin America are hiring qualified employees (62 percent), getting clients (61 percent), and managing cash flow (60 percent); see table 3.14. These problems are at the top of the list for all social classes. However, the average number of problems identified is significantly lower for the more affluent classes. Indeed, upper-class entrepreneurs identify 4.7 initial problems, on average, while middle-class entrepreneurs identify 5.3, and lower-class entrepreneurs identify 5.9.

Compared to upper-class entrepreneurs, middle-class entrepreneurs tend to face more frequent problems related to securing reliable suppliers, purchasing equipment, and managing the company (see table 3.14). Entrepreneurs coming from the lower class tend to face more problems obtaining market information and purchasing equipment and machinery.[29]

The main problems facing middle-class entrepreneurs coincide across regions. However, compared to Latin American entrepreneurs, entrepreneurs in Mediterranean Europe tend to face fewer problems (on average 3.6 in Mediterranean Europe versus 5.3 in Latin America). Looking at each problem by itself, the proportion of middle-class entrepreneurs facing each problem is lower in Spain and Italy than in Latin America. Conversely, East Asian entrepreneurs—mostly Koreans—tend to have more problems acquiring clients, hiring professional managers, and managing their firms (see table 3.15). This may be a function of the greater dynamism observed in East Asian firms. Similarly, getting a balanced cash flow appears to be the main problem mostly for Korean entrepreneurs. East Asian entrepreneurs—especially in Taiwan, China—tend to face fewer problems purchasing machinery and equipment (46 percent in Latin America versus 25 percent in Taiwan, China). This is a function of the scarcity of external financing in Latin America.

To overcome these problems, the majority of entrepreneurs (60 percent) tend to use networks, regardless of their social origins (see table 3.16).

Table 3.14 Main Problems Faced during the First Few Years of Operation, by Social Class, Latin American Sample, 2004 (*percent*)

Problem	Upper class	Middle class	Lower class
Hire qualified employees	62	62	64
Get clients	56	61	67
Attain a balanced cash flow	55	60	65
Get proper suppliers	40**	48	52
Purchase machinery and equipment	39**	46	60**
Adapt products to consumers' needs	35	41	46
Get market information	36	40	49**
Manage the firm	32**	39	41
Attain quality standards	33	35	41
Manage the operations	34	34	39
Manage the relationship with clients	29	34	35
Hire professional managers	18	21	21

Source: Based on the IDB database.
Note: The reference category is always the middle class, which means that differences are calculated for the upper class and lower class with respect to the middle class. Data add up to more than 100 percent because respondents could cite multiple answers.
Significance level: ** = 5 percent.

Table 3.15 Main Problems Faced during the First Few Years of Operation, Interregional Comparison, 2004 (*percent*)

Problem	Latin America	Korea, Rep.	Taiwan, China	Spain	Italy
Hire qualified employees	62	60	62	55	45**
Get clients	61	75**	79**	55	59
Attain a balanced cash flow	60	82**	60	40**	36**
Get proper suppliers	48	70**	57	41	18**
Purchase machinery and equipment	46	42	25**	35**	22**
Adapt products to consumers' needs	41	62**	38	35	25**

(*continued next page*)

Table 3.15 (continued)

Problem	Latin America	Korea, Rep.	Taiwan, China	Spain	Italy
Get market information	40	60**	36	17**	28**
Manage the firm	39	72**	57**	18**	21**
Attain quality standards	35	62**	45	28	14**
Manage the operations	34	62**	34	12**	14**
Manage the relationship with customers	34	60**	38	18**	23**
Hire professional managers	21	65**	66**	12**	11**

Source: Based on the IDB database.

Note: Only data from middle-class entrepreneurs are reported. Data add up to more than 100 percent because respondents could cite multiple answers.

Significance level: ** = 5 percent.

Table 3.16 Use of Networks to Solve Initial Problems, Interregional Comparison, 2004
(*percent*)

Type of network	Latin America	Korea Rep.	Taiwan, China	Spain	Italy
Public institutions	12	20*	30**	13	10
Chambers and unions	13	12	23*	4**	15
Consultancy firms	10	12	19*	8	21**
Suppliers and clients	33	67**	57**	29	16**
Family and friends	24	15*	45**	17	15*
Colleagues	14	40**	40**	12	8*
Universities	11	10	32**	1**	2**
None of the previous (only own efforts)	42	17**	13**	44	48

Source: Based on the IDB database.

Note: Only data from middle-class entrepreneurs are reported. Data add up to more than 100 percent because respondents could cite multiple answers.

Significance level: * = 10 percent, ** = 5 percent.

Middle-class entrepreneurs who decide to contact external sources tend to resort to commercial, institutional, and social networks, in that order.[30]

Although the majority of middle-class entrepreneurs tend to rely on support networks, this strategy is less widespread in Latin America than in other regions. Many more entrepreneurs rely on themselves to solve problems in Latin America (42 percent) than in Korea (17 percent) and Taiwan, China (13 percent). Commercial networks (suppliers, customers, and other entrepreneurs) are the most widely used for assistance with problem solving. Universities and other public institutions are also more frequently relied on mainly in Taiwan, China. Consulting firms are important sources of assistance in overcoming initial problems in Italy.

Conclusions and Policy Implications

Some policy implications emerge from this analysis of the entrepreneurial process and the early stages of firms founded by middle-class entrepreneurs. In general, Latin American middle-class entrepreneurs tend to face less advantageous conditions for acquiring resources and skills than entrepreneurs in the more affluent social classes of their own countries. The latter tend to be exposed to business experience at an earlier age, since they are more likely to belong to families where the father's occupation allows them such contact and since the universities where they study are sounder platforms for developing capabilities and business contacts.

Likewise, Latin American middle-class entrepreneurs tend to be in a disadvantaged position when compared to middle-class entrepreneurs from more developed regions. In Latin America, middle-class entrepreneurs are less exposed to the business world and to entrepreneurial role models. In addition, they tend to rely on a less qualified and less business-specific support network. Moreover, it is more difficult for them to obtain start-up financing.

Firms created by Latin American middle-class entrepreneurs are not as dynamic as those created by the middle class in other regions with regard to exporting and creating jobs. Because of resource constraints, they must downsize the business projects they had planned in order to be able to start them up. In the same vein, Latin American middle-class entrepreneurs face more problems managing the early stage of the venture than their European counterparts and have fewer support networks than their Asian counterparts.

These findings have direct policy implications and offer relevant insights to the formulation of policies designed to democratize the entrepreneurial process and strengthen the contributions of middle-class entrepreneurship to overall economic growth. The recommendations that follow are derived from the study's findings.

- *Improve education.* Entrepreneurial options and processes to develop skills should be promoted through the education system at all levels (starting with primary and secondary school) as a way of avoiding or reducing the disadvantages associated with social origins at the beginning of an entrepreneur's career. At the university level, this implies promoting entrepreneurial skills among students from public institutions, which relatively more middle-class students attend. This, in turn, implies promoting institutional reforms to make this change feasible.

- *Improve technical assistance.* An institutional platform of technical assistance should be developed to support entrepreneurial projects. This platform would assist all entrepreneurs, but it could be especially useful in helping to compensate for the disadvantages that middle-class entrepreneurs face compared with entrepreneurs from a higher social class and other regions of the world.
- *Improve networks.* Strategies to develop networks for entrepreneurs should be promoted as another device to overcome possible disadvantages that middle-class entrepreneurs face. In particular, global contacts and closer relationships with SME owners, executives in large firms, and others in the business world are needed to create new, dynamic firms.
- *Improve financing.* Access to financing for entrepreneurs is a key issue in any effort to equalize opportunities for the middle class to create and grow their business venture. In particular, entrepreneurial capital is needed, and mechanisms should be put in place to connect this financing with the entrepreneurs who need it.

Annex. Methodological Notes

The Inter-American Development Bank (IDB) database used in this study draws from different research projects focused specifically on new, dynamic ventures in Latin America (Kantis, Moori Koening, and Angelelli 2005). To target dynamic young ventures, the study uses the following definitions.

A *young business* is defined as a firm between 3 and 10 years old. This threshold period is intended to focus on ventures that have survived the critical period of early development. The 10-year upper limit serves a dual purpose. First, it ensures that the focus is on ventures whose dynamism has been relatively well established. Second, it minimizes the possibility that the founder might not remember factors that are important to the research, a lapse that Davidsson, Delmar, and Wiklund (2006) term hindsight bias.

A *dynamic enterprise* is defined as one that has at least 15 employees and no more than 300 employees at the time of the study. The *control group*—that is, the group of less dynamic enterprises—is made up of new enterprises with no more than 10 employees. In each country, dynamic enterprises should account for about 70 percent of the enterprises in the panel. This requirement could introduce a degree of selection bias toward these kinds of dynamic new ventures, but this bias is not expected to affect the conclusions about the characteristics of firms created by middle-class entrepreneurs. Each country sample is expected to include 150 young firms. The study does not cover the sizable group of informal microenterprises, which represent a significant proportion of Latin American firms.

In order to capture the context of the entrepreneurial process, the same methodology was applied in each of the various countries and regions studied, and sectors with distinct profiles were included. By gaining access to information on the entrepreneurial process in such diverse contexts, captured using the same methodology, it was possible to identify both the common aspects of enterprise creation and development and the aspects that are specific to each environment.

Enterprises from two types of sectors (conventional and knowledge based) were included. The conventional sector includes manufacturing firms such as food and beverages, furniture, clothing, and metalwork. The knowledge-based activities associated with the new communications and information technologies include software firms as well as Internet-related services, remote voice and data communications, and other branches of applied electronics. In addition, firms from two types of localities (metropolitan areas and local areas with a strong presence of small and medium enterprises) were studied.

This study included only independent firms. Subsidiaries of large firms were removed. Firms were selected at random from enterprise directories and other available information sources, following the previously defined company profile criteria. In Latin America, where registries of businesses that list the date of founding are scarce, a considerable effort was undertaken to create specialized directories of new firms based on information from sources such as municipalities, business chambers, support institutions, universities, foundations, and previous studies.

As the basis for fieldwork, a common questionnaire was designed and used for all the countries. The questionnaire was completed during personal interviews made by qualified interviewers. For consistency, rigorous quality control measures were implemented in accordance with common guidelines in all countries. For example, follow-up calls by telephone were made to ensure that the surveys had been completed by the entrepreneurs themselves. Inconsistencies or ambiguous responses were rejected when it was not possible to resolve or clarify them. For a questionnaire to be used in the study, 90 percent of the answers had to be valid.

The procedures applied for gathering information and the quantitative techniques used adhered to rigorous methodological criteria. That said, some limitations of the study were duly taken into account in interpreting the results. While the definitions adopted for the selection of enterprises were the same, the sources of information used to identify the firms where interviews would take place varied somewhat across countries. Gathering data from various sources made it impossible to estimate the degree of statistical representativeness with precision. In any event, the sources consulted were quite extensive, with a view to limiting biases. Like many growth studies, this sample may suffer from attrition bias: that is, selection bias may be incurred by including only surviving firms. Nevertheless, this bias is not as relevant as it might appear to be (Geroski 1995; McPherson 1996; Weiss 1998).

Notes

1. See, for instance, Kantis, Ishida, and Komori (2002); Kantis, Moori Koening, and Angelelli (2005); Van Praag and Versloot (2007); Henrekson and Johansson (2009); Kelley, Bosma, and Amoros (2010).

2. The uncertainty avoidance index is higher in Latin America (85) than in the rest of emerging countries (for instance, the average of China, the Arab Republic of Egypt, Hungary, India, Malaysia, Poland, the Russian Federation, South Africa, Thailand, and Turkey is 64) and in the most developed countries (62).

3. Tertiary education enrollment rates in Latin American countries are half those of more developed countries and are similar to the average of the emerging economies—48 percent, 70 percent, and 43 percent, respectively (UNESCO 2010).

4. Income disparity, measured by the average income Gini coefficient, is 50 percent higher in Latin American countries than in the most developed countries (World Bank 2010). This feature is shared with the rest of the emerging countries.

5. The business sophistication index is 3.85 for Latin American countries, 4.2 for the average of other emerging economies, and 5.08 for the most developed countries. Additionally, the investment in R&D by firms is 0.1 percent of gross domestic product (GDP) in Latin American countries, 0.4 percent in emerging economies, and 1.3 percent in the most developed countries.

6. Since the size of the data set is rather small, the distinctions by country and subjective classes refer only to differences that are statistically significant and where the number of observations of the pair country-class is larger than 30.

7. Entrepreneurs had to indicate the social class of the household where they were born and educated from the following options: low, middle-low, middle, upper-middle, and high.

8. Although the figures analyzed in this study are not comparable with the information provided by household surveys—since definitions of social origin and entrepreneurship are rather different—it is convenient to consider some information obtained from such surveys, which include a huge number of observations. For instance, according to household surveys, employers tend to belong predominantly to the middle class (for instance, Argentina, 54 percent; Brazil, 60 percent; El Salvador, 46 percent; and Peru, 33 percent), while employees and self-employees belong predominantly to lower classes (more than two out of three in all of the referred countries). For a broader descriptive analysis of the entrepreneurial process based on household surveys, see chapters 4 to 6 of this book.

9. Chile is the only country that shows statistically significant mean differences in this variable. Chilean middle-class entrepreneurs create their first venture when they are 33.8 years old and start to think about it when they are 29.7 years old, on average, while the more affluent Chilean entrepreneurs start their first venture at 28.8 years old and think of becoming an entrepreneur when they are 25.9 years old. Other countries such as Argentina, Ecuador, and Mexico exhibit a similar pattern, but no statistically significant mean differences are evident.

10. This regional trend is also found in Argentina, Chile, Ecuador, Mexico, and Peru. Due to the limited number of observations from the upper classes in Argentina and Mexico, statistics corresponding to these countries should be interpreted with caution.

11. At the country level, these differences are statistically significant in Peru and, to a lesser extent, in Mexico. There are no significant differences between regions. Most middle-class entrepreneurs are well educated.

12. At the country level, statistically significant differences are evident in Chile (59 percent in the upper class and 42 percent in the middle class).

13. Ecuador and Mexico show statistically significant differences in the influence of prior work experience and family context. Argentina also shows this pattern, although the differences are not statistically significant.

14. This is particularly the case in Ecuador, Mexico, and Peru, where statistically significant differences are evident.

15. At the country level, both Chile and Mexico exhibit statistically significant differences in this regard.

16. For instance, the impossibility of continuing one's studies appears to be relevant in Argentina, Chile, and Mexico, whereas being unemployed is statistically significant only in Chile.

17. At the country level, the contribution of upper-class entrepreneurs' families to acquiring negotiation skills is significantly higher in Argentina, Ecuador, and Mexico. Mexican data show significant differences between middle-class and lower-class entrepreneurs in other entrepreneurial factors, such as marketing, administration, and hard work.

18. At the country level, some statistically significant differences are evident. Previous work experience is more prevalent among middle-class than upper-class entrepreneurs in Argentina (problem solving, administration, and hard work), Chile (teamwork, planning, communication, and motivation), Ecuador (negotiation), Mexico (marketing and communication), and Peru (technical knowledge).

19. At the country level, the main statistically significant differences are evident in Argentina (social skills, teamwork, marketing, and motivation), Mexico (creativity), and Peru (technical knowledge, marketing, administration, hard work, and communication).

20. At the country level, differences in the composition of networks are evident in Argentina, Chile, Mexico, and Peru.

21. This characteristic is even more pronounced in Peru, where 36 percent of middle-class firms are located in local areas (versus 9.1 percent of upper-class firms).

22. At the country level, statistically significant differences are only reported in Mexico, where the firms of middle-class entrepreneurs are less likely to be in technology-based industries than the firms of upper-class entrepreneurs (20 percent and 41 percent, respectively).

23. Statistically significant differences are found only in Mexico.

24. This is particularly true in Chile and Peru.

25. The mean export coefficient is 25 percent in Latin America, 38 percent in Italy, 46 percent in Taiwan, China, and 51 percent in Korea.

26. This is particularly noteworthy in Mexico and Peru.

27. This is particularly true in Taiwan, China, where 25 percent of the firms of middle-class entrepreneurs have invested more than $500,000. In Spain, this proportion is around 20 percent.

28. This is the case in all of the countries studied except Peru, where the richest entrepreneurs tend to employ almost 30 people at the beginning (while middle-class firms employ 11).

29. At the country level, some statistically significant differences are worth mentioning. In Chile, middle-class entrepreneurs face more problems than those from the wealthiest class in getting the right suppliers, purchasing equipment and machinery, and managing operations. In Mexico, difficulty in hiring professional managers and managing operations is more frequent among middle-class than

upper-class entrepreneurs. Difficulty in purchasing machinery and equipment is mentioned more frequently by lower-class entrepreneurs in Brazil, Chile, Ecuador, and El Salvador. These findings may reflect firms' lack of access to external financing.

30. At the country level, some differences between middle-class and upper-class entrepreneurs are evident. In Ecuador, middle-class entrepreneurs tend to solve their problems by themselves (66 percent) more often than either upper- or lower-class entrepreneurs (43 percent and 44 percent, respectively). In Chile, they tend to use the support of their suppliers less often (28 percent and 10 percent, respectively). They tend to use public institutions less often in Ecuador (10 percent and 23 percent, respectively) and in Peru (13 percent and 27 percent, respectively). Finally, they tend to use consultants and consultancy firms less often than upper-class entrepreneurs in Mexico (6 percent and 22 percent, respectively).

References

Banerjee, A., and E. Duflo. 2008. "What Is Middle Class about the Middle Classes around the World?" *Journal of Economic Perspectives* 22 (2): 3–28.

Birdsall, N., C. Graham, and S. Pettinato. 2000. "Stuck in the Tunnel: Is Globalization Muddling the Middle Class?" Working Paper 14, Center on Social and Economic Dynamics, Brookings Institution, Washington, DC.

Colombo, M., and L. Grilli. 2005. "Founder's Human Capital and the Growth of New Technology-Based Firms: A Competence-Based View." *Research Policy* 34 (6): 795–816.

Davidsson, P., F. Delmar, and J. Wiklund. 2006. *Entrepreneurship and the Growth of the Firms.* Cheltenham, U.K.: Edward Elgar.

Easterly, W. 2001. "The Middle-Class Consensus and Economic Development." *Journal of Economic Growth* 6 (4): 317–35.

———. 2002. "Does Inequality Cause Underdevelopment: New Evidence." Working Paper 1, Center for Global Development, Washington, DC.

Franco, R., M. Hopenhayn, and A. Leon. 2011. "Crece y cambia la clase media en América Latina: Una puesta al día." Review 103, Comisión Económica para América Latina (CEPAL), Santiago, Chile.

Garnsey, E. 1998. "A Theory of the Early Growth of the Firm." *Industrial and Corporate Change* 7 (3): 523–56.

Geroski, P. 1995. "What Do We Know about Entry?" *International Journal of Industrial Organization* 13 (4): 421–40.

Gimeno, J., T. Folta, A. Cooper, and C. Woo. 1997. "Survival of the Fittest? Entrepreneurial Human Capital and the Persistence of Underperforming Firms." *Administrative Science Quarterly* 42 (4): 750–83.

Henrekson, M., and D. Johansson. 2009. "Gazelles as Job Creators: A Survey and Interpretation of the Evidence." *Small Business Economics* 35 (2): 227–44. doi: 10.1007/s11187-009-9172-z.

Hofstede, G., G. J. Hofstede, and M. Minkov. 2010. *Cultures and Organizations: Software of the Mind,* 3rd ed. New York: McGraw-Hill.

Kantis, H. 2010. "Aportes para el diseño de políticas integrales de desarrollo emprendedor en América Latina." Working Paper, Inter-American Development Bank, Washington, DC.

Kantis, H., and S. Drucaroff. 2009. *Corporate Entrepreneurship*. Washington, DC: Inter-American Development Bank.

Kantis, H., J. Federico, and L. Trajtenberg. 2011. "Entrepreneurship, Economic Mobility, and Entrepreneurial Propensity: A Regional View Based on the Analysis of Selected Latin American Countries." Working Paper 135, Inter-American Development Bank, Washington, DC.

Kantis, H., M. Ishida, and M. Komori, eds. 2002. *Entrepreneurship in Emerging Economies: The Creation and Development of New Firms in Latin America and East Asia*. Washington, DC: Inter-American Development Bank.

Kantis, H., V. Moori Koening, and P. Angelelli. 2005. *Developing Entrepreneurship: Experience in Latin America and Worldwide*. Washington, DC: Inter-American Development Bank.

Kelley, D., N. Bosma, and J. E. Amoros. 2010. *Global Entrepreneurship Monitor: 2010 Executive Report*. London: Global Entrepreneurship Research Association. http://www.gemconsortium.org.

LAVCA (Latin American Private Equity and Venture Capital Association). 2010. *Scorecard: The Private Equity and Venture Capital Environment in Latin America*. New York. http://lavca.org/2010/04/21/2010scorecard/.

Lora, E., and F. Castellani. 2011. "Strengthening Mobility and Entrepreneurship: A Case for the Middle Classes." Research Department, Inter-American Development Bank, Washington, DC.

McPherson, M. 1996. "Growth of Micro and Small Enterprises in Southern Africa." *Journal of Development Economics* 48 (2): 253–77.

Pressman, S. 2007. "The Decline of the Middle Class: An International Perspective." *Journal of Economic Issues* 41 (1): 181–99.

Schoar, A. 2010. "The Divide between Subsistence and Transformational Entrepreneurship." *Innovation Policy and the Economy* 10 (1): 57–81.

Torche, F., and L. López Calva. Forthcoming. "Stability and Vulnerability of the Latin American Middle Class." in *Dilemmas of the Middle Class around the World,* edited by Katherine Newman. New York: Oxford University Press.

UNDP (United Nations Development Programme). 2010. Human Development Index Database. New York. http://hdr.undp.org/en/statistics/hdi/.

UNESCO (United Nations Educational, Scientific, and Cultural Organization). 2010. *UNESCO Science Report 2010*. Paris: UNESCO Publishing.

Van Praag, M., and P. Versloot. 2007. "What Is the Value of Entrepreneurship? A Review of Recent Research." *Small Business Economics* 29 (4): 351–82.

Veciana, J. 2005. *La creación de empresas: Un enfoque gerencial*. Colección de Estudios Económicos 33. Barcelona: Caja de Ahorros y Pensiones de Barcelona.

WEF (World Economic Forum). 2010. *The Global Competitiveness Report 2010–2011*. Geneva: WEF.

Weiss, C. 1998. "Size, Growth, and Survival in the Upper Austrian Farm Sector." *Small Business Economics* 10 (4): 305–12.

World Bank. 2010. Ease of Doing Business Rankings 2010. Washington, DC. http://www.doingbusiness.org/rankings.

4

The Role of Entrepreneurship in Promoting Intergenerational Social Mobility in Mexico

Viviana Vélez-Grajales and Roberto Vélez-Grajales

The degree of upward social mobility—the ability to move from a lower social class to a higher one—is an important indicator of a society's success. It is a sign of equal opportunity among children of families with different socioeconomic status. Equality of opportunity, in turn, is necessary to ensure that people's position in the social hierarchy is the result of a merit-based competitive process rather than determined by their socioeconomic origin.[1] A good indicator of the performance of redistributive policies is whether individuals' life achievements depend more on their talent and effort or more on their physical or socioeconomic characteristics (Vélez-Grajales, Campos-Vazquez, and Fonseca Godínez 2012).

As Serrano and Torche (2010) contend, social mobility should be promoted for three main reasons: justice, efficiency, and social cohesion. The argument for justice is normative: individuals should earn what they deserve, as in a meritocracy. The argument for efficiency is economic: lack of social mobility creates barriers to an optimal allocation of human resources. The argument for social cohesion is consensual: social mobility reduces the probability of social conflict.

This chapter analyzes the role played by entrepreneurship in promoting social mobility in Mexico. To design policies that might enhance social mobility across generations, it would be useful to know the extent to which family background determines individuals' occupational choices and how these choices affect their income. Becoming an entrepreneur can depend not only on specific individual characteristics such as talent or effort, but also on factors such as family wealth or membership in a family of entrepreneurs. If family background affects the probability of an individual becoming an entrepreneur, public policies should seek to overcome this barrier.

Mexico presents a good case study. Intergenerational social mobility is relatively low in Mexico (Cortés, Escobar, and Solis 2007; Serrano and Torche 2010). Moreover, as Torche (2010) shows, it is significantly lower at the extreme ends of Mexico's socioeconomic distribution.[2] At the same time entrepreneurial activity is constrained by lack of credit, which is one reason why Mexican entrepreneurs do not take advantage of scale economies to increase the added value of their activity. Lecuona Valenzuela (2009) shows that even though commercial banks allocated 42 percent of their credit portfolios to entrepreneurial activities in 2007, on average, only 11 percent—amounting to 0.7 percent of gross domestic product (GDP)—was available to small clients, and almost 80 percent was concentrated on the 300 major clients of each bank. In this context, the question is whether entrepreneurial activity is a good vehicle for social mobility.

This chapter analyzes three areas. First, it characterizes Mexican entrepreneurs and analyzes whether they experience greater upward social mobility than the self-employed or employees. Second, it identifies possible intergenerational determinants of entrepreneurship. Finally, it estimates the effect of entrepreneurial activity on income. For the analysis, retrospective socioeconomic data are taken from the Mexican Social Mobility Survey 2006 (MSMS-2006), which is conducted by the Centro de Estudios Espinosa Yglesias (CEEY). This survey collects current socioeconomic information on respondents and retrospective information on their parents. The analysis is conducted for two birth cohorts of respondents: 1942–64 and 1965–81.

Results show that entrepreneurial activity is a good vehicle for upward mobility. The magnitude of increase in entrepreneurs' social mobility, however, varies with their individual characteristics and family background. Results suggest that, although entrepreneurs with lower-income parents experience upward mobility, they have more difficulty reaching the top end of the socioeconomic distribution than those with parents in the middle- or high-income part of the socioeconomic distribution. Moreover, the individual's decision to become an entrepreneur is strongly determined by the father's occupation; it is not necessarily related to the individual's initial wealth or educational attainment. Finally, the mean effect of entrepreneurial activity on income is positive in general and relatively larger for individuals with parents at the extreme ends of the socioeconomic distribution.

Data Source and Entrepreneurs' Profile

There is little consensus about what constitutes entrepreneurship. Scholars have proposed various definitions, which depend largely on the research questions they seek to answer. Early works concerned with defining entrepreneurship can be classified into two thematic groups. The first group looks at the functions of entrepreneurs in the economy. These include managers of the uncertainties of the market, innovators, risk takers, and coordinators of factors of production. The second focuses on the characteristics of entrepreneurs as individuals. Behavioral scientists, among others, have claimed that entrepreneurs possess special traits that influence their participation in entrepreneurship, such as leadership, and that entrepreneurial characteristics tend to run in families.

More recent studies in empirical economics try to model the decision to become an entrepreneur and to understand the evolution of small businesses (Landström, Harirchi, and AstrÖm 2012). Many of them equate entrepreneurship with self-employment, based on the argument that the self-employed fulfill one or more of the roles of entrepreneurs in the economy, such as risk takers. Others consider entrepreneurs to be only those who employ workers. According to Parker (2004), "The self-employed are often taken to be individuals who earn no wage or salary but who derive their income by exercising their profession or business on their own account and at their own risk. Likewise, partners of an unincorporated business are usually classified as self-employed. It is sometimes helpful to partition the self-employed into employers and own-account workers (the latter of which work alone) or into owners of incorporated or unincorporated businesses."

In this chapter, we distinguish employers from own-account workers. Entrepreneurs are individuals who own a business or are partners of a business and employ workers. Self-employed are own-account workers. Figure 4.1 shows the occupational distribution of male workers between 24 and 65 years old in Mexico. Since 2005, the proportion of entrepreneurs has fluctuated between 6 and 8 percentage points, while that of self-employed has fluctuated between 20 and 27 percentage points.

The MSMS-2006 is a nationally representative, fully probabilistic, stratified multistage survey. The sample is representative only for men, but it also includes a sample of women. The respondents are individuals between 25 and 64 years old. The most relevant information for the purpose of this chapter concerns the education and employment of respondents and their fathers. Respondents are asked about the characteristics of their current job, their first job, and their father's job when they were 14 years old. The survey also asks about the characteristics of respondents' households and their father's household.

For our purposes, only those men who completed the interview are included: 6,312 individuals. Only 8.3 percent are entrepreneurs—that is,

Figure 4.1 Occupational Distribution of Male Workers
Ages 24–65 in Mexico, 2005–12

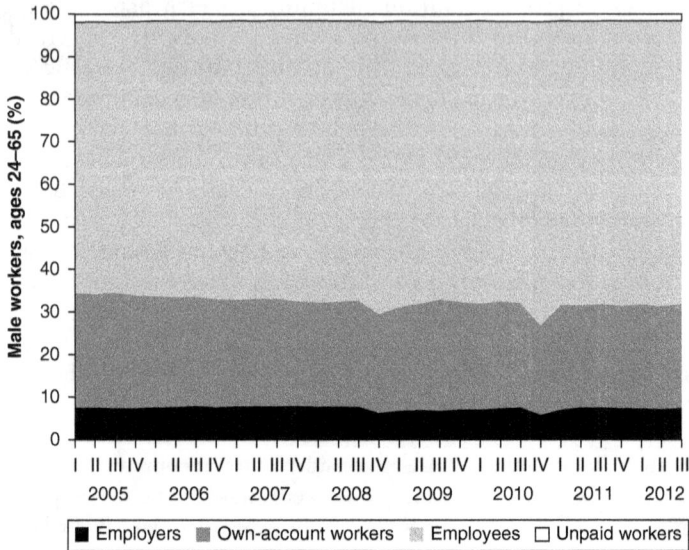

Source: Based on data from the *Encuesta Nacional de Ocupación y Empleo*
2005–12.
    Note: I = first quarter, II = second quarter, III = third quarter, IV = fourth
quarter.

they reported being owners or partners of a business.[3] Almost 60 percent
of respondents are employees in the private or public sector, and 30 percent
are self-employed. The rest did not report their occupation (figure 4.2).[4]

On average, the household monthly income for all respondents is
Mex$5,390 (Mexican pesos) or $677 (2005 purchasing power parity
[PPP]).[5] For entrepreneurs, the mean household monthly income is higher:
Mex$7,300, or $917 (2005 PPP) (figure 4.3).

Socioeconomic classes are defined with regard to household income.
Middle-class individuals are defined as those from households with a daily
income between $10 and $50 (2005 PPP), following López-Calva and
Ortíz-Juárez (2011).[6] According to this definition, 21 percent of individuals are considered lower class, 71 percent are middle class, and 8 percent
are upper class (see figure 4.4).

A total of 7.6 percent of middle-class individuals report being entrepreneurs; this figure is 5.7 percent for the lower class and 16.9 percent for the
upper class (see figure 4.5).

Figure 4.2 Type of Employment of the Sample in Mexico, 2006

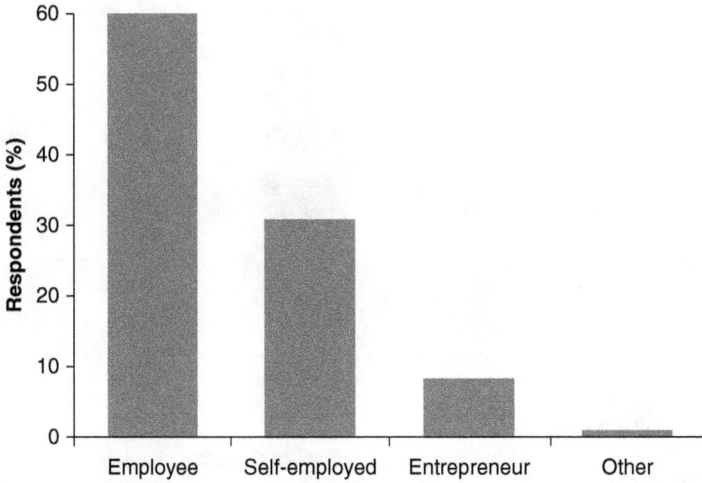

Source: MSMS-2006.

Figure 4.3 Mean Monthly Household Income of Sample in Mexico, 2006

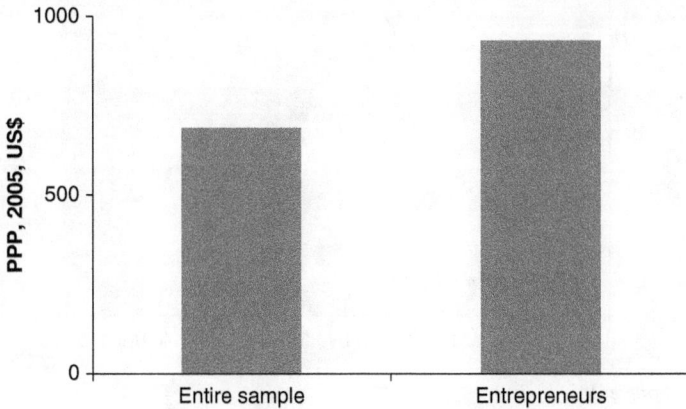

Source: MSMS-2006.

Figure 4.4 Class Distribution of the Entire Sample in Mexico, 2006

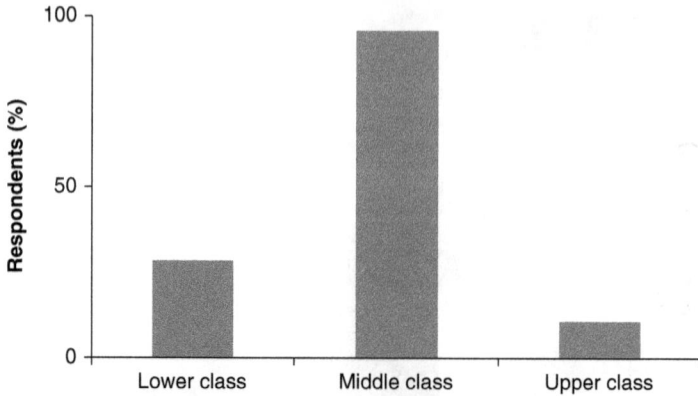

Source: MSMS-2006.

Note: Middle class individuals are defined as those from households with a daily income between $10 and $50 (2005 PPP [purchasing power parity]).

Figure 4.5 Proportion of Entrepreneurs in Each Income Class in the Sample in Mexico, 2006

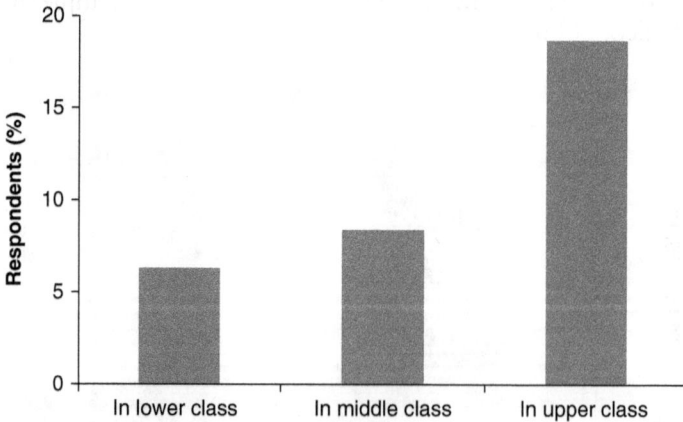

Source: MSMS-2006.

Note: Middle class individuals are defined as those from households with a daily income between $10 and $50 (2005 PPP [purchasing power parity]).

Entrepreneurship and Intergenerational Mobility

Social mobility refers to changes in the position of individuals in the social hierarchy. For this chapter, such changes are measured across generations—that is, the focus is on changes experienced by individuals in relation to their parents or intergenerational mobility. Numerous studies support this kind of analysis (Solon 1992, 2002; Behrman, Gaviria, and Székely 2001; Mazumder 2005; Jantti et al. 2006).

Social mobility is multidimensional and can be measured by combining different dimensions of well-being. Torche (2010) argues that following such a strategy allows for more accurate identification of differences across the entire socioeconomic distribution, including the extreme ends.[7] Intergenerational mobility is measured here by calculating the intergenerational persistence of household wealth.[8] In the long run, wealth can increase households' consumption and reduce their vulnerability, as Torche and Spilerman (2010) argue. Also, wealthier households face fewer restrictions and can make long-term investments, such as in educating their children.

To measure wealth, we constructed an index of household assets. An advantage of using an asset-based index instead of expenditures or income is that individuals' wealth is predicted largely by their ability to accumulate assets (Sahn and Stifel 2003).[9]

Indexes are computed for both the household assets of the respondents and those of their parents.[10] Three types of assets are considered: durables, household characteristics, and access to credit.[11] Examples of durables are cars, televisions, telephones, and books. Household characteristics include having a toilet, access to hot water, and electricity. Variables associated with access to credit include ownership of a bank account and ownership of a credit card. The set of asset variables available in the data is not the same for respondents and their parents.

Respondents were born over a period of 39 years, from 1942 to 1981. Because it is probable that the value of assets changed over time, indexes were estimated separately for two groups of respondents: those who were born from 1942 to 1964 and those who were born from 1965 to 1981. Indexes for the parents of each group of respondents were also estimated.[12] Fathers of the second generation of respondents were born, on average, 18 years later than those of the first generation, which is consistent with the difference of 20 years in the average year of birth between the two generations of respondents.

Next, the proportions of respondents, or children, who experienced upward, downward, or no mobility with respect to their parents, were calculated. Figure 4.6 presents the results for the entire sample and the subsample of entrepreneurs for the two birth cohorts. As shown in the left-side panel of panel a, for example, 24 percent of respondents in the first bar, 50 percent in the second, and 30 percent in the third did not experience

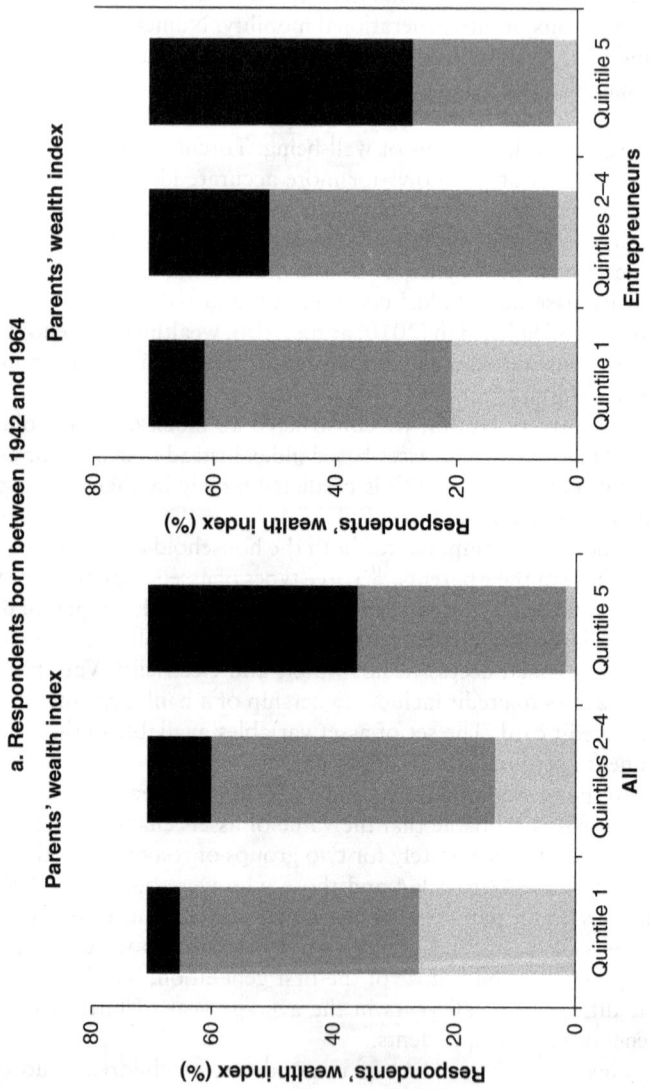

Figure 4.6 Proportion of Respondents with Upward or Downward Mobility with Respect to Parents' Position, 2006

a. Respondents born between 1942 and 1964

Parents' wealth index

Parents' wealth index

Respondents' wealth index (%)

Respondents' wealth index (%)

Quintile 1   Quintiles 2–4   Quintile 5
All

Quintile 1   Quintiles 2–4   Quintile 5
Entrepreneurs

(continued next page)

88

Figure 4.6 (continued)

b. Respondents born between 1965 and 1981

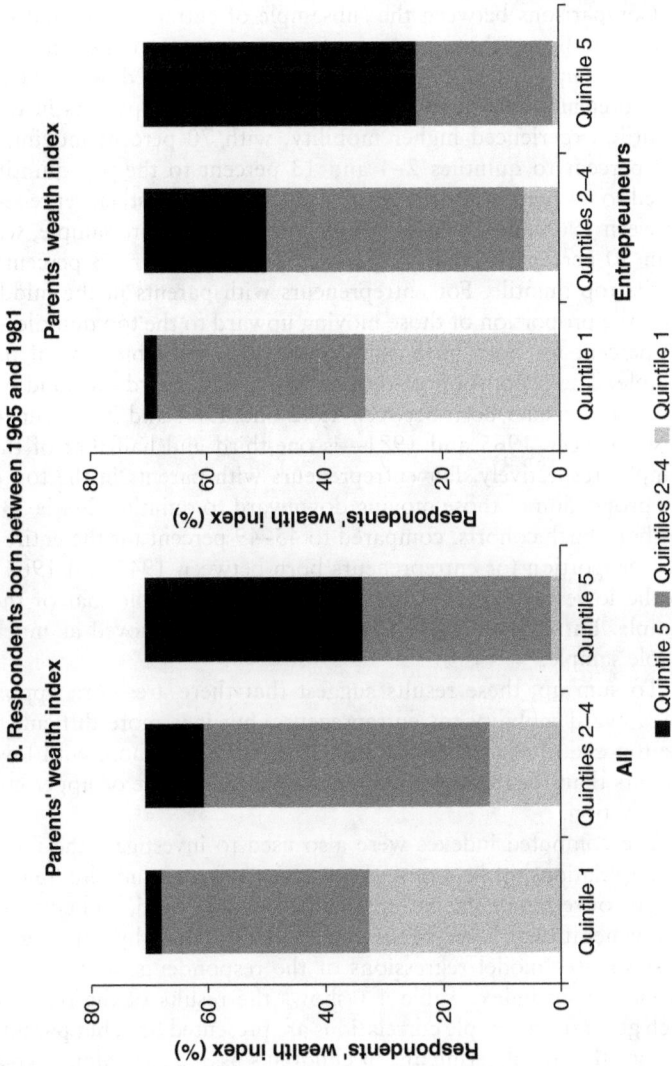

Source: Based on data from the MSMS-2006.

relative mobility—that is, respondents stayed in the same quintile as their parents. In the extremes, 8 percent of respondents with parents in the lowest quintile moved up to the top quintile of the asset index distribution, and only 3 percent of respondents with parents in the top quintile moved down to the lowest quintile.

Comparisons between the subsample of entrepreneurs and the entire sample indicate that, in general, entrepreneurs experience a higher degree of upward mobility and a lower degree of downward mobility. Entrepreneurs born between 1942 and 1964 with parents in the lowest quintile experienced higher mobility, with 70 percent moving upward (57 percent to quintiles 2–4 and 13 percent to the top quintile) compared to 64 percent for the entire sample. In contrast, entrepreneurs born between 1965 and 1981 moved as much as the entire sample, with more than 50 percent moving to quintiles 2–4 and around 3 percent moving to the top quintile. For entrepreneurs with parents in the middle quintiles, the proportion of those moving upward to the top quintile—around 30 percent for both birth cohorts—is almost double that of the entire sample. The proportion of those moving downward—around 5 percent for entrepreneurs born between 1942 and 1964 and 9 percent for those born between 1965 and 1981—is one-third and half that of the whole sample, respectively. For entrepreneurs with parents in the top quintile, the proportion of those moving downward to quintiles 2–4 is 33 percent for both birth cohorts, compared to 45–49 percent for the entire sample. The proportion for entrepreneurs born between 1942 and 1964 moving to the lowest quintile—around 6 percent—is double that of the whole sample. Entrepreneurs of the other birth cohort moved as much as the whole sample.

To sum up, these results suggest that there are more opportunities for upward mobility for entrepreneurs, but it is more difficult to reach the top end of the socioeconomic distribution for those with lower-class parents than for those with parents from the middle or upper end of the distribution.

The computed indexes were also used to investigate the intergenerational relationship in terms of assets for parents and children for three groups of respondents: entrepreneurs, self-employed, and employed. The intergenerational asset persistence was estimated by running ordinary least squares model regressions of the respondents' asset index on the parents' asset index. Table 4.1 shows the results of the regressions for each generation. Simple correlations are presented first, but parental assets are not the sole determinant of children's assets; they alone explain only around 25 to 40 percent of their variation. When controlling for age and education of respondents, the estimated asset persistence falls and the regression explains a higher percentage of the variation in children's assets.

For the generation of respondents born between 1942 and 1964, the correlation between parents' wealth and children's wealth is higher for

Table 4.1 Intergenerational Asset Persistence in Mexico, by Birth Cohort, 2006

Indicator	All	Entrepreneurs	Self-employed	Employed
Respondents born between 1942 and 1964				
Simple correlation	0.49 (0.014)	0.47 (0.044)	0.54 (0.025)	0.44 (0.019)
R^2	0.28	0.29	0.30	0.25
Number of observations	2,964	286	1,019	1,636
Correlations controlling for age and years of education of respondent	0.3 (0.015)	0.28 (0.049)	0.37 (0.029)	0.26 (0.020)
R^2	0.41	0.41	0.40	0.40
Number of observations	2,960	286	1,018	1,634
Respondents born between 1965 and 1981				
Simple correlation	0.56 (0.014)	0.63 (0.055)	0.57 (0.026)	0.51 (0.018)
R^2	0.34	0.39	0.38	0.29
Number of observations	2,795	201	744	1,829
Correlations controlling for age and years of education of respondent	0.39 (0.015)	0.49 (0.057)	0.43 (0.028)	0.35 (0.018)
R^2	0.48	0.50	0.51	0.46
Number of observations	2,792	201	744	1,826

Source: Based on data from the MSMS-2006.

the self-employed than for entrepreneurs and employees. For the generation of respondents born between 1965 and 1981, entrepreneurs' wealth
is determined to a higher degree by their parents' wealth. If the complement of the intergenerational asset persistence (1 – intergenerational asset
persistence) is used as a measure of mobility, intergenerational mobility
decreased over the years more for entrepreneurs than for the self-employed.

Initial Conditions and Relationship to Entrepreneurship

The positive relationship between initial household wealth and entrepreneurship in industrial countries has been interpreted as evidence of liquidity or credit constraints for entrepreneurship (see Quadrini 1999; Hurst
and Lusardi 2004). Based on data availability, this section investigates the
factors that may be important for becoming an entrepreneur in Mexico,
including parents' socioeconomic class.

Taking these classes into account, the probability of being an entrepreneur, self-employed, or an employee is estimated using a multinomial
probit model. To establish causality, predetermined variables are used as
independent variables. These include respondents' and parents' education, parents' socioeconomic class defined according to the wealth index,
father's occupation, and regional variables such as size of the city where
respondents were raised. Wealth variables can be expected to explain to
some extent the ability of some individuals to obtain the capital needed to
become entrepreneurs.

It is interesting to see how the same variables affect different occupational choices. Table 4.2 shows the marginal effects for selected variables.
Those related to the father's occupation have the largest marginal effect
on the decision to become an entrepreneur. Having a father who is an
entrepreneur increases the probability of becoming an entrepreneur by
0.1382, compared to having a father who is self-employed. Also, having
a father who worked in a large firm, as opposed to a small or medium
enterprise (SME), increases the probability by 0.0444.[13] An unexpected
finding is that the parents' socioeconomic class does not significantly
affect an individual's decision to become an entrepreneur; neither does the
number of years of schooling.[14] These results suggest that entrepreneurship in Mexico is strongly determined by the father's occupation and not
necessarily by the individual's initial wealth or educational attainment.[15]
The sample of entrepreneurs in the analysis includes only individuals who
are still entrepreneurs, not those who failed at entrepreneurial activity.
Therefore, having a father who is an entrepreneur may increase the entrepreneurship survival or success rate.

For the self-employed and employees, the father's occupation is the
variable that has the greatest effect on the son's choice of occupation.

Table 4.2 Probability of Being an Entrepreneur, an Employee, or Self-Employed in Mexico, 2006

Indicator	Entrepreneur	Employee	Self-employed
Sociodemographic characteristics			
Age	0.0105***	−0.0184***	0.0078
Age squared	−0.0104***	−0.017***	−0.0066
Years of schooling	−0.0006	−0.0114**	−0.0108**
Years of schooling squared	0.0085	−0.0209	0.0123
1 if speaks an indigenous language or belongs to indigenous group, 0 otherwise	−0.0084	−0.0749**	0.0833***
1 if lived in an urban area when 14 years old, 0 otherwise	0.0117	0.0294*	−0.0411***
1 if did not attend school when 14 years old, 0 otherwise	−0.0073	−0.0057	0.0203
First job[a]			
1 if worked in a microenterprise, 0 otherwise	0.0239**	−0.1673***	0.1434***
1 if worked in a large enterprise, 0 otherwise	−0.0088	0.0064	0.0024
Parents' socioeconomic class[b]			
1 if parents were in the first quintile of the wealth index distribution, 0 otherwise	−0.0029	−0.0266	0.0296*
1 if parents were in the fifth quintile of the wealth index distribution, 0 otherwise	−0.006	−0.0498**	0.0437**

(continued next page)

Table 4.2 (continued)

Indicator	Entrepreneur	Employee	Self-employed
Father's occupation^c			
1 if father worked as an entrepreneur, 0 otherwise	0.1382***	0.0342	−0.1724***
1 if father worked as an employee, 0 otherwise	0.0055	0.1938***	−0.1993***
1 if father worked as a domestic worker, 0 otherwise	0.0317	0.0668	−0.0984
Father's employment, by size of enterprise^d			
1 if father worked in a small enterprise, 0 otherwise	−0.014	0.0175	−0.0034
1 if father worked in a large enterprise, 0 otherwise	0.0444***	−0.0516	0.0071
Number of observations	4,717	4,717	4,717

Source: Based on data from the MSMS-2006.

Note: Multinomial probit estimates, marginal effects. The other covariates included in the regression are number of siblings, number of siblings squared, father's years of schooling, father's years of schooling squared, dummies for if he lived with his father or mother at age 14, ranked middle level with respect to his classmates at age 14, ranked high level with respect to his classmates at age 14, worked in the United States legally, and worked in the United States illegally and if father worked in the United States, in the agriculture sector, in the industry sector, in the construction sector, in the trade sector, in the transport sector, and in the services sector. SME = small and medium enterprise.

a. *Reference variable:* 1 if worked in an SME enterprise, 0 otherwise.
b. *Reference variable:* 1 if parents were in quintiles 2–4 of the wealth index distribution, 0 otherwise.
c. *Reference variable:* 1 if father worked as self-employed, 0 otherwise.
d. *Reference variable:* 1 if father worked in an SME enterprise, 0 otherwise.
Significance level: * = 10 percent, ** = 5 percent, *** = 1 percent.

In both cases, the probability increases at around 0.19 when the father has the same occupation. Some of the positive determinants of the decision to become an employee are negative ones for the decision to become self-employed. For instance, while having worked in a microenterprise as opposed to an SME for the first job decreases the probability of being an employee, it increases the probability of being self-employed. Speaking an indigenous language or belonging to an indigenous group negatively affects the decision to become an employee, while it positively affects the decision to be self-employed. Having a father who is an entrepreneur decreases the probability of becoming self-employed, but not the probability of becoming an employee. It could be that when a family business is established, next-generation family members have the option of becoming an employee of the enterprise or another firm within the father's business network.

Entrepreneurship and Profits

To measure the effect of entrepreneurship on earnings, the income of entrepreneurs was compared to that of non-entrepreneurs. Because two outcomes cannot be observed at the same time for a given individual, mean effects were estimated. The parameter of interest is what in the evaluation literature is called treatment on the treated.[16] The idea is to pair each treated individual with similar nontreated individuals, so that, after conditioning for a set of observable characteristics, the income distribution observed for the nontreated individuals can be substituted for the missing income distribution of the treated individuals. Matching methods assume that the nontreated outcome is independent of treatment conditional on observable characteristics. In this way, the difference in the mean values of the income outcomes can be attributable to entrepreneurship. It is assumed, then, that selectivity in entrepreneurship depends only on observable characteristics.

The set of observable characteristics used to do the matching includes individual characteristics that are not affected by the choice of becoming an entrepreneur, such as age, years of schooling, whether the individual lived in a city when younger, and years of work experience. It also includes characteristics of the individual's parents, such as years of schooling, socioeconomic class, and whether the father was an entrepreneur, self-employed, or employed worker.[17]

The effects of being an entrepreneur on individual income were estimated for four groups of individuals: entrepreneurs in general and entrepreneurs with parents from each socioeconomic class.[18] Figure 4.7 presents the estimated impacts.[19] For the group of all entrepreneurs, entrepreneurship increases income by 17 percent. The effect is also positive when estimations are done for entrepreneurs with parents from different socioeconomic classes. The effect observed for entrepreneurs with parents who belong to the first (lower-class) quintile (47 percent) and the fifth (upper-class) quintile (29 percent) are higher than those observed for entrepreneurs with middle-class parents (13 percent).[20]

In order to make comparisons, the same exercise was undertaken for the group who are self-employed (see figure 4.8). In this case, self-employment increases income by only 1.5 percent. When estimations were done for the self-employed with parents from different socioeconomic classes, a positive difference in earnings (8 percent) is evident only for those with parents in the fifth quintile. Contrary to the case of entrepreneurs, the observed effect is negative (–14 percent) for the self-employed with parents in the first quintile and negligible for those with parents in the second to fourth quintiles.[21] However, it cannot be concluded that self-employment leads to different levels of earnings, except for the self-employed with parents in the first quintile, because the differences are not statistically significant.

The results suggest that entrepreneurs are more successful than non-entrepreneurs. The positive effect of entrepreneurial activity on income suggests that entrepreneurs have distinct characteristics that make them succeed in entrepreneurial life. This argument is supported by the finding

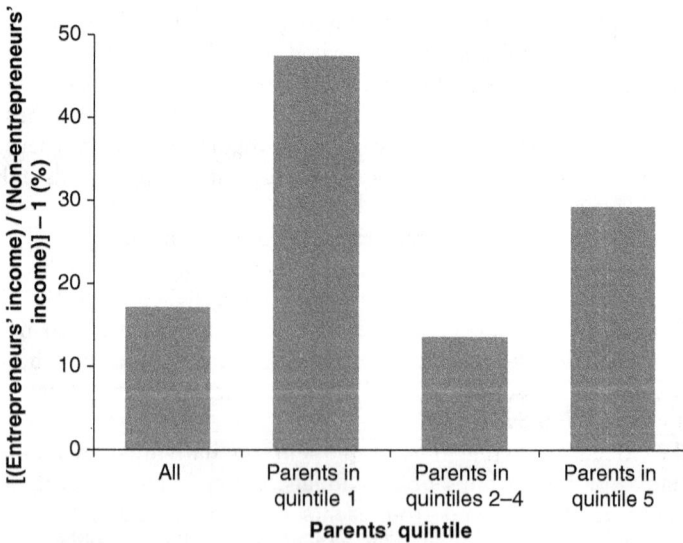

Figure 4.7 Income of Entrepreneurs Compared to Non-Entrepreneurs in Mexico, 2006

Source: Based on data from the MSMS-2006.
Note: Positive values refer to higher incomes for entrepreneurs.

Figure 4.8 Income of Self-Employed Compared to Workers Who Are Not Self-Employed in Mexico, 2006

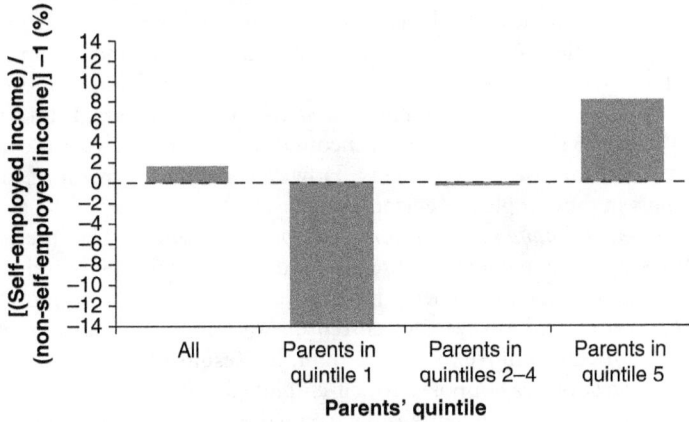

Source: Based on data from the MSMS-2006.
Note: Positive values refer to higher incomes for self-employed workers.

that an alternative activity such as self-employment does not seem to have an impact on income. Assuming that family credit constraints restrict entrepreneurial entry and that entrepreneurs are equally distributed across socioeconomic classes, one could further conclude that entrepreneurial success is affected by entry barriers. The implications of the results are twofold. On the one hand, the finding that the relative effect on income is higher for those with parents in the lowest quintile suggests that entrepreneurs are successful once barriers to entrepreneurial activities, such as lack of credit, are eliminated. On the other hand, the finding that the effect on income is bigger for entrepreneurs with parents in the fifth quintile than for those with parents in the second to fourth quintiles suggests that the success or survival rate decreases when entrepreneurs encounter barriers to entrepreneurial activities, such as lack of credit.

Conclusions

A good indicator for the performance of redistributive policies is that individuals' life achievements depend more on their talent and effort and less on their physical or socioeconomic characteristics, as Vélez-Grajales, Campos-Vazquez, and Fonseca Godínez (2012) argue. This chapter has analyzed the role played by entrepreneurship in promoting social mobility in Mexico. The study was done within the scope of the intergenerational social mobility theory—that is, the focus is on the differences in socioeconomic characteristics between individuals and their parents. Within this retrospective context, socioeconomic characteristics of parents and their relative position in the social hierarchy were explored as possible determinants of the achievements of adult children (survey respondents) and, in particular, the achievements of entrepreneurs. The main findings follow.

Entrepreneurs have higher incomes than non-entrepreneurs. Data from the MSMS-2006 show that monthly income is 35 percent higher for entrepreneurs than for non-entrepreneurs. However, only 8.3 percent of male individuals in the sample are entrepreneurs.

Entrepreneurs have more options for upward mobility. The intergenerational transition matrixes for the asset indexes of respondents and their parents suggest that entrepreneurs have more options for upward mobility than other workers. However, for entrepreneurs with lower-class parents, it is more difficult to move to the top quintile. Results of the econometric analysis suggest that, as opposed to self-employed and employed individuals, the wealth of entrepreneurs is determined to a higher degree by their parents' wealth, at least for the younger generation (those born between 1965 and 1981).

The father's occupation is an important determinant of the son's likelihood of becoming an entrepreneur. Estimates of the determinants of the decision to become an entrepreneur show that the probability of becoming an entrepreneur increases when the respondent's father was an entrepreneur. In addition, the probability of becoming an entrepreneur is higher for a respondent whose father worked in a large firm as opposed to an SME or a microenterprise. These results suggest that, in Mexico, the decision to become an entrepreneur is strongly determined by the father's occupation and not necessarily by the individual's initial wealth or educational attainment.

Entrepreneurs with parents in the high or low ends of the income distribution have bigger gains in income. Estimates of the mean effect of entrepreneurial activity on income using the propensity score matching method suggest that entrepreneurship increases income by 17 percent overall for the group of all entrepreneurs. When the exercise is broken down by socioeconomic class, the effects observed for entrepreneurs with parents in the extreme quintiles (the first and fifth quintiles) are significantly higher than those observed for entrepreneurs with middle-class parents.

Some policy lessons can be obtained from these results. First, earnings are higher for entrepreneurs than for non-entrepreneurs. However, if the rate of entrepreneurship is close to the reported 8.3 percent, the size of public programs intended to consolidate or create enterprises should be designed and targeted accordingly. They should not be mass programs.

Second, entrepreneurship can be a good vehicle for social mobility. However, entry barriers to entrepreneurial activities remain and should be identified and eliminated.

Finally, the estimated effects of entrepreneurial activity on income also suggest that entrepreneurs are exceptional individuals, or outliers. This result supports the necessity of designing well-focused public programs to support entrepreneurship.

The analysis has some limitations. The most important one is that it is not possible to identify all entrepreneurs who were engaged in entrepreneurial activities before the survey was conducted. Therefore, the results might be biased toward successful entrepreneurs. Further analysis should be done to derive policy implications. For example, it is important to analyze whether credit constraints limit the options to increase the number of successful entrepreneurs. In any case, not all individuals have the potential to become entrepreneurs, just as not all individuals have the potential to become professional piano players or professional baseball players.

Notes

1. Following the capabilities approach proposed by Sen (1985, 1987), equality of opportunity should be measured in terms of effective freedom—that is, the available options. However, equality of opportunity does not assure equality of results (UNDP 2010).
2. Torche (2010) estimates a multidimensional index of intergenerational well-being using information from the Mexican Social Mobility Survey 2006. Results show that around 50 percent of male Mexican household heads with parents in the lowest quintile stayed in the same quintile. Moreover, only 4 percent reached the top quintile. In contrast, no household heads with parents in the top quintile fell to the lowest one.
3. This percentage is slightly higher than the one obtained with the *Encuesta Nacional de Ocupación y Empleo* because the sample for our analysis contains a higher proportion of heads of household.
4. On average, men in the sample used for the analysis are 42 years old, with a standard deviation of 11 years. More than 90 percent of them are heads of household, 6 percent are a son of the head of household, and the rest are deemed other relatives. On average, they have eight years of schooling, which corresponds to the second year of junior high school, and 77 percent completed primary school. More than 2 percent reported being unemployed, and more than 3 percent reported being retired. Those with a job are distributed in the following seven sectors of the economy: services (19 percent); industry (19 percent); trade (18 percent); agriculture (12 percent); other services, such as automotive services and domestic repairs (12 percent); construction (11 percent); and transport (8 percent).
5. The 2005 PPP factor is 7.64. The factor is taken from the World Development Indicators, http://data.worldbank.org/indicator/PA.NUS.PRVT.PP.
6. López-Calva and Ortíz-Juarez determine the $10 lower bound based on the probability of falling into poverty in three countries: Chile, Mexico, and Peru. In the case of Mexico, nonpoor individuals with a 10 percent probability of falling into poverty have a daily income level of $9.70 (2005 PPP). In a similar exercise only for entrepreneurs, which Ortíz-Juarez provided to the authors, the lower threshold is equal to $10.63 (2005 PPP). However, this estimation is based on a limited number of observations.
7. In addition to wealth, the literature analyzes social mobility with regard to several other dimensions. Measures of income mobility are the most common, as

are years of schooling, because accumulating human capital through education is considered one of the main vehicles for ascending the social ladder. Social class is studied in the sociological literature. Torche (2009) argues that this approach can capture the value of several market assets, such as specific skills, job occupation, sector of economic activity in which individuals work, and education. The most commonly used classification for social mobility and stratification studies is the Comparative Analysis of Social Mobility in Industrialized Nations (CASMIN), a social class grouping defined by Erikson and Goldthorpe (1992). Social mobility can also be measured through social perception. Huerta (2010) affirms that self-perception or the perception of others about an individual's traits and intentions is a main determinant of individuals' well-being.

8. The most studied relationship in the literature for measuring intergenerational social mobility relates the earnings of parents to those of children (Behrman and Taubman 1990; Solon 1992). Because the MSMS-2006 contains information on income only for the respondents' generation, it is not possible to estimate intergenerational earning elasticities.

9. This requires selecting a set of weights to obtain an index of the form, $A_i = \gamma_1 a_{i1} + \ldots + \gamma_K a_{iK}$, where A_i is the asset index, a_{iK} are the specific assets, and γ_S are the weights. The weights were estimated through the principal components analysis method. Then correlations between the indexes of parents and children were estimated. This was done for the entire sample and also for the samples of entrepreneurs, employees, and self-employed. The principal components analysis technique is used to reduce the dimension of a set of variables by constructing fewer new variables that capture the variation in the original set. The new variables are linear combinations of the original variables. The first principal component is the combination that explains the largest amount of variation, the second principal component is the combination that best explains the remaining variability, and so on. In this investigation, the asset index is the first principal component.

10. Following the notation in Filmer and Pritchett (2001), the formula of the index for each household Aj can be written as $A_j = f_i \cdot \dfrac{a_{ji} - a_1}{s_1} + \cdots + f_N \cdot \dfrac{a_{jN} - a_N}{s_N}$, where f_i is the weight in the linear combination for asset i; a_{ji} is the value assigned to asset i; and a_i and s_i are the mean and standard deviation, respectively, of the ith asset variable over all households.

11. Most of the variables are binary. The value 1 represents ownership or access, and 0 represents lack of the asset. Therefore, a move of the variable from 0 to 1 results in a discrete change of $\dfrac{f_i}{s_i}$ in the index.

12. As in Filmer and Pritchett (2001), the internal coherence of the asset index is tested by comparing the average asset ownership across households with different levels of wealth.

13. Respondents were asked about the number of workers in their firm. The options were 1 person, 2–4, 5–9, 10–100, and more than 100. Given these options, it is not possible to define firms with 10–50 employees as small and those with 51–250 employees as medium. Therefore, SMEs are defined as enterprises with 10–100 workers, without distinguishing between small and medium enterprises.

14. The number of years of schooling increases by class. Lower-class entrepreneurs have an average of 5.6 years of education, middle-class entrepreneurs have 8.1 years, and upper-class entrepreneurs have 12.6 years.

15. This does not mean that education is not an important determinant of success for entrepreneurs. When returns to school are estimated using a Mincer earnings model, the coefficient of years of education is 0.08 (with a standard error of 0.011).

16. The impact on income for entrepreneurs is obtained in the following way: $E(\Delta|T=1) = E(Y_1 - Y_0|X, T=1) = E(Y_1|X, T=1) - E(Y_0|X, T=0)$, where X denotes

a set of conditioning variables, $T = 1$ if an individual is an entrepreneur (treated), and $T = 0$ if an individual is not an entrepreneur (nontreated). The first expectation, $E(Y_1|X,T = 1)$, can be estimated, but the data for the second expectation, $E(Y_0|X,T = 0)$, are missing. Matching estimators are used to impute that expectation.

17. Matching on many variables could generate the problem that, for some combinations of characteristics of treated individuals, no nontreated pairs are available. To reduce the "high dimensionality problem" that arises when Z is large, the propensity score theorem of Rosenbaum and Rubin (1983) was applied. It states that when matching on $Pr(T = 1|Z)$ is valid, then matching on the propensity score is also valid. This is the conditional probability of becoming an entrepreneur.

18. The mean effect of entrepreneurship on income was calculated using the

estimator: $\Delta Y = \dfrac{1}{N}\sum_{i \in N}\left(Y_i - \dfrac{1}{J}\sum_{j \in J} Y_j \right)$, where N is the number of entrepreneurs

and J is the number of propensity score matched non-entrepreneurs.

19. Only the estimates using a neighborhood radius of 0.002 are reported. It is important to point out that the simple mean difference in incomes is higher than the estimated propensity score matching effect for every group of entrepreneurs, except for the first quintile. This suggests that, in general, the simple difference in means overestimates the size of the effects.

20. To assess the quality of the matching, a statistical test for the difference of population means was performed. It consists of comparing the average values of the covariates used to estimate the probability of being an entrepreneur (propensity score model) between treated and nontreated groups. With p-values greater than 0.05, the null cannot be rejected at 5 percent. In this case, for every variable, the possibility that the means are the same after the matching is performed cannot be rejected.

21. As for entrepreneurs, a statistical test for the difference of population means was performed to assess the quality of the matching for the self-employed. Also in this case, for every variable, the possibility that the means are the same after the matching was performed cannot be ruled out.

References

Behrman, J. R., A. Gaviria, and M. Székely. 2001. "Intergenerational Mobility in Latin America." Working Paper 452, Inter-American Development Bank, Washington, DC.

Behrman, J. R., and P. Taubman. 1990. "The Intergenerational Correlation between Children's Adult Earnings and Their Parents' Income: Results from the Michigan Panel Survey of Income Dynamics." *Review of Income and Wealth* 36 (2): 115–27.

Cortés, F., A. Escobar, and P. Solís, eds. 2007. *Cambio estructural y movilidad social en México*. Mexico City: El Colegio de México.

Erikson, R., and J. H. Goldthorpe. 1992. *The Constant Flux: A Study of Class Mobility in Industrial Societies*. Oxford, U.K.: Clarendon Press.

Filmer, D., and L. Pritchett. 2001. "Estimating Wealth Effects without Expenditure Data—or Tears: An Application to Educational Enrollments in States of India." *Demography* 38 (1): 115–32.

Huerta, J. E. 2010. "El rol de la migración y las redes sociales en el bienestar económico y la movilidad social percibida." In *Movilidad social en México: Población, desarrollo y crecimiento*, edited by J. Serrano and F. Torche. Mexico City: Centro de Estudios Espinosa Yglesias.

Hurst, E., and A. Lusardi. 2004. "Liquidity Constraints, Household Wealth, and Entrepreneurship." *Journal of Political Economy* 112 (2): 319–47.

Jantti, M., K. Roed, R. Naylor, A. Bjorklund, B. Bratsberg, O. Raum, E. Osterbacka, and T. Eriksson. 2006. "American Exceptionalism in a New Light: A Comparison of Intergenerational Mobility in the Nordic Countries, the UK, and the US." IZA Discussion Paper Series 1938, Institute for the Study of Labor, Bonn.

Landström, H., G. Harirchi, and F. Aström. 2012. "Entrepreneurship: Exploring the Knowledge Base." *Elsevier Research Policy* 41 (7): 1154–81.

Lecuona Valenzuela, R. 2009. "El financiamiento a las PyMES en México: La experiencia reciente." *Economía UNAM* 6 (17): 69–91.

López-Calva, L. F., and E. Ortíz-Juárez. 2011. "A Vulnerability Approach to the Definition of the Middle Class." Policy Research Working Paper 5902, World Bank, Washington, DC.

Mazumder, B. 2005. "Fortunate Sons: New Estimates of Intergenerational Mobility in the United States Using Social Security Earnings Data." *Review of Economics and Statistics* 87 (2): 235–55.

Parker, S. C. 2004. *The Economics of Self-Employment and Entrepreneurship.* Cambridge, U.K.: Cambridge University Press.

Quadrini, V. 1999. "The Importance of Entrepreneurship for Wealth Concentration and Mobility." *Review of Income and Wealth* 45 (1): 1–19.

Rosenbaum, P. R., and D. B. Rubin. 1983. "The Central Role of the Propensity Score in Observational Studies for Causal Effects." *Biometrica* 70 (1): 41–55.

Sahn, D. E., and D. Stifel. 2003. "Exploring Alternative Measures of Welfare in the Absence of Expenditure Data." *Review of Income and Wealth* 49 (4): 463–89.

Sen, A. 1985. *Commodities and Capabilities.* Amsterdam: North-Holland.

———. 1987. *The Standard of Living.* Cambridge, U.K.: Cambridge University Press.

Serrano, J., and F. Torche, eds. 2010. *Movilidad social en México: Población, desarrollo y crecimiento.* Mexico City: Centro de Estudios Espinosa Yglesias.

Solon, G. R. 1992. "Intergenerational Income Mobility in the United States." *American Economic Review* 82 (3): 393–408.

———. 2002. "Cross-Country Differences in Intergenerational Earnings Mobility." *Journal of Economic Perspectives* 16 (3): 59–66.

Torche, F. 2009. "Sociological and Economic Approaches to the Intergenerational Transmission of Inequality in Latin America." Working Paper HD-09-2009, Regional Bureau for Latin America and the Caribbean, United Nations Development Programme, New York.

———. 2010. "Cambio y persistencia de la movilidad intergeneracional en México." In *Movilidad social en México: Población, desarrollo y crecimiento*, edited by J. Serrano and F. Torche. Mexico City: Centro de Estudios Espinosa Yglesias.

Torche, F., and S. Spilerman. 2010. "Influencias intergeneracionales de la riqueza en México." In *Movilidad social en México. Población, desarrollo y crecimiento*, edited by J. Serrano and F. Torche. Mexico City: Centro de Estudios Espinosa Yglesias.

UNDP (United Nations Development Programme). 2010. *Regional Human Development Report for Latin America and the Caribbean 2010: Acting on the Future—Breaking the Intergenerational Transmission of Inequality.* New York: UNDP.

Vélez-Grajales, R., R. Campos-Vazquez, and C. E. Fonseca Godínez. 2012. "El concepto de movilidad social: Dimensiones, medidas y estudios en México." In *Movilidad social en México: Constantes de la desigualdad,* edited by R. Campos-Vázquez, J. E. Huerta Wong, and R. Vélez-Grajales. Mexico City: Centro de Estudios Espinosa Yglesias.

5

Entrepreneurship, Entrepreneurial Values, and Public Policy in Argentina

José Anchorena and Lucas Ronconi

An entrepreneurial spirit has long been viewed as a positive factor for economic growth (Schumpeter [1911, 1934] 1989; Schmitz 1989; King and Levine 1993; Wennekers and Thurik 1999). A large middle class has been considered to be the cradle of entrepreneurship (Landes 1998; Maddison 2007). The usual argument posits that middle-class individuals have the resources and values to postpone gratification and reap the long-term benefits of innovation. Linking these two perspectives together suggests that a large middle class promotes economic growth through a more dynamic entrepreneurial environment.

Within this context, Argentina is particularly puzzling. It has long been described as having a large middle class (Altimir 1986). Since the early twentieth century, Argentina and Uruguay have had the largest middle classes in Latin America (Torrado 1992). According to the literature, this attribute should have translated into high economic growth in subsequent decades. However, Argentina performed poorly in the second half of the twentieth century. Questioning why the link between a large middle class and economic growth broke down, this chapter tentatively proposes that public policy in the second half of the twentieth century made a difference and that, if a large middle class is a necessary condition for economic catch-up, it is not sufficient. Public policy incentives are such that too few within the Argentine middle class become productive entrepreneurs.

Argentina is home to many entrepreneurs, as documented by Ardagna and Lusardi (2008), among others. The type of entrepreneurship that dominates the landscape, however, is not conducive to economic growth. As Ardagna and Lusardi put it, there are many "necessity" entrepreneurs, but few "opportunity" entrepreneurs. "Necessity" entrepreneurs choose entrepreneurship because they lack a decent salaried alternative, not because they see a business opportunity. As we show in this chapter, many entrepreneurs (considering as such business owners and the self-employed) work in low-productivity, informal occupations and engage in rent seeking. Thus it is important to characterize entrepreneurship by both its quantity and its quality. Taking a long-term perspective, Baumol (1990) distinguishes between productive, unproductive, and destructive entrepreneurship.[1] Only the first type is conducive to economic growth, according to the theories of Schumpeter ([1911, 1934] 1989) and Aghion and Howitt (1992).

What kind of public policies pushed middle-class individuals out of productive entrepreneurship? First, the broken link between the middle classes and entrepreneurship is partly due to a disastrous monetary and financial policy, which keeps the financial sector highly undeveloped. According to World Bank Indicators, credit to the private sector in Argentina amounts to 14 percent of gross domestic product (GDP), compared with 53 percent in Brazil, 97 percent in Chile, and 152 percent in Organisation for Economic Co-operation and Development (OECD) countries. Savings are not channeled through the financial sector to highly productive investments with high microlevel indivisibilities and uncertainty (Acemoglu and Zilibotti 1997). Second, the bureaucracy is highly inefficient in promoting business creation and reducing its costs, as De Soto (1986) argues about Peru. Third, the tax system is highly discontinuous, meaning that the marginal rates for business have drastic jumps in size. This policy has contributed to a segmented business distribution: a few large, formal, high-productivity businesses and many small, informal, low-productivity businesses.[2] As a consequence, entrepreneurs have no incentive to increase the size of their business. Fourth, intrusive and complex labor and tax codes have deterred formal job creation. Last, fiscal federalism that provides abundant rents through transfers to provincial governments, which use them to obtain local political support by offering attractive public employment (Gervasoni 2010), has crowded out entrepreneurship.

This chapter has four objectives. First, it describes entrepreneurs in Argentina: their demographics, schooling, employment conditions, size of their firm, income, and intergenerational characteristics.[3] This characterization provides measures of the quantity and quality of entrepreneurs. Second, it describes entrepreneurial values and analyzes the extent to which Argentine society supports those values.[4] Third, it summarizes the main policy obstacles faced by entrepreneurs. Finally, it assesses how public employment policies affect entrepreneurship.

Although the chapter is mainly descriptive, it provides a collection of stylized facts to advance the knowledge on entrepreneurship in developing countries and its relationship to public policy. Given the scant amount of research on these issues, the collection of facts and statistical analyses in this chapter is intended to serve as a guide for future formal modeling and deeper empirical analysis. Since no single source of information covers all of the topics discussed in this chapter, several data sets were used: three Argentine household surveys, the World Values Survey, two firm-level surveys, and administrative data on registered firms. Although these data sets provide valuable information, many measurement problems remain, particularly regarding the "quality" of entrepreneurship.

Who Is an Entrepreneur?

There are three main interrelated classical definitions of entrepreneur. Two of them emphasize the characteristics of entrepreneurs, such as risk taking and innovation, and the third emphasizes the role of entrepreneurs as a factor of production. The first definition was put forward by Knight (1929) and somewhat formulized by Kihlstrom and Laffont (1979): the entrepreneur has a "peculiar twofold function of (a) exercising responsible control and (b) securing the owners of productive services against uncertainty and fluctuation in their incomes." The essence of this definition is that the entrepreneur is the bearer of all risks, which implies that his income is highly unpredictable. Neither a top manager nor the owner of capital is an entrepreneur per se. According to Knight (1929), "The nearest approach to an entrepreneur only would be a man who borrowed all the resources for operating a business and then hired a manager and gave him an absolutely free hand."

The second definition, proposed by Schumpeter ([1911, 1934] 1989), indicates that an entrepreneur is a person who "carries out new combinations" of productive factors. A new combination can be (a) an introduction of a new good, that is, one with which consumers are not familiar; (b) the introduction of a new production method; (c) the opening of a new market; (d) the acquisition of a new source of supplies of primary or semi-manufactured products; and (e) the new organization of an industry, such as a monopoly position. Like Knight, Schumpeter distinguished the entrepreneur from the capitalist and the manager, but did not emphasize the uncertainty of the situation. Rather, he emphasized the role of the entrepreneur as a creator of value.

The third definition (but the oldest one), attributed to Say (1880) and incorporated by modern classical theory, poses that an entrepreneur is "one who undertakes an enterprise, especially a contractor, acting as intermediary between capital and labour."

These definitions overlap in some cases. For example, the last definition seems to consider a manager as an entrepreneur even if he does not bear risk or create value, but merely manages the "current flow of circulation."

Another person can bear a lot of risk but not create anything of value, such as by operating in a risky environment (for example, a gambler). Conversely, an employed person may not bear risk but may create value for the firm (for example, a creative scientist hired by a firm).

An important question is whether these concepts are well captured by the typical measure of entrepreneurship as independent or self-employed workers. This measurement is likely to produce two types of errors: it excludes employees who are actually engaged in entrepreneurial activities (error I) and includes as entrepreneurs some self-employed workers who are not (error II). The typical case of error I are individuals who conduct a nonprofit activity that puts their reputation on the line and their creative mind at work (such as the so-called social entrepreneurs). That person may be taking risk, may be innovating, and may be coordinating factors of production, but may still be classified as an employee. The typical case of error II is an individual who works alone but carries out a routine task, say, a taxi driver. In other words, entrepreneurship is a function pursued by individuals regardless of their type of employment.

The lack of appropriate data, however, forces researchers to use self-employment as a proxy for entrepreneurship. In what follows, entrepreneurs are classified as independent workers, be they employers or self-employed, who manage, or work in, a business of two or more people. A distinction is made between employer-entrepreneurs (those who hire workers) and self-employed entrepreneurs (those who do not hire workers). Further distinctions are made between formal and informal entrepreneurs, innovative and rent-seeking entrepreneurs, and high- and low-productivity entrepreneurs.

While these categories are likely to suffer from the two types of errors described above, they are dictated by data availability. Future research should focus on measuring entrepreneurship based on the functions and activities of the population and organizations.

Stylized Facts of Entrepreneurship in Argentina

The description of entrepreneurship in this section is based on the Permanent Household Survey (EPH), which has been conducted since 1974 in 31 urban agglomerates distributed all over Argentina, covering about 65 percent of the total population.[5] First, the main facts in 2010 are described using the whole sample. Second, taking advantage of a one-time special survey conducted in the fourth quarter of 2005 in Greater Buenos Aires (an urban conglomerate that accounts for roughly a third of the country's population), the distinction between "necessity" and "opportunity" entrepreneurs is discussed. Third, the evolution of the main variables of interest since 1974 is described.

Main Facts

Ten main facts are related to entrepreneurship in Argentina in 2010. Most of the statistical details are presented in the annex.

- *Fact 1.* Nearly one-fourth of the employed population over 14 years of age are independent workers (22.7 percent), of which 4.5 percent are employers (henceforth employer-entrepreneurs or entrepreneurs 1), 4.7 percent are self-employed and work with at least one more person (self-employed entrepreneurs or entrepreneurs 2), and 13.5 percent are the "pure" self-employed, who work alone. Therefore, entrepreneurs (1 and 2) represent 9.2 percent of the employed population (table 5A.1).[6]
- *Fact 2.* Many entrepreneurs become so out of necessity rather than opportunity: 22.5 percent of employer-entrepreneurs and 45.5 percent of self-employed entrepreneurs are so by necessity (table 5A.2).
- *Fact 3.* Informality, defined by the lack of business registration for tax purposes, is pervasive among entrepreneurs, although it is much higher for self-employed entrepreneurs (54.4 percent) than for employer-entrepreneurs (11.5 percent, table 5A.3).
- *Fact 4.* The majority of employer-entrepreneurs are male. This predominance is somewhat less pronounced among the self-employed—both the "pure" and the self-employed entrepreneurs—and considerably less so among employees.[7]
- *Fact 5.* The mean age is higher for entrepreneurs and self-employed than for employees.[8]
- *Fact 6.* On average, employer-entrepreneurs have more education than employees, who, in turn, have more education than self-employed workers (either pure or self-employed entrepreneurs). In all four categories, dispersion is large, but it is smaller for employees (see figure 5.1).[9]
- *Fact 7.* Both types of entrepreneurs work longer hours on average than either the pure self-employed or employees. A large share of self-employed workers would have preferred to work more hours than they did in the previous month.
- *Fact 8.* Most entrepreneurs work in small businesses. On average, employer-entrepreneurs manage businesses of nine workers (the median is only four), while self-employed entrepreneurs work in firms of three persons, on average (with medians of only two). On average, employees work in firms of around 120 employees, although the median is only 18.[10]
- *Fact 9.* A large share of entrepreneurs own or rent equipment or machinery, although the share is larger for employer-entrepreneurs than for self-employed entrepreneurs. The share is, however, much smaller for the purely self-employed. Almost none of the self-employed owns equipment or machinery valued at higher than

Figure 5.1 Schooling Distribution in Argentina, by Occupational Status and Type of Worker, 2010

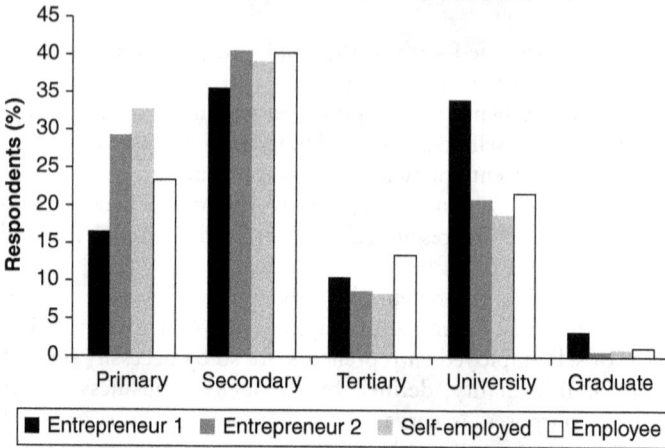

Source: Permanent Household Survey.

Figure 5.2 Income Distribution in Argentina, by Occupational Status and Type of Worker, 2010

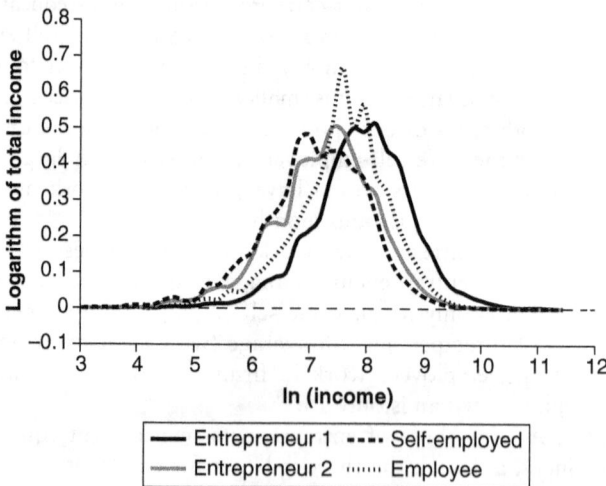

Source: Permanent Household Survey.

$15,000, and only slightly more than 5 percent of entrepreneurs own equipment or machinery.[11]

- *Fact 10*. Employer-entrepreneurs have, on average, higher incomes than employees, and they have, on average, higher incomes than both purely self-employed and self-employed entrepreneurs (see figure 5.2).

Necessity versus Opportunity Entrepreneurs

Based on the EPH special survey on informality for 2005, an entrepreneur is classified as a "necessity entrepreneur" in either of two cases: first, if she answered the question, "Why do you devote yourself to this business/firm/activity?" with "I did not find a job as an employee," and second, if she answered the question, "If you could choose, would you be an employee or an independent worker?" with the first option (an employee). The rest of the independent workers are classified as "opportunity entrepreneurs."

Using these definitions, slightly more than one-third of entrepreneurs are "necessity" entrepreneurs, and less than two-thirds are entrepreneurs by "opportunity" (see figure 5.3). There is not much difference between the two groups as to average age and hours worked, but "opportunity" entrepreneurs are significantly more educated and have more capital, larger firms, and higher income (see table 5A.2).

Figure 5.3 Income Distribution in Argentina, by Type of Entrepreneur, 2010

a. Opportunity versus necessity entrepreneurs

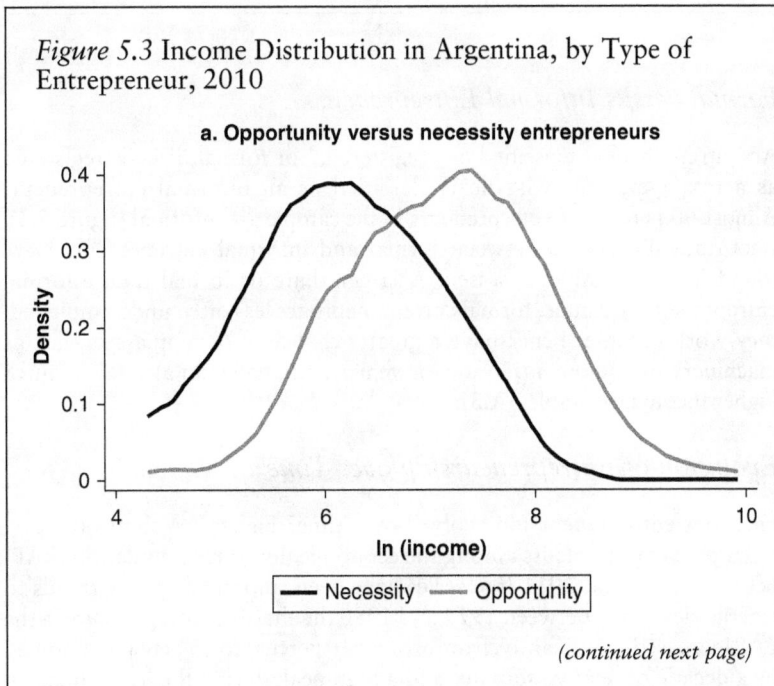

In (income)

— Necessity   — Opportunity

(continued next page)

Figure 5.3 *(continued)*

b. Formal versus informal entrepreneurs

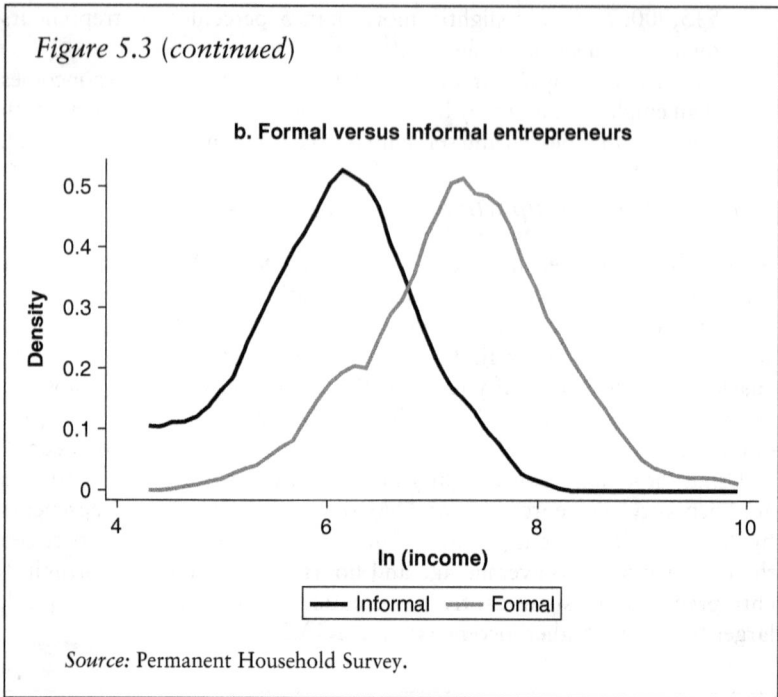

Source: Permanent Household Survey.

Formal versus Informal Entrepreneurs

An entrepreneur is classified as "registered," or formal, if he is registered as a taxpayer; otherwise he is classified as an informal entrepreneur. Almost 40 percent of entrepreneurs in the sample are informal (figure 5.3). Important differences between formal and informal entrepreneurs were found in the variables assessed. A larger share of formal than informal entrepreneurs are male, formal entrepreneurs are less often underemployed, they work in larger firms, have a greater chance of owning assets such as machinery or equipment, locale, or vehicle, and have, on average, a much higher income (see table 5A.3).

Evolution of Entrepreneurship over Time

How has entrepreneurship evolved over time? Figure 5.4 shows the percentage of entrepreneurs among the economically active population (EAP) between 1974 and 2011 (the series have been smoothed for the trends to emerge clearly).[12] Between 1974 and 1980 the share of entrepreneurs in the EAP increased significantly, from around 10 percent to 13 percent, followed by a decade of relative stability and a high peak during the hyperinflation

Figure 5.4 Entrepreneurship as a Share of the Economically Active Population in Argentina, 1974–2011

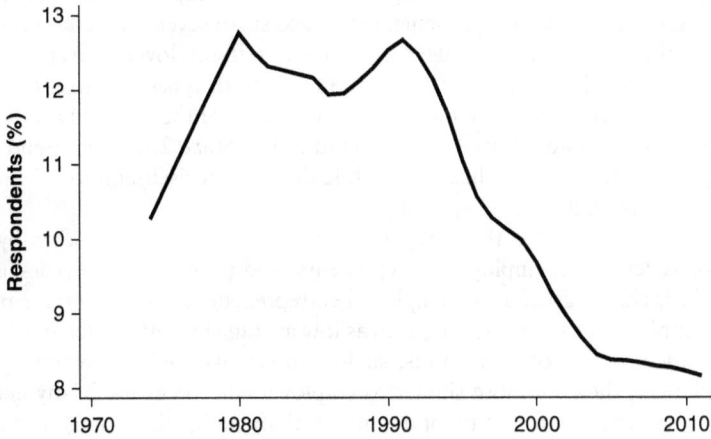

Source: Permanent Household Survey.

Figure 5.5 Types of Entrepreneurship as a Share of the Economically Active Population in Argentina, 1974–2011

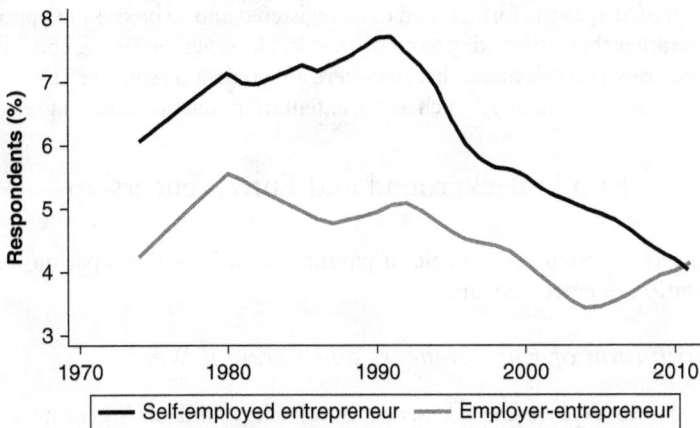

Source: Permanent Household Survey.

years of 1989–92. From then on, the share decreased from more than 13 percent to a historic low near 8 percent in 2011.

Between 1974 and 1980, the share of both types of entrepreneurs increased, as shown in figure 5.5, which separates employer-entrepreneurs from self-employed entrepreneurs. In the next six or seven years, the number of employer-entrepreneurs decreased, while self-employed entrepreneurs increased. In the critical period of 1988–92, both types of entrepreneurship increased. During the modernization period of the 1990s, both types of entrepreneurs decreased until around 2004. Since 2005, the trend for employer-entrepreneurs has risen, while the trend for self-employed entrepreneurs has fallen.

Summing up, the three types of independent workers—employer-entrepreneurs, self-employed entrepreneurs, and pure self-employed—have different characteristics. Self-employed entrepreneurs are similar to the pure self-employed in some respects, such as low average income or lack of health insurance, but in other respects, such as hours worked or ownership of machinery, they are more similar to employer-entrepreneurs. Many entrepreneurs are so by necessity, or are informal, or both, which suggests a low average quality of entrepreneurship, in the sense that their social value added is probably low. Moreover, most of the necessity and informal entrepreneurs are self-employed, which suggests that frictions in the economy impede self-employed entrepreneurs from becoming either formal employees or formal entrepreneurs. During the second half of the 1970s the percentage of entrepreneurs in the EAP increased, in the 1990s it decreased dramatically, and in the most recent decade it decreased little. However, a significant change in composition occurred during the last 10 years, with an increase in the share of employer-entrepreneurs and a reduction in the number of self-employed entrepreneurs. This could indicate a recent improvement in the "quality" of entrepreneurs, as the former tend to be registered and to be seeking opportunities rather than attempting to satisfy needs. However, no strong conclusion can be drawn on this matter because there are no data on some key aspects of entrepreneurial "quality," such as the extent of innovation and rent seeking.

Family Background and Entrepreneurship

This section discusses the role of parental wealth and occupation in the formation of entrepreneurs.

Distribution of Entrepreneurs and Parental Wealth

In order to explore the socioeconomic background of Argentine entrepreneurs, it would be ideal to have a longitudinal survey to determine if actual entrepreneurs were born in high-, middle-, or low-income families. Unfortunately, none of the available surveys in Argentina provides such information. The Social Development Survey (EDS), however, is a cross-section that includes recall questions. Each person over the age of 25 answers questions about the income of her or his parents and their employment status when the respondent was 15 years old.[13]

Based on the self-assessed wealth of their parents, respondents can be classified in three income groups:[14] 20 percent of the current entrepreneurs come from a high-income family, 65 percent from a middle-income family, and 15 percent from a low-income family (see figure 5.6). Based on these numbers, the middle class seems to be the cradle of the majority of entrepreneurs, but the shares do not differ markedly from those for the whole population.[15]

The relationship between parental wealth and current occupation is statistically significant, as shown in table 5.1: those born in higher-income families are more likely to become entrepreneurs, and those born in lower-income families are more likely to work as either an employee or as self-employed. However, the differences are small: 13 percent of those born in a high-income family become entrepreneurs compared to 12 percent and 7 percent of those from middle- and low-income families, respectively. Thus parental wealth is a predictor of entrepreneurial activity, but not a very strong one.

However, individuals whose parents owned a business are substantially more likely to become entrepreneurs than those whose parents did not own a business (see table 5.2). Although the relationship is not perfect, it is stronger than the correlation between parental wealth and entrepreneurship: the probability of becoming an entrepreneur is 15.8 percentage points higher if the parents owned a business, but only between 1.5 and 6.3 percentage points higher if the parents were high income (relative to middle class and low income).[16]

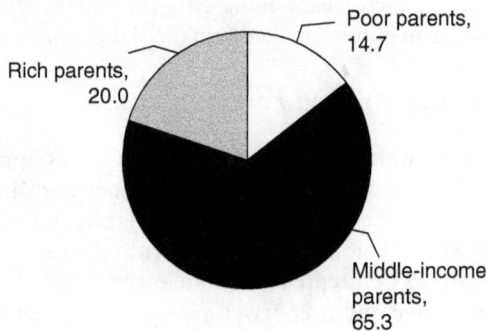

Figure 5.6 Distribution of Entrepreneurs in Argentina, by Parental Wealth, 1997

Poor parents, 14.7

Rich parents, 20.0

Middle-income parents, 65.3

Source: Social Development Survey.

Table 5.1 Relationship between Parental Wealth and Current
Occupation in Argentina, 1997

Current occupation	Low income, % (1)	Middle income, % (2)	High income, % (3)	Difference, % points (1) – (3)	Difference, % points (2) – (3)
Entrepreneur	7.1	11.9	13.4	–6.3***	–1.5**
Self-employed	18.7	15.5	17.7	1.0	–2.2***
Employee	74.3	72.6	68.9	5.4***	3.7***
Total	100	100	100	n.a.	n.a.

Source: Social Development Survey.
Note: Respondents were asked to self-assess the wealth of their parents when they
were 15 years old. n.a. = not applicable.
Significance level: ** = 5 percent, *** = 1 percent.

Table 5.2 Relationship between Parental Occupation and Current
Occupation in Argentina, 1997

Current occupation	Yes, %	No, %	Difference, % points
Entrepreneur	25.0	9.2	15.8***
Self-employed	14.7	14.8	–0.1
Employee	60.3	76.0	–15.7***
Total	100	100	n.a.

Source: Social Development Survey.
Note: Respondents were asked whether their parents owned a firm when they were
15 years old. n.a. = not applicable.
Significance level: *** = 1 percent.

Parental occupation is thus a better predictor of entrepreneurship than
parental wealth, suggesting that the intergenerational transmission of values is an important factor explaining entrepreneurial activity. Parental
wealth, however, is an important determinant of the skills of entrepreneurs.

Skills of Entrepreneurs and Parental Wealth

Entrepreneurs who were born in low-income families appear to be, on
average, much less productive than entrepreneurs born in middle- and
high-income families: their earnings are less than half, and they are less
likely to hire workers. This may be due in part to their shortage of human
and social capital, since entrepreneurs from lower-income families have on
average between three and four fewer years of schooling than entrepreneurs from higher-income families (table 5.3).

Regrettably, the EDS does not collect information on whether a business is formally registered or the extent to which it devotes resources

Table 5.3 Human Capital and Productivity of Entrepreneurs in Argentina, by Parental Wealth, 1997

| Variable | *Wealth of your parents when you were 15 years old (self-assessed)* | | | *Difference* | |
	Low income (1)	*Middle income (2)*	*High income (3)*	*(1)–(2)*	*(2)–(3)*
Monthly income ($)	407	1,190	1,085	–783***	106
Share of employer entrepreneurs (%)	18.4	42.6	37.0	–24.2***	5.6**
Years of schooling	7.4	10.6	11.6	–3.2***	–1.0***
Receives credit from government (%)	0	3.0	6.3	–3.0*	–3.3*
Main client is public sector (%)	5.4	11.6	11.4	–6.2*	0.2
Works in the street or at home (%)	43.9	18.7	19.8	25.3***	–1.1

Source: Social Development Survey.
Note: Respondents were asked to self-assess the wealth of their parents when they were 15 years old.
Significance level: * = 10 percent, ** = 5 percent, *** = 1 percent.

to innovation. However, it does gather information on a few characteristics of the business, such as sales to the public sector and access to government programs that provide credit or assistance to small businesses. This information reveals that entrepreneurs who were born in middle- and high-income families are more likely to benefit from the government than entrepreneurs from low-income families. This could be due to their personal relationships with government authorities and favoritism in the allocation of public funds. Thus entrepreneurs from higher-income families are endowed with more human and social capital, allowing their businesses to be more profitable.[17]

Values and Entrepreneurship

Having characterized the number, income, social origins, and human and social capital of entrepreneurs in Argentina, we now characterize the values of both the society at-large and the entrepreneurial class. Two questions are addressed in this section. What are typical entrepreneurial values worldwide? Does the Argentine society support those values?

The 2005–07 waves of the World Values Survey (WVS), a data set with more than 50,000 interviews in more than 50 countries, are used to that end. In what follows, any person who is self-defined in the WVS

as an "employer/manager of an establishment" is considered an entrepreneur (all others, including inactive people, are considered "non-
entrepreneurs").[18] The WVS asks about the "qualities that children can
be encouraged to learn at home." Respondents have to choose up to 5 of
10 alternatives: independence, hard work, sense of responsibility, imagination, tolerance and respect for other people, thrift (saving money and
things), determination and perseverance, religious faith, unselfishness, and
obedience. We use the answers to this question to identify the values of the
society at-large and those of entrepreneurs and to compare Argentina with
other countries from that angle.

Weber (1905) wrote the seminal study on the relationship between values
and economic progress. He hypothesized that the Protestant ethic, which
emphasizes hard work, thriftiness, patience, and perseverance, was the cultural and spiritual basis for the development of capitalism. It is natural to
associate those values with entrepreneurs, given the central role of these
values in capitalist systems. However, the world has changed dramatically
in the last 100 years, and the values that underlie entrepreneurship might
have changed accordingly. Rather than deciding a priori which values are
entrepreneurial, we have opted to infer them from the self-assessed values
of entrepreneurs and non-entrepreneurs worldwide. The overall conclusion is that, worldwide, entrepreneurs place more emphasis—relative to
non-entrepreneurs—on responsibility, tolerance and respect, independence,
determination and perseverance, and imagination (see table 5.4). They value
obedience, religious faith, and thriftiness less than non-entrepreneurs, and
there is no significant difference between both groups as to unselfishness
and hard work.

This classification seems plausible. Some of the inferred entrepreneurial
values are similar to those cited by Weber, such as responsibility, independence, and perseverance. Weber and others also view obedience and
religious faith as detrimental to the capitalist spirit insofar as they deter
rational economic behavior vis-à-vis traditional and nonscientific behavior. Meanwhile, tolerance has long been associated with nascent capitalism, emphasized by economic historians in the case of, for example, the
vibrant seventeenth-century Dutch economy.[19]

An important empirical fact is that the differences in values are larger
between societies than between entrepreneurs and non-entrepreneurs
within a particular society. Figure 5.7 shows the proportion of respondents
indicating that "independence" is an important value that children should
be taught at home. Two facts are worth noting. First, as most points are
below the 45 degree line, on average entrepreneurs value independence
more than non-entrepreneurs. Second, the values of entrepreneurs and
non-entrepreneurs correlate highly within societies.

The values of entrepreneurs can be determined in two ways. The first
is through societal values, which can directly influence those of entrepreneurs: it is hard for a small group to have values radically different from

Table 5.4 Share of Respondents Worldwide Saying That
Entrepreneurial Value Is Important for Children to Learn at
Home, 2005–07

Value	Entrepreneurs, % (1)	Non-entrepreneurs, % (2)	Difference, % points (1) – (2)	Type of value inferred
Responsibility	77.9	71.8	6.1***	Entrepreneurial
Tolerance and respect	74.7	70.3	4.4***	Entrepreneurial
Hard work	54.7	55.9	–1.1	Neutral
Independence	60.1	51.0	9.1***	Entrepreneurial
Obedience	34.4	43.0	–8.6***	Non-entrepreneurial
Religious faith	32.0	41.4	–9.4***	Non-entrepreneurial
Thrift	36.2	38.8	–2.6***	Non-entrepreneurial
Determination and perseverance	45.1	37.3	7.8***	Entrepreneurial
Unselfishness	34.8	34.1	0.7	Neutral
Imagination	30.2	22.8	7.4***	Entrepreneurial

Source: World Values Survey.
Notes: The observations are from 4,019 entrepreneurs and 78,973 non-entrepreneurs.
Significance level: *** = 1 percent.

those of the society in which it lives. The second is through intergenerational influence: in a dynamic economy, a large proportion of descendants of non-entrepreneurs become entrepreneurs and vice versa. Given this background, what values characterize Argentine society?

It is convenient to compare Argentina with other countries from Latin America that share some historic and cultural traits (Brazil, Chile, Colombia, Mexico, Peru, and Uruguay) and with two countries rich in natural resources with populations of European descent (Australia and New Zealand).[20] In general, the values of Argentine society are better aligned with entrepreneurship than those of the rest of Latin America, although this group is heterogeneous. Table 5.5 shows that Argentine society promotes six values supportive of entrepreneurship more than the rest of Latin America. These are higher independence, lower obedience, lower religious faith, lower thriftiness, higher determination and perseverance, and higher imagination.

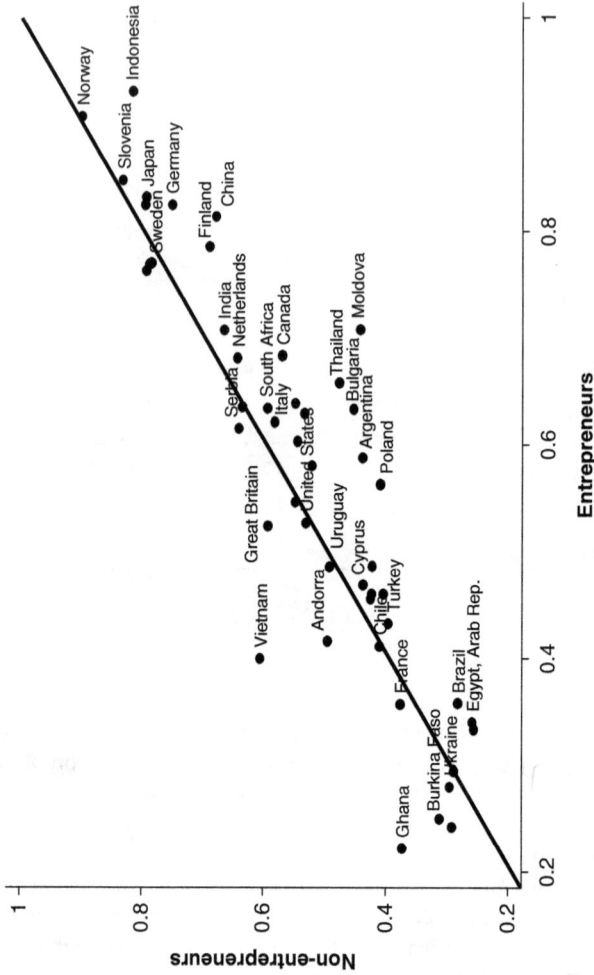

Figure 5.7 Proportion of Entrepreneurs and Non-entrepreneurs Worldwide Indicating That the Value of Independence Is Important for Children to Learn at Home, 2005–07

Source: World Values Survey.

Table 5.5 Societal Values in Argentina, Other Latin American Countries, and Australia and New Zealand, 2005–07

Value	% mentioning			Difference: Argentina versus		Values for or against entrepreneurship: Argentina versus	
	Argentina	Other Latin America	Australia and New Zealand	Other Latin America	Australia and New Zealand	Other Latin America	Australia and New Zealand
Responsibility	84.1	85.6	71.5	-1.5	12.6***	—	For
Tolerance and respect	83.5	82.2	91.9	1.3	-8.4***	—	Against
Hard work	68.4	34.3	47.0	34.1***	21.4***	—	—
Independence	59.8	40.1	61.7	19.7***	-1.9	For	—
Obedience	53.4	58.0	32.2	-4.6**	21.2***	For	Against
Religious faith	36.7	48.6	19.1	-11.9***	17.6***	For	Against
Thrift	23.9	39.3	31.0	-15.4***	-7.1**	For	For
Determination and perseverance	37.5	33.1	51.9	4.4**	-14.4***	For	Against
Unselfishness	15.1	53.4	49.8	-38.3***	-34.7***	—	—
Imagination	37.5	25.4	43.8	12.1***	-6.3**	For	Against
Summary for or against entrepreneurship relative to other society						6	-3

Source: World Values Survey.

Notes: Latin America refers to the following countries: Brazil, Chile, Colombia, Mexico, Peru, and Uruguay. If an entrepreneurial value (as defined in table 5.4) is significantly higher in Argentina than in the other country-region, it is computed as supporting entrepreneurship; if it is lower, it is computed as working against entrepreneurship. The opposite applies to non-entrepreneurial values. — = not available.

Significance level: ** = 5 percent, *** = 1 percent.

Australia and New Zealand hold values more aligned with entrepreneur-ship than Argentina: higher tolerance, higher independence, lower obedi-ence, lower religious faith, and higher determination and perseverance. Only with respect to responsibility and thrift does Argentine society have values more aligned with entrepreneurship than the two other countries.

Some caution is required in interpreting these results. First, the "feeling of responsibility" is rather vague, as several distinct interpretations are possible. It can be interpreted as "individual responsibility" by which the individual is responsible for his actions and their consequences. It can also be interpreted as the person declaring that he or she feels responsible for the family or society. In Latin America "responsibility" may be interpreted as being responsible for family, while in other parts of the world it may well be interpreted as having "individual responsibility" or being responsible for the well-being of society at-large. The entrepreneurial value is more related to the latter interpretation than to "family" responsibility; therefore, it is not clear what can be gained from the results with respect to this value.

Second, thriftiness is not an entrepreneurial value in the sense that, once financial markets are developed, it is no longer a necessary condition for founding an enterprise. However, for a society to flourish economically, someone in the society, though not necessarily the entrepreneur, must save, so it is still valuable in the aggregate. But in places such as Argentina where financial markets are underdeveloped, thriftiness again becomes a neces-sary condition for entrepreneurship. So it is not clear that low values of thriftiness in a society are an incentive for entrepreneurship.

Summing up, we find that the Argentine society overall promotes entre-preneurial values, but does so less than some successful, natural-resource-abundant economies, such as Australia and New Zealand. Argentine society places relatively little value on determination and perseverance and relatively high value on obedience. Although an exploration of the long-run determinants of these values must be left for future study, we conjecture that the periodic financial crises that Argentina has suffered have damaged the value of perseverance, while the country's authoritarian past has increased the value of obedience.

Values are shaped by history and public policy, and they are trans-mitted intergenerationally. In turn, they shape public policy because the electorate supports governments and institutions that reflect their values. We therefore turn to a discussion of the policies that promote or hinder entrepreneurship.

Entrepreneurship and Public Policy

Public policies may influence the quantity and quality of entrepreneurial activity. They may affect the supply and demand side of entrepreneurship, the availability of resources, skills, and knowledge, and the decision-making process. Several authors have analyzed these links, including Acs and Szerb (2007), Audretsch, Grilo, and Thurik (2007), Baumol, Litan, and Schramm (2007), and Lundström and Stevenson (2005), although much of the literature focuses on developed countries.

This section uses firm-level data from Argentina's Enterprise Survey to analyze how public policies affect the costs and benefits of registration (according to entrepreneurs' opinions), to provide additional measures of the "quality" of entrepreneurs (by describing access to financial instruments, the extent of innovation, and rent-seeking activities), and to describe the main policy obstacles according to the opinions of business people.

The Enterprise Survey is a firm-level survey that provides information on the business environment, sales, finance, and other characteristics of firms. The survey is administered to business owners and senior managers. Two separate surveys were conducted in Argentina in 2010: one for registered firms (FES) and the other for unregistered firms (IES). The former included 1,054 firms located in Buenos Aires, Chaco, Córdoba, Mendoza, and Rosario, while the latter included 384 firms in Buenos Aires and Chaco.[21]

Benefits and Costs of Registration

Almost 10 percent of registered firms begin operations informally and become registered later on, while 5.3 percent of informal firms are registered at start-up but stop paying taxes and complying with regulations at some point. This suggests that the formal or informal status of a firm changes little over time, although there is some transition both in and out of formality.

The owners of informal businesses mentioned that registering a business helps to gain access to loans and financing (51.2 percent), to attract customers (38.2), and to gain access to government services (36.2). Many reported that they would like to register their business (41.2 percent). When asked why they do not do so, however, they mentioned the expected cost of paying taxes and the complexity of the registration process (table 5.6).[22] The majority of owners of formal firms reported that the reason for registering is to comply with the law (table 5.7).

Access to Financial Instruments

As expected, access to financial instruments is limited among unregistered firms. Only 1.3 percent of firms have a bank account and 5.5 percent have a loan (table 5.8). Almost every registered firm, however, has a business savings or checking account. What is more surprising is that only half of all registered firms have a loan. This is presumably because of the negative effect of inflation and political instability on Argentina's financial markets.

Table 5.6 Reasons for Not Registering a Business in Argentina, 2010

Reason	% of firms
Time, fees, and paperwork to complete registration	35.0
Taxes that need to be paid if registered	71.1
Inspections that would take place if registered	16.4
No benefit for the business from being registered	39.1

Source: Enterprise Survey, Informal Firms.

Table 5.7 Most Important Factor Motivating the Decision to Register in Argentina, 2010

Factor	% of firms
Don't know	4.3
Fewer gifts or informal payments to officials	0.1
More access to government programs or services	0.8
Better access to financing	2.8
Better access to skilled workers	0.4
Customers or suppliers only deal with registered firms	15.0
Comply with the law	71.7
Other reasons not included above	5.0

Source: Enterprise Survey, Registered Firms.

Table 5.8 Access to Financial Instruments, 2010
(% of firms)

Indicator	Unregistered firms (IES)	Registered firms (FES)
Has a business bank account	1.3	98.4
Has a loan	5.5	49.8
Has a loan from a bank	1.3	48.5

Source: Enterprise Survey, Informal Firms and Registered Firms.

As the literature suggests, a highly developed financial system is important for the emergence of a successful entrepreneurial economy (Kauffman Foundation 2007). This is an area where Argentina has much room for improvement.

Innovation and Rent Seeking among Formal Firms

As argued by Acs, Braunerhjelm, and Audretsch (2009) and others, economic growth is strongly influenced by research, inventions, and their spillovers, and entrepreneurs play a fundamental role in linking these variables. The FES (but not the IES) includes several variables that provide information about innovation activities among Argentine firms. More than 70 percent of formal entrepreneurs reported that the idea giving rise to the business was to modify or develop a new product; almost 40 percent reported using a service to support innovation in the past three years, and 62 percent said that they envisage using them in the next three years (table 5.9). Innovation activity is presumably less prevalent among informal firms.

Rent-seeking activities are a topic of interest because anecdotal evidence suggests that many business people in Argentina devote a considerable part of their time to lobbying the government for subsidies or special treatment. Destructive entrepreneurship plays a major role in the decline of economies, as Baumol (1990) argues in his seminal work. However,

Table 5.9 Innovation and Rent Seeking among Formal Firms in Argentina, 2010

Variable	% of firms
Innovation	
Was motivated to create the business to modify or develop a new product	70.6
Used any services or programs to support innovation during last three years	39.1
Foresees using services or programs to support innovation in next three years	62.2
Has an internationally recognized quality certification	33.4
Rent seeking	
% of senior management's time spent on dealing with requirements imposed by government regulations	20.3
% of firms reporting that an informal payment or gift is usually paid to secure a government contract	23.9

Source: Enterprise Survey, Registered Firms.

measuring rent seeking is not easy, in part because neither government officials nor businessmen are likely to report their actual behavior, even in an anonymous survey such as the FES. Taking these caveats into account, the FES shows that almost one-fourth of business people reported that a typical firm bribes government officials to secure a contract and that about 20 percent of senior management's time is devoted to complying with government regulations, which presumably includes lobbying for special treatment (table 5.9).

Although there is no information on rent seeking among informal firms in Argentina, anecdotal evidence suggests that it is much less prevalent than among formal firms. This is an important aspect to consider when discussing the optimal distribution of firm size in an economy. Recent work by the Inter-American Development Bank (IDB 2010) suggests that low productivity, particularly among firms in the service sector, is a major problem in Latin America, and this is because the region is populated by too many small, informal, and unproductive firms. Although many of these small firms compete by evading regulations and are unable to exploit economies of scale, the argument made by the IDB should be weighed against the inefficiencies and inequities that could be generated by a corporate model. The evidence suggests that, in Argentina, large registered firms do innovate and exploit economies of scale, but they also lobby the government for special treatment, fostering uncompetitive markets and corruption.

Obstacles and Policies

According to formal entrepreneurs, taxes, political instability, and corruption are the three main problems for their business (see table 5.10). Informal entrepreneurs point to lack of access to credit and crime as their main problems (see table 5.11). Crime is relatively unimportant for formal entrepreneurs but is important for informal firms, and corruption is a major concern for formal but not for informal firms. These results require some interpretation. Since there are economies of scale in private security (security services require a modicum of infrastructure and personnel), formal firms—which are bigger—can more easily afford the fixed costs than informal firms. Because formal firms have their own security, they consider crime and theft to be relatively unimportant. Additionally, many unregistered firms are street vendors, who are more exposed to theft. The differences of opinion on corruption could be due to the fact that government officials target larger firms because they have more resources to pay bribes.

Some caution is necessary before deriving any policy recommendations from these findings. While policies should be designed with the objective of increasing entrepreneurs' social contribution to society, entrepreneurs are concerned about the impact of these obstacles on profits. There is some overlap. For example, political instability and corruption inhibit long-term

Table 5.10 Major Obstacles for Registered Firms in Argentina, 2010

Obstacle	% of firms
Tax rates	63.3
Political instability	60.4
Corruption	56.9
Inadequately educated labor force	56.6
Labor regulations	47.9
Courts	44.7
Telecommunications	44.6
Access to finance or loans	43.2
Electricity supply	43.1
Tax administration	40.5
Practice of competitors in informal sector	39.6
Crime, theft, disorder	28.6
Access to land	26.2
Transport	26.2
Business license and permits	21.5
Customs and trade regulations	15.9

Source: Enterprise Survey, Registered Firms.

Table 5.11 Biggest Obstacle for Unregistered Firms in Argentina, 2010

Obstacle	% of firms
Access to finance or loans	36.4
Crime, theft, disorder	28.8
Electricity supply	14.0
Access to land	10.4
Corruption	6.0
Water supply	4.4

Source: Enterprise Survey, Informal Firms.

investment and promote rent seeking and hence reduce businesses' profits and social welfare. Crime and lack of credit are another example. But some potentially important policies are not listed. Public employment policies, for example, could inhibit nascent entrepreneurial activity, and established firms are not likely to consider them to be an obstacle.

Effect of Public Employment Policies on Entrepreneurship

The effects of public employment policy on entrepreneurship have been relatively ignored in the empirical literature, with the exception of Alesina, Danninger, and Rostagno (2001), who studied Italy. Argentina is a federal country with large differences in public employment across regions. Public employment is relatively high in cities located in Patagonia and the northern region and relatively low in the Pampas region (see table 5.12). The two extreme cases are Viedma, a city located in Patagonia, where 27.3 percent of the population between 18 and 65 years old were public employees in 2010, and Rosario, located in the Pampas region, where only 7.5 percent of the population were public employees. With 12 percent of its population in the public sector, the City of Buenos Aires has a moderate level of public employment, given that it is the seat of the national government.

Differences in public employment across provinces are explained in part by fiscal federalism. The government transfers a disproportionate amount of resources to provinces with overrepresentation in the national legislature, and governors use these resources to obtain local political support by offering attractive public employment (Gervasoni 2010).

Public employment increased from 10 percent of the population in 2003 to 11 percent in 2010 but with considerable heterogeneity across cities. While it increased by more than 30 percent in Resistencia and Mar del Plata, it declined more than 15 percent in San Luis and Rosario.

Public employees are relatively well paid. Their hourly wages are about 30 percent higher than those of workers with similar levels of education in the private sector.[23]

Theoretically, public employment can have a positive or a negative impact on entrepreneurship. Increasing the number of public employees can foster entrepreneurship in the long run if those employees level the playing field, provide public goods, solve coordination failures, promote competitive markets, and keep red tape at a minimum. Public employment can crowd out entrepreneurship if working conditions in the public sector are too generous, a short-run effect, or if public employees introduce policies that deter entrepreneurs from pursuing otherwise profitable opportunities, a long-run effect.

Public employment can affect not only the quantity, but also the quality of entrepreneurs. Increases in public employment can foster formality among entrepreneurs if public employees increase enforcement or simplify registration procedures. But if higher corporate taxes are levied to cover the public sector payroll, firms may be drawn to the informal sector. Depending on the policies implemented, public employees can also increase or reduce the productivity of firms and affect the size distribution of firms and the use of labor.

Table 5.12 Public Employment per Capita in Argentina,
by Urban Agglomerate, 2010

Urban agglomerate	Public employees (% of population)	Urban agglomerate	Public employees (% of population)
Viedma, C. Patagones	27.3	Concordia	14.2
Río Gallegos	26.9	Corrientes	13.9
Ushuaia, Río Grande	24.1	Salta	13.2
Santa Rosa, Toay	21.5	Gran Tucumán, Tafí Viejo	13.0
Gran Catamarca	21.3	Gran San Juan	12.2
La Rioja	20.9	San Luis, Chorrillo	12.0
Rawson, Trelew	20.8	City of Buenos Aires	12.0
Gran La Plata	20.5	Gran Mendoza	11.3
Neuquén, Plottier	18.8	C. Rivadavia, Rada Tilly	10.7
Jujuy, Palpalá	18.6	Gran Córdoba	9.8
Gran Paraná	18.2	Mar del Plata, Batán	9.7
Formosa	17.6	Río Cuarto	9.5
Gran Resistencia	17.2	Bahía Blanca, Cerri	9.3
Santiago del Estero, La Banda	15.2	Greater Buenos Aires	8.0
Gran Santa Fe	14.5	San Nicolás, V. Constitución	7.9
Posadas	14.4	Gran Rosario	7.5

Source: Permanent Household Survey.
Note: C = Comodoro, V = Villa.

Given the characteristics of the available data and exploiting the variation in the variables of interest across provinces over time, estimates are
presented below of the short- and long-run effects of public employment on
the quantity of entrepreneurs and on two measures of "quality": whether
the entrepreneur has registered the firm and whether the entrepreneur

hires workers. Before presenting the results, it is important to point out four limitations of the analysis. First, the estimates presented should be interpreted more as correlations than as causal effects, since—despite our efforts—endogeneity cannot be ruled out. Second, there is no direct link between entrepreneurship and welfare. That is, finding that public employment reduces entrepreneurship does not necessarily imply that public employment reduces welfare. Third, although entrepreneurship is clearly linked to economic growth, this relationship is crucially shaped by the "quality" of entrepreneurs (the analysis performed only covers some measures of quality). Fourth, exploiting variation across provinces can capture some of the long-run effects of public employment on entrepreneurship, but not those due to national policies, which are the same across provinces.

The relation between public employment and entrepreneurship across the 32 urban agglomerates in the data set is depicted in figure 5.8, which presents averages for the period from 2003 to 2010.[24] Each data point represents a city or urban agglomerate. Cities with a higher number of public employees per capita tend to have fewer entrepreneurs per capita (pairwise correlation –0.4 and statistically significant at the 5 percent level).

The negative relationship between public employment and entrepreneurship is not enough to claim that public employment has a negative causal effect on entrepreneurship, since a third factor could be driving the correlation. In particular, cultural differences may be driving the

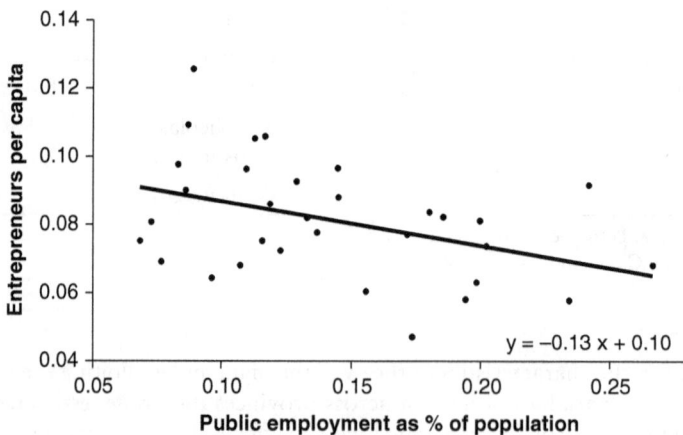

Figure 5.8 Public Employment and Entrepreneurship in 32 Urban Agglomerates in Argentina, 2003–10 (Average)

$y = -0.13 x + 0.10$

Source: Permanent Household Survey.

cross-city variation. In order to test in a more formal way the relationship between public employment and entrepreneurship across cities and through time, the following statistical model was estimated:

$$Entrepreneurship_{it} = \alpha_i + \tau_t + \beta Public\ Employment_{it} + Z_{it}\pi + \varepsilon_{it}, \qquad (5.1)$$

where *Entrepreneurship* is the share of entrepreneurs in the EAP in city *i* and quarter-year *t*, *Public Employment* is the share of the population that works in the public sector, *Z* is a vector of covariates, and α and τ are time dummies and city fixed effects. The data set is the EPH, which covers 29 urban agglomerates from the third quarter of 2003 to the fourth quarter of 2010 and three additional agglomerates from the third quarter of 2006 to the fourth quarter of 2010. Because the survey was not conducted during the third quarter of 2007, the total number of quarter-year city cells is 892. The sample is restricted to the population between 18 and 65 years old.

The results are presented in table 5.13, where column 1 shows a regression that includes only quarter-year dummies to control for national unobserved shocks that could affect both public employment and entrepreneurship. Column 2 includes a set of labor force characteristics (sex, age, educational attainment, share of the population that is foreign born, and share that is migrant) and a measure of the business cycle (unemployment rate in the city) and column 3 includes city fixed effects in order to control for time-invariant heterogeneity across cities (thus relaxing the assumption of random effects in the previous regressions). This removes all cultural, institutional, or other differences across cities that change little over time, preventing them from biasing the estimates.

The results indicate that a 1 percentage point increase in public employment as a share of the population produces between an 0.1 and a 0.14 percentage point reduction in entrepreneurship as a share of the EAP, or between an 0.07 and 0.10 percentage point reduction in entrepreneurs as a share of the population.[25] Is this reduction a large crowding-out effect? To answer this question, it is useful to compare the results with the following hypothetical situation. Assume that people who enter public employment are randomly selected from the EAP. Then, a 1 percent increase in public employment produces a 0.1 percentage point reduction in entrepreneurship because entrepreneurs represent 10 percent of the workforce not employed in the public sector. Therefore, our findings are almost as large as those that would occur under random selection, implying a substantial crowding-out effect. It appears that governments are not targeting unemployed workers as potential hires (the rationale for anticyclical public employment policies); instead they are offering a sufficiently attractive compensation package to attract entrepreneurs into the public sector. As we show below using individual panel data, when public employment is created, some entrepreneurs do abandon their firms and take those jobs.

Table 5.13 Effect of Public Employment on the Quantity of Entrepreneurship in Argentina, 2003–10

	Contemporaneous effect			Long-run effect	
Variable	(1)	(2)	(3)	(4)	(5)
Public employment	−0.108***	−0.121***	−0.139**	−0.546**	−0.556**
	(0.037)	(0.040)	(0.052)	(0.208)	(0.207)
Labor force and business cycle	No	Yes	Yes	No	Yes
Quarter-year dummies	Yes	Yes	Yes	—	—
City fixed effects	No	No	Yes	—	—

Source: Permanent Household Survey.
Note: Number of observations is 892 in columns 1–3 and 29 in columns 4–5. The dependent variable is the number of entrepreneurs in each quarter-year-city over the economically active population in columns 1–3 and the change in entrepreneurship between 2003 and 2010 in columns 4–5; public employment is the number of public employees over the population in columns 1–3 and the change between 2003 and 2010 in columns 4–5. Robust standard errors are in parentheses. — = not available.
Significance level: ** = 5 percent; *** = 1 percent.

The negative short-run effect could be more than compensated for in the long run if the newly hired public employees would implement policies that foster entrepreneurship, such as, for example, providing public goods or promoting competitive markets, but they also might implement policies that inhibit entrepreneurship. To estimate the long-run effects of public employment on entrepreneurship, the following model was tested:

$$\Delta Entrepreneurship_i = \beta \Delta PublicEmployment_i + \Delta Z_i \pi + \varepsilon_i, \qquad (5.2)$$

where $\Delta Entrepreneurship$ is the change in the share of entrepreneurs in the EAP in city i between the fourth quarter of 2010 and the third quarter of 2003 (that is, between the last and first available surveys), and $\Delta Public$ $Employment$ is the change in the share of the population that worked in the public sector during the same period. By analyzing changes over a seven-year period, we can test whether public employment has fostered or inhibited entrepreneurship in the long run.[26]

The results are also presented in table 5.13: the regression in column 4 does not include any controls, while that in column 5 includes the same controls as before. The results indicate that a 1 percentage point increase in public employment as a share of the population produces a 0.55 percentage point reduction in entrepreneurship as a share of the EAP or a 0.37 percentage point reduction as a share of the population. That is, the effect in absolute value terms is more than three times larger than the contemporaneous effect, suggesting that the policies implemented by newly hired public employees hamper entrepreneurship. Because public employment increased by 0.9 percentage point during the last decade, it can be tentatively concluded that the policy has produced, in the long run, a reduction of approximately 0.33 percentage point in entrepreneurship or 6 percent of the initial stock of entrepreneurs.

A useful feature of the EPH is that individuals were followed over 1.5 years. That is, individuals surveyed for the first time in the first quarter of 2004 were surveyed again in the second quarter of 2005. This longitudinal characteristic of the data allows us to count the number of people who effectively change occupations from entrepreneurship to public employment, providing additional evidence of the short-run crowding-out effect.

For that purpose, it is useful to compute the transition probabilities (between the third quarter of 2003 and the fourth quarter of 2010) of those individuals who were entrepreneurs the first time they were surveyed. The majority of entrepreneurs, 51.5 percent, had the same occupation a year and a half later, 18.9 percent became "pure" self-employed, 15.5 percent became private sector employees, 8.9 percent left the labor force, 1.8 percent became family workers, 1.2 percent were unemployed, and 2.1 percent shut down their businesses and entered public employment.[27]

Summing up, public employment appears to have a crowding-out effect on the quantity of entrepreneurs in the short run and an even larger effect in the long run. These results suggest that the public sector in Argentina offers a sufficiently good compensation package to attract entrepreneurs into public employment and that the policies implemented do not foster entrepreneurship.

Finally, how does public employment policy affect the "quality" of entrepreneurs? Two measures of quality can be assessed: whether the entrepreneur has registered the firm and whether the entrepreneur hires workers.[28] The latter is obtained from the EPH by distinguishing between employer-entrepreneurs and self-employed entrepreneurs—that is, between those who do and those who do not have employees working in their firm. Since the former are not available in the EPH, administrative data from the Ministry of Labor is used instead.[29] The data indicate the total number of registered firms in each province during the fourth quarter between 2003 and 2009.

The same models as in table 5.13 were estimated, but using as dependent variables employer-entrepreneur, self-employed entrepreneur, and registered firm, all as a share of the EAP. Table 5.14 presents the results, with one panel for each dependent variable.

The results suggest that the negative contemporaneous crowding-out effect of public employment policies over the quantity of entrepreneurs occurs mainly by a reduction in the number of small and informal firms. In the long run, however, public employment produces a statistically significant reduction in the number of employer-entrepreneurs, but not in the number of self-employed entrepreneurs or in the number of registered firms. Our interpretation of these results is that public employment crowds out entrepreneurs who are somewhere in the middle of the "quality" spectrum. Without public employment, these people would have started a small and informal firm, but later on would have hired some workers, although the firm would have remained informal.

Conclusions

This chapter has covered a range of aspects related to entrepreneurship in Argentina and its relationship to public policies, using information from household surveys, firm surveys, and administrative data. The aim has been to provide a collection of stylized facts and to identify the main bottlenecks facing entrepreneurs, in the hope that the findings will serve as a guide for future research. The main findings are presented here.

The total number of independent workers in Argentina (in 2010) represents 22.7 percent of the employed population. However, many of them apparently perform routine tasks and can hardly be considered entrepreneurs. Properly measuring entrepreneurship—particularly its "quality"— is difficult with the available data because entrepreneurship refers to the functions and activities of individuals and organizations, and such

Table 5.14 Effect of Public Employment on the Quality of Entrepreneurship in Argentina, 2003–10

Variable	Contemporaneous effect			Long-run effect	
	(1)	(2)	(3)	(4)	(5)
a. Dependent variable: employer-entrepreneur					
Public employment	−0.015	−0.025	−0.038	−0.265**	−0.257**
	(0.021)	(0.025)	(0.030)	(0.129)	(0.100)
b. Dependent variable: self-employed entrepreneur					
Public employment	−0.097***	−0.094***	−0.101**	−0.281	−0.299
	(0.028)	(0.028)	(0.041)	(0.243)	(0.192)
c. Dependent variable: registered firm					
Public employment	0.001	−0.045**	0.006	0.034	−0.026
	(0.020)	(0.022)	(0.019)	(0.039)	(0.072)
Labor force and business cycle	No	Yes	Yes	No	Yes
Quarter-year dummies	Yes	Yes	Yes	—	—
City fixed effects	No	No	Yes	—	—

Source: Permanent Household Survey.

Note: Number of observations is 892 in columns 1–3, panels a–b; 161 in columns 1–3, panel c; 29 in columns 4–5, panels a–b; and 23 in columns 4–5, panel c. — = not available.

Significance level: ** = 5 percent, *** = 1 percent.

information is rarely available. To confront this problem, entrepreneurs are considered only those independent workers who manage or work in a firm with two or more people, leaving out the solo self-employed. Using this proxy, about 9 percent of the employed population are entrepreneurs.

A large share of individuals categorized as entrepreneurs are likely to be engaged in activities that are not conducive to economic growth: 37 percent are necessity entrepreneurs and 39 percent have not registered their business. These two types of entrepreneurs use little machinery and have low human capital and productivity. Furthermore, among formal entrepreneurs, almost one-fourth reported that a typical firm bribes government officials to secure a contract, and about 20 percent of senior management's time is devoted to dealing with government regulations, including lobbying for special treatment.

Two types of entrepreneurs must be distinguished: employer-entrepreneurs and self-employed entrepreneurs who do not hire but do work with other people. As a percentage of the employed population, the number of both types of entrepreneurs has fallen since 1980. However, during the last half decade the number of employer-entrepreneurs has increased as a share of total entrepreneurship. As these entrepreneurs tend to be more formal and opportunity driven than self-employed, the quality of entrepreneurship may have improved. However, more research is necessary, particularly an analysis of the evolution of innovation and rent seeking, before any firm conclusions can be drawn in this regard.

Exploring the relationship between parental wealth and entrepreneurship reveals that people born in wealthier families receive a better education, have more access to a network of influential people, and have parents who can finance their start-ups, which is important when access to credit is very limited, as in Argentina. These advantages are important in explaining differences in earnings among entrepreneurs: those born in middle- and upper-class families earn over two times more than entrepreneurs from lower-class families. However, there is only a small positive correlation between parental wealth and the probability of becoming an entrepreneur.

Parental occupation is a stronger predictor of entrepreneurship. The probability of becoming an entrepreneur is almost three times greater among individuals whose parents were entrepreneurs. This is because entrepreneurs inculcate values in their children, such as responsibility, tolerance, respect, independence, determination, perseverance, and imagination, that are conducive to entrepreneurship.

Differences in values are larger between societies than between entrepreneurs and non-entrepreneurs within a particular society. In this sense, the values of society at-large are as important for entrepreneurship as the values of entrepreneurs. The values of the Argentine population are better aligned with entrepreneurial activity than those of Latin America as a whole, but they are less conducive to entrepreneurial pursuits than those of Australia and New Zealand.

Whether public employment crowds entrepreneurship in or out is a relevant issue in a country such as Argentina, where public employment is relatively high in some northern and Patagonian provinces that largely benefit from the federal fiscal regime. Public employment has been increasing in the last decade, and it is relatively well paid compared to work in the private sector. According to the estimates presented in this chapter, public employment has a large crowding-out effect on entrepreneurship in both the short and long run.

Furthermore, public employment crowds out entrepreneurs who are somewhere in the middle of the "quality" spectrum—that is, people who, were it not for public employment, would have started a small and informal firm and later on would have hired some workers.

Overall, the evidence suggests that there is much to be done if Argentina wants to become an entrepreneurial economy. Although some improvements could be made by fostering certain cultural values, such as perseverance, or by redistributing wealth so that people born in poor families could become productive entrepreneurs, the main bottleneck in Argentina is inadequate public policy. Political and macroeconomic instability, lack of a developed financial market, inefficient bureaucracy, corruption, a complex tax system, and the use of public employment as a political instrument are the main culprits.

Annex. Tables Characterizing Entrepreneurship in Argentina

Table 5A.1 Characteristics of the Workforce in Argentina, 2010, and in Greater Buenos Aires, Fourth Quarter of 2005

Variable	Argentina, 2010	Greater Buenos Aires, 2005 4Q
Employed persons age 15 or more (%)		
Independent	22.7	23.5
Entrepreneur 1	4.5	3.5
Entrepreneur 2	4.7	6.1
Self-employed	13.5	14.0
Employee	77.3	76.5
Male (%)		
Entrepreneur 1	73.0	78.8
Entrepreneur 2	63.4	60.2
Self-employed	65.8	65.4

(continued next page)

Table 5A.1 (continued)

Variable	Argentina, 2010	Greater Buenos Aires, 2005 4Q
Employee	55.9	54.8
Inactive	29.7	27.1
Age (mean, in years)		
Entrepreneur 1	46.9	49.2
Entrepreneur 2	43.5	44.9
Self-employed	45.2	45.3
Employee	38.1	38.1
Inactive	46.9	49.1
Hours worked (weekly)		
Entrepreneur 1	49.6	51.9
Entrepreneur 2	46.9	49.9
Self-employed	38.3	37.5
Employee	40.9	41.7
Wanted more hours? (%)		
Entrepreneur 1	10.1	9.8
Entrepreneur 2	16.0	15.4
Self-employed	31.9	41.9
Employee	15.4	23.7
Size of firm (mean [median] number of workers)		
Entrepreneur 1	9.3 (4)	14.2 (4)
Entrepreneur 2	2.9 (2)	2.6 (2)
Employee	122.0 (18)	112.8 (18)
Size of firm: entrepreneur 1 (%)		
Small (≤5)	72.5	67.7
Medium (>5 and <40)	23.7	29.6
Large (≥40)	3.8	2.7
Size of firm: entrepreneur 2 (%)		
Small (≤5)	96.7	95.3
Medium (>5 and <40)	3.1	4.7
Large (≥40)	0.2	0.0

Table 5A.1 (continued)

Variable	Argentina, 2010	Greater Buenos Aires, 2005 4Q
Size of firm: employee (%)		
Small (≤5)	23.7	24.4
Medium (>5 and <40)	35.9	37.0
Large (≥40)	40.5	38.6
Owns or rents machinery or tools? (%)		
Entrepreneur 1	87.0	85.9
Entrepreneur 2	77.0	73.2
Self-employed	59.0	48.0
Owns or rents locale? (%)		
Entrepreneur 1	85.0	91.4
Entrepreneur 2	65.0	71.7
Self-employed	33.0	28.7
Owns or rents vehicle? (%)		
Entrepreneur 1	49.0	43.5
Entrepreneur 2	31.0	32.0
Self-employed	23.0	20.6
Annual income (mean, $)		
Entrepreneur 1	13,044	10,370
Entrepreneur 2	6,513	3,611
Self-employed	5,840	3,270
Employee	7,863	3,847

Source: Permanent Household Survey.

Note: Entrepreneur 1 = employers. Entrepreneur 2 = persons who report being self-employed but who work with at least one additional person. Self-employed (or "pure" self-employed) = persons who work by themselves. Q = quarter.

Table 5A.2 Characteristics of Necessity and Opportunity
Entrepreneurs in Greater Buenos Aires, Fourth Quarter of 2005

Variable and occupation	Necessity	Opportunity
Entrepreneurs (%)		
Entrepreneur 1	22.5	77.5
Entrepreneur 2	45.5	54.5
Male (%)		
Entrepreneur 1	69.8	81.4
Entrepreneur 2	57.2	62.6
Age (mean, in years)		
Entrepreneur 1	50.6	48.8
Entrepreneur 2	45.0	44.7
Hours worked (weekly)		
Entrepreneur 1	52.0	51.9
Entrepreneur 2	49.2	50.5
Wanted more hours? (%)		
Entrepreneur 1	26.4	5.0
Entrepreneur 2	17.2	13.9
Size of firm (mean [median] number of workers)		
Entrepreneur 1	6.6 (3)	17.2 (4)
Entrepreneur 2	2.7 (2)	2.5 (2)
Size of firm: entrepreneur 1 (%)		
Small	82.2	63.5
Medium	14.8	33.9
Large	3.0	2.6
Size of firm: entrepreneur 2 (%)		
Small	92.0	98.0
Medium	8.0	2.0
Large	0.0	0.0
Owns or rents machinery or tools? (%)		
Entrepreneur 1	76.7	88.5
Entrepreneur 2	69.0	76.7

Table 5A.2 (continued)

Variable and occupation	Necessity	Opportunity
Owns or rents locale? (%)		
Entrepreneur 1	90.2	91.7
Entrepreneur 2	65.8	76.5
Owns or rents vehicle? (%)		
Entrepreneur 1	50.0	41.6
Entrepreneur 2	24.1	38.5
Annual income (mean, $)		
Entrepreneur 1	4,974	11,776
Entrepreneur 2	2,045	4,927

Source: EPH special survey.

Table 5A.3 Characteristics of Formal and Informal Entrepreneurs in Greater Buenos Aires, Fourth Quarter of 2005

Variable and occupation	Informal	Formal
Entrepreneurs (%)		
Entrepreneur 1	11.5	88.5
Entrepreneur 2	54.4	45.6
Male (%)		
Entrepreneur 1	74.4	78.8
Entrepreneur 2	51.3	67.2
Age (mean, in years)		
Entrepreneur 1	51.5	48.9
Entrepreneur 2	43.2	47.5
Hours worked (weekly)		
Entrepreneur 1	50.2	52.8
Entrepreneur 2	48.5	52.0
Wanted more hours? (%)		
Entrepreneur 1	24.4	5.9
Entrepreneur 2	17.9	11.6

(continued next page)

Table 5A.3 (continued)

Variable and occupation	Informal	Formal
Size of firm (mean [median] number of workers)		
Entrepreneur 1	7.4 (2)	13.0 (4)
Entrepreneur 2	2.5 (2)	2.6 (2)
Size of firm: entrepreneur 1 (%)		
Small	87.3	66.4
Medium	6.5	32.1
Large	6.2	1.6
Size of firm: entrepreneur 2 (%)		
Small	93.6	97.5
Medium	6.4	2.5
Large	0.0	0.0
Owns or rents machinery or tools? (%)		
Entrepreneur 1	78.4	88.6
Entrepreneur 2	66.9	80.5
Owns or rents locale? (%)		
Entrepreneur 1	83.3	93.6
Entrepreneur 2	67.1	76.4
Owns or rents vehicle? (%)		
Entrepreneur 1	39.2	43.6
Entrepreneur 2	19.5	43.7
Annual income (mean, $)		
Entrepreneur 1	2,627	11,132
Entrepreneur 2	2,039	5,867

Source: EPH special survey.

Notes

1. Hirschleifer (2001) also develops this topic.
2. A recent publication (IDB 2010) shows the predominance of small firms in Latin America, including Argentina, with low aggregate productivity, especially in the service sector.
3. Similar characterizations have been done by Evans and Leighton (1989) for the United States and Blanchflower and Shadforth (2007) for the United Kingdom.
4. On the relationship between values, entrepreneurship, and economic performance for a cross-section of countries, see Phelps (2011) and Freytag and Thurik (2010).

5. The coverage has increased over time. Some important methodological changes were introduced in 2003 (see http://www.indec.gov.ar).

6. The population of Argentina was 40.1 million in 2010. Of these, 29.9 million were older than 15, of which 18.3 million made up the economically active population (applying EPH percentages to the whole population, which may be imprecise because it includes the rural population that is not surveyed). Within the EAP, 1.3 million were unemployed and 17 million were employed. Of those who were employed, 695,000 were employers (entrepreneurs), 3.1 million were self-employed (of which 723,000 were self-employed entrepreneurs and 2.4 million were solo self-employed), and 13.2 million were employees (of which 10.5 million were private employees and 2.7 million were public employees). The total number of entrepreneurs, according to our classification, was around 1.4 million.

7. It is not clear why male predominance is higher for independent workers than for employees. It could be related to either income or physical security, perhaps associated with the "brawn versus brain" explanation (Rendall 2010). For big firms, the fact that employers are predominantly male may be related to discrimination.

8. Analyzing the whole distribution suggests a lifecycle explanation. The density function of age for employees is highest in the late 20s and then diminishes quickly. The density function of age for self-employed and entrepreneurs grows more slowly but stays high for a longer period, until their late 50s. In fact, some entrepreneurs start as employees or self-employed during their 20s and then become entrepreneurs in their 30s and 40s.

9. All educational categories include people who either completed or did not complete the level. Graduate refers to a master's or Ph.D. degree.

10. Why do so few entrepreneurs own a medium- or large-size firm (say, larger than 40 employees)? First, the nonresponse rate can be especially high for medium- and large-firm owners. Second, there may simply be too few medium and large firms. A more focused and less representative survey of individuals, along the lines of Kantis, Ishida, and Kamori (2002), may be more useful for understanding some aspects of entrepreneurship. It is difficult to get an absolute number of firms. A rough estimate can be obtained by adding the number of employer-entrepreneurs (assuming a one-to-one relationship between employer and firm) and the number of self-employed entrepreneurs divided by the average number of co-workers (as they do not hire employees, all workers in those firms must be self-employed entrepreneurs). This calculation gives 944,000 businesses for Argentina in 2010. Dividing the number of private employees by the number of employer-entrepreneurs gives a mean firm size of 16.1, 73 percent higher than the number reported in table 5A.1 (9.3). This difference can be attributed to underrepresentation of medium and large firms in the EPH and underreporting of the number of workers by employer-entrepreneurs, presumably due to labor taxes and regulations.

11. We suspect that underreporting could be a problem with these figures.

12. Due to the methodological changes made to the EPH survey in 2003, the data before 2003 have been rescaled to make them comparable with post-2003 data.

13. The EDS is a household survey conducted in more than 100 localities in 1997 by the National Institute of Statistics and includes 75,374 individuals. The EPH does not include recall questions.

14. See Castellani and Parent (2011) for a discussion about defining and measuring the middle class, and Lora and Fajardo (forthcoming) for mismatches between subjective and objective measures of middle class.

15. We restrict the population to those between 18 and 64 years old: 16.4 percent of the employed population comes from a high-income family, 60.4 percent from a middle-income family, and 23.2 percent from a low-income family.

16. We ran a probit regression (controlling for age, sex, schooling, and province dummies) and found that having parents who owned a business increases the probability of being an entrepreneur by 12 percent while having parents who were rich (that is, equal to 1 if high income and 0 if middle and low income) increases the probability of being an entrepreneur by only 1 percent.

17. An interesting fact is the nonlinear correlation between parental wealth and the analyzed variables. There appears to be a dividing line between entrepreneurs born in lower- and middle-income families, but no major differences between entrepreneurs born in middle- and high-income families. We leave this issue for further work.

18. The share of entrepreneurs in the sample is of 4.8 percent for the world, 3.4 percent for Argentina, 2.7 percent for other Latin American countries (Brazil, Chile, Colombia, Mexico, Peru, and Uruguay), and 17.8 percent for Australia and New Zealand.

19. For example, Maddison (2006, 82) writes, "Dutch institutions favoured economic growth. Religious tolerance encouraged skilled immigration." We believe that the ascent of imagination as a value of entrepreneurs and the demise of hard work and thriftiness (thriftiness is significantly more valued by non-entrepreneurs) are related to how capitalism evolved. Financial markets have separated the agents of saving from those of investing, and therefore entrepreneurs do not need to be frugal themselves; they can use the frugality of others to set up their projects. The increasing importance of human capital and innovation in modern capitalism makes imagination a scarce factor compared to hard work per se. This classification makes sense from an anecdotal point of view. For example, the great entrepreneur Steve Jobs, in his 2005 commencement speech at Stanford, did not recommend thriftiness and hard work; instead, he emphasized independence, imagination, and perseverance.

20. The question is an open one, allowing respondents to give up to five answers. To compare across countries, we considered only those respondents who mentioned exactly five values.

21. According to the National Economic Census of 2004/05 and the National Agricultural Census of 2008, there are almost 1 million firms in Argentina (see http://www.indec.gov.ar), but other estimates suggest that the figure is 1.6 million (Claves Información Competitiva 2010). The discrepancy is due to the difficulty in estimating the number of unregistered firms. The number of registered firms in 2009 was 616,000 (see http://www.trabajo.gov.ar).

22. For evidence of the effects of recent simplification reforms on registration in Latin America, see Bruhn (2008) and Kaplan, Piedra, and Seira (2006) for Mexico; Fajnzylber, Maloney, and Montes-Rojas (2009) for Brazil; and Ronconi and Colina (2011) for Argentina. De Soto (1986) is a seminal work in this area.

23. It is 33 percent higher for those with primary education, 39 percent higher for those with secondary education, and 27 percent higher for those with college or more.

24. For three cities, San Nicolas, Viedma, and Rawson, the average is from 2006 to 2010.

25. The ratio of EAP to total population in the sample is 0.697.

26. We also considered analyzing whether the effects of public employment on entrepreneurship vary by the jobs of public employees. For example, if the newly hired employees work as researchers or as professors at public universities, the effects on entrepreneurship could be positive in the long run due to the spillover effects of their research. The data and identification strategy we use, however, do not allow a proper analysis. First, only 5 percent of public employees in the sample report having such a job, making the estimates unreliable. Second, any spillover effect is likely to affect the whole country and not only the city where the job is located.

27. This figure is likely to be a biased estimate of the causal effect of public employment on entrepreneurship. For example, it ignores the individuals who were considering starting a new business but did not start the project because they chose to enter public employment. Similarly, an increase in public employment might attract employees from the private sector, which may cause some transition from entrepreneurship to private employment.

28. Entrepreneurs who have registered their business and entrepreneurs who hire workers tend to have higher productivity. These are, however, imperfect proxies of quality because some aspects (such as rent seeking) are not observable and could be correlated with formality and firm size.

29. The data can be obtained from http://www.trabajo.gov.ar.

References

Acemoglu, D., and F. Zilibotti. 1997. "Was Prometheus Unbounded by Chance? Risk, Diversification, and Growth." *Journal of Political Economy* 105 (4): 709–51.

Acs, Z. J., P. Braunerhjelm, and D. B. Audretsch. 2009. "The Knowledge Spillover Theory of Entrepreneurship." *Small Business Economics* 32 (1): 15–30.

Acs, Z. J., and L. Szerb. 2007. "Entrepreneurship, Economic Growth, and Public Policy." *Small Business Economics* 28 (2–3): 109–22.

Aghion, P., and P. Howitt. 1992. "A Model of Growth through Creative Destruction." *Econometrica* 60 (2): 323–55.

Alesina, A., S. Danninger, and M. Rostagno. 2001. "Redistribution through Public Employment: The Case of Italy." *IMF Staff Papers* 48 (3): 447–73.

Altimir, O. 1986. "Estimaciones de la distribución del ingreso en la Argentina, 1953–1980." *Desarrollo Económico* 100 (25): 521–66.

Ardagna, S., and A. Lusardi. 2008. "Explaining International Differences in Entrepreneurship: The Role of Individual Characteristics and Regulatory Constraints." NBER Working Paper 14012, National Bureau of Economic Research, Cambridge, MA.

Audretsch, D. B., I. Grilo, and A. R. Thurik. 2007. "Explaining Entrepreneurship and the Role of Policy: A Framework." In *Handbook of Entrepreneurship Policy*, edited by D. B. Audretsch, I. Grilo, and A. R. Thurik. Northampton, MA: Edward Elgar.

Baumol, W. 1990. "Entrepreneurship: Productive, Unproductive, and Destructive." *Journal of Political Economy* 98 (5): 893–921.

Baumol, W. J., R. E. Litan, and C. J. Schramm. 2007. *Good Capitalism, Bad Capitalism, and the Economics of Growth and Prosperity.* New Haven, CT: Yale University Press.

Blanchflower, D. G., and C. Shadforth. 2007. "Entrepreneurship in the UK." *Foundations and Trends in Entrepreneurship* 3 (4): 257–364.

Bruhn, M. 2008. "License to Sell: The Effect of Business Registration Reform on Entrepreneurial Activity in Mexico." Policy Research Working Paper 4538, World Bank, Washington, DC.

Castellani, F., and G. Parent. 2011. "Being 'Middle Class' in Latin America." Working Paper 305, Organisation for Economic Co-operation and Development, Development Centre, Paris.

Claves Información Competitiva. 2010. "Estructura productiva PyME." Claves Información Competitiva, Buenos Aires.

De Soto, H. 1986. *El otro sendero*. Lima: Editorial Printer Colombiana for the Instituto Libertad y Democracia.

Evans, D., and L. Leighton. 1989. "Some Empirical Aspects of Entrepreneurship." *American Economic Review* 79 (3): 519–34.

Fajnzylber, P., W. Maloney, and G. Montes-Rojas. 2009. "Does Formality Improve Micro-Firm Performance? Quasi-Experimental Evidence from the Brazilian SIMPLES Program." IZA Discussion Paper 4531, Institute for the Study of Labor, Bonn.

Freytag, A., and A. R. Thurik. 2010. *Entrepreneurship and Culture*. New York: Springer Publishing.

Gervasoni, C. 2010. "A Rentier Theory of Subnational Regimes." *World Politics* 62 (2): 302–40.

Hirschleifer, J. 2001. *The Dark Side of the Force*. Cambridge, MA: Cambridge University Press.

IDB (Inter-American Development Bank). 2010. *The Age of Productivity: Transforming the Economies from the Bottom Up*. Washington, DC: IDB.

Kantis, H., M. Ishida, and M. Kamori. 2002. *Entrepreneurship in Emerging Economies: The Creation and Development of New Firms in Latin America and East Asia*. Washington, DC: Inter-American Development Bank.

Kaplan, D., E. Piedra, and E. Seira. 2006. "Are Burdensome Registration Procedures an Important Barrier on Firm Creation? Evidence from Mexico." SIEPR Discussion Paper 06-13, Stanford Institute for Economic Policy Research, Stanford, CA.

Kauffman Foundation. 2007. "On the Road to an Entrepreneurial Economy: A Research and Policy Guide." Working Paper, Ewing Marion Kauffman Foundation, Kansas City, MO.

Kihlstrom, R., and J. J. Laffont. 1979. "A General Equilibrium Entrepreneurial Theory of Firm Formation Based on Risk Aversion." *Journal of Political Economy* 87 (4): 719–48.

King, R., and R. Levine. 1993. "Finance, Entrepreneurship, and Growth." *Journal of Monetary Economics* 32 (3): 513–42.

Knight, F. 1929. *Risk, Uncertainty, and Profit*. Boston, MA: Hart, Schaffner, and Marx.

Landes, D. 1998. *The Wealth and Poverty of Nations: Why Some Are So Rich and Some So Poor*. New York: W. W. Norton.

Lora, E., and J. Fajardo. Forthcoming. "Latin American Middle Classes: The Distance between Perception and Reality." *Economía*.

Lundström, A., and L. Stevenson. 2005. *Entrepreneurship Policy: Theory and Practices*. International Studies in Entrepreneurship. New York: Springer Publishing.

Maddison, A. 2006. *The World Economy*. Paris: Organisation for Economic Co-operation and Development.

———. 2007. *Contours of the World Economy, 1–2030 AD: Essays in Macro-Economic History*. Oxford, U.K.: Oxford University Press.

Phelps, E. 2011. "Economic Culture and Economic Performance: What Light Is Shed on the Continent's Problem?" In *Perspectives on the Performance of the Continental Economies,* edited by E. Phelps and H. W. Sinn. Cambridge, MA: MIT Press.

Rendall, M. 2010. "Brain Versus Brawn: The Realization of Women's Comparative Advantage." IEW Working Paper 491, Institute for Empirical Research in Economics, University of Zurich.

Ronconi, L., and J. Colina. 2011. "Labor Registration Simplification in Argentina: Achievements and Pending Issues." IDB-WP-277, Inter-American Development Bank, Washington, DC.

Say, J. B. 1880. *A Treatise on Political Economy*. Philadelphia: Claxton, Remsen, and Haffelfinger.

Schmitz, J. 1989. "Imitation, Entrepreneurship, and Long-Run Growth." *Journal of Political Economy* 97 (3): 721–39.

Schumpeter, J. (1911, 1934) 1989. *The Theory of Economic Development: An Inquiry into Profits, Capital, Credit, Interests, and the Business Cycle*. Repr. of 1934 trans., New Brunswick, NJ: Transaction Publishers.

Torrado, S. 1992. *Estructura social de la Argentina, 1945–1983*. Buenos Aires: Ediciones de La Flor.

Weber, M. 1905. *The Protestant Ethic and the Spirit of Capitalism*. New York: Unwin Hyman.

Wennekers, S., and R. Thurik. 1999. "Linking Entrepreneurship and Growth." *Small Business Economics* 13 (1): 27–56.

6

The Effect of Social Capital on Middle-Class Entrepreneurship in Ecuador

Xavier Ordeñana and Elizabeth Arteaga

Many governments in Latin America have developed special programs to encourage entrepreneurship, hoping it will contribute to growth, employment, and economic welfare.[1] However, the effect of entrepreneurship on these economic variables is not obvious, especially in developing countries where entrepreneurship has a strong component based on necessity. Furthermore, it is difficult to identify the "type" of entrepreneurship that public policy should foster.

Some authors, such as Amorós and Cristi (2010), find that entrepreneurial activities enhance human development, contributing to poverty reduction; they argue that public support for entrepreneurship is justified. Others, such as Shane (2009), find that promoting a large number of start-ups is not an effective public policy. Using data for the United States and other developed countries, Shane shows that many start-up firms do not create many jobs or contribute significantly to economic growth. He recommends financing a few high-growth start-ups, since those are likely to have important economic spillovers.

In the same vein, Acs and Amorós (2008) find that competitiveness and gross domestic product (GDP) per capita are negatively correlated with entrepreneurship rates in Latin America and argue that competitiveness in Latin America has not been oriented toward improving innovation and entrepreneurship. However, they do not advocate "laissez-faire" as the best policy. Instead, they propose a twofold strategy: (a) reducing necessity-based entrepreneurship to achieve the *efficiency-driven* stage (when firms must begin to develop more efficient production processes and to improve product quality because wages have risen and they cannot increase prices)[2] and (b) promoting innovative entrepreneurship to reach the *innovation-driven* stage (when wages have risen so much that firms can only sustain those higher wages and the associated standard of living if they can compete with new or unique products, services, models, and processes).

Both sides of this debate share the idea that a kind of entrepreneurship exists that can generate growth and job creation—which is crucial to economic performance—and that should be promoted by public policy. According to Acemoglu and Zilibotti (1997), these entrepreneurs can be found in the middle class. Others authors stress the spillover effect of the middle class. For example, Kharas (2010) focuses on the role of consumption and the range of goods and services demanded by the middle class. Thus a convenient starting point is to observe a country's middle class.

Ecuador's Middle Class, Mobility, and the Role of Entrepreneurship

Nearly half (49.9 percent) of the Ecuadorian population can be labeled middle class, according to the most recent data available from the National Institute of Statistics and Census (INEC).[3] Since the economic crisis of 1999 and the subsequent dollarization, the middle class has enjoyed some favorable conditions that have positively affected its consumption behavior.

Middle-class purchasing power increased from 2007 to 2011, according to a recent report on the Ecuadorian middle class (Revista Líderes 2011). This increase has been the result of growth in the number of government employees (bureaucrats) and public sector wages. The middle class has also benefited from real estate conditions. Valdez (2011) refers to Ecuador's middle class as "spoiled," because middle-class buyers benefited as real estate sales rose 20 percent in Quito and 14 percent in Guayaquil in 2010. The considerable increase in real estate public loans extended by the Social Security Institute (IESS) explains most of this change.

A strong middle class generates consumer power and social stability, according to Solimano (2008). Easterly (2001) finds that a higher share of income for the middle class and a low degree of ethnic division (a condition he calls the "middle-class consensus") are associated with higher income and higher growth. The middle class is indeed growing in Latin America (Franco, Hopenhayn, and León 2011), and consumption of goods such as cars and mobile phones is rising.

A strong middle class can also have an important effect on poverty reduction (see Ravallion 2009) and thus improve inequality measures. As in most of Latin America, inequality is a concern in Ecuador. The richest 20 percent of the population held more than 50 percent of the wealth during the first decade of the twenty-first century (Canelas 2010). Income inequality generates social and political instability, which in turn reduces investment and growth (Alesina and Perotti 1996).

The type and degree of entrepreneurship are related to the social hierarchy and mobility prevailing in a society. Using data from Latinobarómetro, the *Latin American Economic Outlook* (OECD 2010b) highlights two interesting results: most entrepreneurs perceive themselves as upper class rather than middle class, and there is no significant difference among upper-, middle-, and lower-class respondents regarding their attitudes toward entrepreneurship. Analyzing a set of 129 countries, Solimano (2008) finds a negative (although weak) correlation between the share of small and medium enterprises (SMEs) in employment and output and the share of the middle class.

Using U.S. data, Quadrini (2000) finds that a higher savings rate for entrepreneurs compared with workers generates upward wealth mobility for entrepreneurs and downward mobility for employees. Given all of these links between entrepreneurship, growth, and social mobility, this chapter zeroes in on Ecuador and reviews the state of entrepreneurship there.

Entrepreneurship in Ecuador

Insights on the characteristics of entrepreneurs and entrepreneurial activities in Ecuador can be gleaned from the Global Entrepreneurship Monitor (GEM) project, in which Ecuador has participated since 2004.[4] The 2012 GEM report for Ecuador finds that 21.3 percent of the population is involved in early-stage entrepreneurship: that is, they are planning to start a new business or are running one that is up to 42 months old. Ecuador ranks 8 (out of the 59 countries surveyed) with regard to early-stage entrepreneurial activity. Some 5.9 percent of entrepreneurs start their business out of necessity and 15.4 percent to pursue an opportunity. The ratio of opportunity-based to necessity-based entrepreneurs in Ecuador is similar to the ratio in other countries in Latin America (2.6), but lower than in the innovation-driven economies (4.81).

More than 50 percent of entrepreneurs earn more than $400 a month:[5] specifically, 72 percent of opportunity-based and 28 percent of necessity-based entrepreneurs cross that threshold. Men (54.6 percent) and women (45.4 percent) participate in roughly equal shares in entrepreneurial activity. Male participation is higher in opportunity- than in necessity-based entrepreneurship.

Education is a key factor favoring business start-ups in Ecuador, as in other parts of the world (see, for example, Kantis, Angelelli, and Moori 2004). GEM finds a significant effect of different types of education (primary, secondary, and specific business training) on entrepreneurship in the last three years of analysis (2008, 2009, and 2010). Furthermore, when comparing entrepreneurs with and without education, the percentage of opportunity-based entrepreneurs is significantly higher in the former. This difference is not present among necessity-based entrepreneurs.

As in most developing countries, the main motivation for opportunity-based entrepreneurs is preserving or enhancing income.[6] This suggests that, in general, opportunity entrepreneurship is related to the middle-class quest for stability—as suggested by Torche and López-Calva (2010)—rather than a sign of economic growth.

Regarding the impact of entrepreneurship on job creation, 98 percent of entrepreneurs created between 0 and 5 jobs. Only 6.3 percent of early-stage entrepreneurs had high expectations of creating jobs (few expected their business to employ more than 10 people within five years of starting up or to increase the number of jobs from their current level by 50 percent).[7] This suggests that Ecuadorian entrepreneurs have some self-limitations or face external constraints in the business environment that restrict the potential of start-ups. The lack of job creation might limit the upward mobility of entrepreneurs.

Middle-Class Entrepreneurship

While Ecuadorian entrepreneurship in general has been the subject of research, the role of middle-class entrepreneurs in promoting economic mobility has not been investigated. Thus this study seeks to characterize middle-class entrepreneurship and assess its role in economic and social mobility.

The first challenge is to define the middle class. Pressman (2007), in his international study of the middle class, offers three definitions: a sociological one, referring to attitudes (interest in good education, having a career, using reasoning rather than violence); an economic one (some middle range of the overall income distribution); and a personal one, based exclusively on self-perception. Kharas (2010), in a study of the middle class in developing countries, defines the middle class as those who live on between $10 and $100 a day in terms of purchasing power parity (PPP).[8] Castellani and Parent (2011) propose household income of between 50 and 150 percent of the median income. This definition is the first choice of this chapter, although middle-class characteristics generally accepted in the literature, such as patience and the "spirit of capitalism," cited by Doepke and Zilibotti (2005), are not necessarily observed in Ecuadorian data in that range.[9] Ecuadorian market research firms, such as the IPSA Group (2010), use alternative measures for the middle class that include much higher average incomes (around $1,500) and access to higher education. This study also explores the $10 to $50 a day definition in terms of purchasing power parity, which translates into monthly household income of between $612 and $2,500.

Dynamic Entrepreneurship

An exploratory study of dynamic businesses in Ecuador conducted by Arteaga and Lasio (2009) provides insights on business growth.[10] Based on a study of 150 companies in the manufacturing, corporate services, and knowledge-based sectors, the study finds that companies, across all sizes, have, on average, only 1 percent growth in sales and 20 percent growth in employment in their first three years of operation. Furthermore, businesses that are 4 to 10 years old have 24 percent growth in sales and 15 percent growth in employment in their third year of operation, on average. Only 17 percent of the companies are considered *dynamic*.[11] Among dynamic entrepreneurs, 80 percent are males with a university degree (Kantis, Angelelli, and Moori 2004), and the typical dynamic Latin American entrepreneur is young, highly educated, and middle class.[12]

Although Arteaga and Lasio (2009) confirm the low growth potential of new businesses in Ecuador, they do not find important limitations (at least self-perceived limitations). Entrepreneurs attribute the main competencies of dynamic entrepreneurs (problem solving, negotiation, and networking skills) to experience rather than university training.[13] GEM results show that 85 percent of Ecuadorian early-stage entrepreneurs believe that they have the entrepreneurial skills and expertise they need.

Government agencies, universities, chambers of commerce, and other actors do not seem to give appropriate support to developing business skills and providing financing and market information, according to Arteaga and Lasio (2009). The study points out three factors that increase the probability of dynamic behavior in an Ecuadorian company: writing a business plan, having support from a consulting company, and using a network of colleagues to solve problems and find resources.

These results are supported by GEM data, which consistently find that the political, institutional, and social contexts are perceived as limiting factors for entrepreneurship. Respondents cited legal uncertainty, corruption, lack of agreement between the government and the private sector, lack of tax incentives, and lengthy bureaucratic paperwork as among the issues negatively affecting entrepreneurship. They also mentioned government policies as a limiting factor, including excess regulation, lack of a sound commercial policy, lack of incentives for industry, and paternalistic employment laws.[14] Another important limitation observed in GEM data is the lack of financial support, specifically in venture capital, angel investment, or seed capital.

Social Capital

The use of networks by entrepreneurs is important in both the start-up and development stage, according to Ferri, Deakins, and Whittam (2009) in their study of social capital in the entrepreneurial context. The observed weakness in Ecuadorian institutions and specialized agencies might reflect a fragile network for Ecuadorian entrepreneurs. This study uses the concept of social capital as defined by Nahapiet and Ghoshal (1998, 243), which considers social capital to be "the knowledge embedded within, available through, and utilized by interactions among individuals and their networks of interrelationships." Meanwhile, Xu (2011) and Burt (1992) consider social capital as the networks of contacts and their resources.

Several authors have addressed the importance of social capital as one of the "vital factors" affecting entrepreneurship, in addition to human capital, personality, goals, and environment. Zorn (2004) concludes that entrepreneurial capital is composed of human and social capital and has a strong positive impact on entrepreneurial dynamics.

The appropriate use of personal relationships can transform the entrepreneur's personal network into an effective tool to enhance firm performance, according to Bratkovic, Antoncic, and Ruzzier (2009). They also suggest that the growth of firms can be influenced by strategic use of the entrepreneur's resource-based social capital.

Ferri, Deakins, and Whittam (2009) conclude that an entrepreneur's social capital is a key asset for organizational growth, and it can be gathered through family membership, social relations and networks, and affiliations with formal and informal institutions. Nahapiet and Ghoshal (1998) suggest that social contacts provide information and knowledge— both of which are essential to creating a new venture—and emphasize the role of the immediate family in shaping the available opportunities.

New entrepreneurs have difficulty establishing relationships with new contacts and rely on ties of friendship, which limits their networks. Consequently, these entrepreneurs have fewer opportunities to access diverse resources. It is thus important to determine whether Ecuadorian entrepreneurs have adequate access to their network and whether this affects firm performance—specifically its dynamism.

Data and Methodology

To explore the role that social capital may play in the dynamism of Ecuadorian firms, this chapter uses both primary and secondary data. The primary data are obtained from a survey that we constructed and administered to entrepreneurs.[15] The secondary data are compiled from publicly available sources such as the Superintendency of Companies (the number of enterprises by economic sector and location); the INEC V Living Conditions Survey report (median income of Ecuadorian households by area and province); the Latinobarómetro report for 2010 (including the distribution of wealth, perception of the current economic situation, the impact of the economic crisis, education level, and entrepreneurial attitudes, activities, and aspirations); and the GEM Ecuador reports (perceived constraints); see Superintendency of Companies (2009);

INEC (2005); Corporación Latinobarómetro (2011); and Lasio, Arteaga, and Caicedo (2009, 2010). The 2003–10 National Survey of Employment and Unemployment (ENEMDU) is central to our analysis. The methodology used in this study to assess each research objective is described next.

Characterization of Entrepreneurs

For starters, the data obtained from the survey are used to gauge the differences between middle-class and upper-class entrepreneurs. "Typical" middle-class and upper-class entrepreneurs are defined, and the internal and external factors that hinder the entrepreneurial process are analyzed.

Dynamic Businesses

Data obtained from the survey are used to determine the impact of middle-class entrepreneurship on the economy. As a proxy for impact, we use the "success" of the middle-class businesses. In particular, we are interested in determining what factors affect the probability of "success." The analysis draws on several studies. Kantis, Angelelli, and Moori (2004) find that family background, work experience, and education differ for dynamic and less dynamic enterprises. Autio (2007) finds that household income, labor status, and entrepreneurial attitudes are significantly associated with high-growth entrepreneurship. Unger et al. (2011) find that human capital (education, experience, knowledge, and skills) has an important effect on entrepreneurial success. Networking and use of a business plan also affect the probability of dynamism in the firm (Arteaga and Lasio 2009). Building on these works, the following model of business growth is defined:

$$BG_i = \alpha + \beta_1 HI_i + \beta_2 Ed_i + \beta_3 F_i + \beta_4 Exp_i$$
$$+ \beta_5 EST_i + \beta_6 SC_i + \gamma X_i + \varepsilon_i, \tag{6.1}$$

where the dependent variable is a measure of potential business growth and the independent variables are, in order, household income, education level, family background, experience, business-specific training, and social capital, followed by a group of control variables X_i. The measure of potential business growth is an increase in the number of employees.

Intergenerational Mobility

We are also interested in determining whether entrepreneurial characteristics (personal characteristics of the entrepreneur as well as specific features of the enterprise and local business environment) can affect the probability of upward intergenerational mobility. A report on intergenerational social mobility (OECD 2010a) shows that parental or socioeconomic background influences the economic performance of descendants. It also finds that education and redistributive government policies have a positive effect on mobility.

Based on data from our survey, the following model is used to estimate the probability that an entrepreneur will experience upward mobility:

$$M_i = \propto + \beta_1 E_i + \beta_2 S_i + \beta_3 Age_i + \beta_4 H_i + \beta_5 F_i + \delta Z + \varepsilon_i, \qquad (6.2)$$

where M_i is a dummy variable for upward mobility that measures whether the entrepreneur has moved from one social stratum to another (income), and the independent variables are education, savings rate, age, household size, family background, and a set Z of entrepreneurial characteristics (such as the sector of the enterprise).

Data Construction: The Survey

Ordeñana and Villa (forthcoming) find some interesting results relating entrepreneurship to (intragenerational) mobility using the ENEMDU databases. To analyze some issues that are not considered in those or other available databases, we sought to tackle issues such as intergenerational mobility and business growth. The sampling procedure and the questionnaire are described next.

Sampling

The primary data for this study come from surveys of 203 entrepreneurs. These businesses are located in three cities (Guayaquil, Quito, and Cuenca), where 85.7 percent of Ecuadorian enterprises are concentrated (Superintendency of Companies 2009). The enterprises are up to 10 years old. The sample size was calculated with a 95 percent confidence level and a 7 percent sampling error. The sampling framework was selected from the databases of three Ecuadorian institutions: the Superintendency of Companies, the Internal Revenue Service, and the IESS.

Questionnaire

The questionnaire had five sections: (a) entrepreneurs and businesses characteristics; (b) entrepreneurial motivations, attitudes, and competencies; (c) financing; (d) innovation; and (e) entrepreneurial environment.

Entrepreneurs and Businesses Characteristics

This section of the questionnaire included the following variables: the entrepreneur's gender; age (number of years); education level (ordinal scale: primary, secondary, university, postgraduate); social origin (ordinal scale: lower, middle, and upper class); entrepreneurial experience (number of previously founded enterprises); labor experience (nominal scale: national organization employee, multinational employee, consultant, other); business age (number of years); business size (number of employees); and proportion of sales in foreign markets (percentage of total sales). Education level, social origin, business size, entrepreneurial experience, and proportion of sales in foreign markets are measured according to Kantis, Angelelli, and Moori (2004).

Entrepreneurial Motivations, Attitudes, and Competencies

To analyze entrepreneurial attitudes, the questionnaire contained six dichotomous (yes/no) questions about entrepreneurial intentions, perceived opportunities, knowledge and skills to start a business, fear of failure, starting a business as a career choice, and starting a business to gain status and respect. To measure entrepreneurial motivations, one question (nominal scale: independence, increase in income, unemployment) was included from the GEM Adult Population Survey (Kelley, Bosma, and Amorós 2011). The importance of entrepreneurial competencies (making decisions, networking, oral and written communication, and the like) was measured with a four-point Likert scale (Arteaga and Lasio 2009).

Financing

This section of the questionnaire included the variables of initial investment (in dollars) and the use of various financing sources, such as personal savings, relatives' and friends' savings, and bank loans (four-point Likert scale).

Innovation

To measure the level of innovation of goods and services offered by the entrepreneur, two questions about the age of technology used (ordinal scale: less than one year, between one and five years, more than five years) and the number of competitors (ordinal scale: many business competitors, few business competitors, no business competitors) were included from the GEM Adult Population Survey (Kelley, Bosma, and Amorós 2011).

Entrepreneurial Environment

To measure the entrepreneurial environment, the following variables were analyzed: use of planning tools (business plan, sales and costs forecasts, internal rate of return calculation, others); main problems during the entrepreneurial process (access to financing, bureaucracy, taxes and government regulations, information about competitors, hiring of human resources); external support to solve problems (public agencies, consultants, chambers, colleagues, family, friends, universities); sources of training in entrepreneurship (primary or secondary school, university, seminary, government agencies, online courses); and main constraints (financing alternatives, entrepreneurship policy, labor code characteristics, judicial system).

Following Arteaga (2011), dichotomous scales (yes/no) were used to measure planning tools, main problems encountered during the entrepreneurial process, and external support used to solve problems. To determine where the entrepreneurs received training in businesses creation, some of the questions from the education section of the GEM Adult Population Survey were included. For the constraints to the entrepreneurial process, the list of alternatives was elaborated using the results of the National Experts Survey (NES) from GEM Ecuador (Lasio, Arteaga, and Caicedo 2009, 2010). The strategies to mitigate the constraints were investigated with open-ended questions.

Main Results

Based on the survey described, a profile for middle- and upper-class entrepreneurs was first defined. *Middle-class entrepreneurs* are predominantly male (68 percent) and, on average, are 42 years old, have a four-member household, are college educated (50 percent), and come from a middle-class (59 percent) and lower-class (33 percent) background. Before becoming an entrepreneur, they worked at a national company (43 percent) or as an independent professional (30 percent). *Upper-class entrepreneurs* are predominantly male (75 percent) and on average are 44 years old, have a four-member household, and come from the middle class (58 percent). Some 55 percent of them previously worked for a national firm and 20 percent were independent professionals.

For both middle- and upper-class entrepreneurs, the main motivations for starting a business are to be independent (86 percent) or to improve their economic status (85 percent). The most important skills for middle-class entrepreneurs are achieving goals, creative thinking, and decision making (see figure 6.1). Upper-class entrepreneurs highly value decision making, problem solving, and creative thinking. Middle-class entrepreneurs mentioned achieving goals and communication skills significantly more often than upper-class entrepreneurs.

Tables 6.1 and 6.2 show the external and internal factors hindering the entrepreneurial process, respectively, for both middle- and upper-class entrepreneurs. Among the external factors, paperwork and tax policy are common problems for both middle- and upper- class entrepreneurs (table 6.1). Middle-class business people have more difficulty obtaining adequate financing and inputs than upper-class entrepreneurs, but upper-class entrepreneurs have more difficulty obtaining access to information about competitors.

When analyzing the internal factors that hinder the entrepreneurial process, both middle-class and upper-class entrepreneurs claim to have

Figure 6.1 Key Skills of Entrepreneurs in Ecuador, by Social Class, 2011

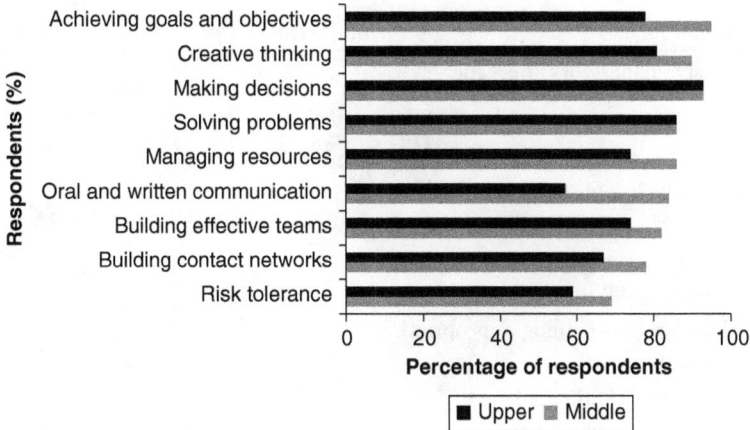

difficulty managing functional areas of the firm: finance, human resources, and advertising or marketing (probably related to the fact that they find it difficult to hire human resources). Another important internal factor is the difficulty of networking, a common problem for Latin American markets, according to Schött (2011).

Regarding the sources of support to deal with internal and external difficulties, 40 percent of middle-class entrepreneurs solve their problems on their own, compared to 51 percent of upper-class entrepreneurs, and 34 percent of middle-class entrepreneurs resort to friends and family, compared to 27 percent of upper-class entrepreneurs (see table 6.3). This finding reinforces the low level of networking shown in the previous tables.

Table 6.4 presents the sources of education for both starting and managing a business. Most entrepreneurs get entrepreneurial training from a university education. Specifically, 34 percent of middle-class entrepreneurs said that they learned their entrepreneurial skills from their university studies (compared with 36 percent of upper-class entrepreneurs). However, when it comes to managing a business, 32 percent (for both middle- and upper-class entrepreneurs) said that they learned the needed skills in private seminars or short courses.

Regardless of social class, few entrepreneurs use government agencies to start or manage a business (between 1 and 2 percent). This may suggest that the recent initiatives taken by the Ecuadorian government (such as Emprende Ecuador) are being used by new entrepreneurs or the self-employed rather than by established entrepreneurs (those identified in this study).

Table 6.1 External Factors That Hinder the Entrepreneurial
Process in Ecuador, by Social Class, 2011
(*% of respondents*)

External factors	Middle class	Upper class	Proportions difference
Extensive paperwork (bureaucracy)	55	51	4*
Tax policy	40	43	-3*
Difficulties in obtaining financing	38	28	10*
Difficulties in obtaining human resources	35	39	-4*
High costs of materials, human resources, and inputs	27	22	5*
Difficulties in obtaining appropriate suppliers	19	20	-1*
Difficulties in finding adequate facilities	18	10	8*
Duties on imports	13	12	1*
Difficulties in access to information about competitors	11	29	-18***
Difficulties in access to information about the target or potential market size	9	9	0*
Lack of infrastructure for basic services (communications, electricity)	9	8	1*
Difficulties in obtaining information and telecommunications infrastructure	6	10	-4*

Significance level: * = 10 percent, *** = 1 percent.

Finally, the *average firm owned by a middle-class entrepreneur* is a
family business (69 percent) with six years of continuous operation. Firms
are focused on the domestic market, mainly in wholesale or retail commerce (30 percent) or in business services such as real estate and consulting companies (25 percent). They have an average of four employees
and annual sales of $100,000. The initial investment averaged $10,000,
funded mainly by the entrepreneur's own resources (73 percent); only
25 percent received funds from family and friends. Most of these results
are similar to those found consistently in GEM reports for Ecuador.

The *average firm owned by an upper-class entrepreneur* is also a family business with an average of eight years of continuous operation. It is

Table 6.2 Internal Factors That Hinder the Entrepreneurial
Process in Ecuador, by Social Class, 2011
(*% of respondents*)

Internal factors	Middle class	Upper class	Proportions difference
Managing human resources	40	30	10*
Lack of networking, which caused difficulties in getting customers	36	35	1*
Lack of knowledge in managing advertising and marketing	33	40	–7*
Managing finance issues	28	24	4*
Managing the business tax aspects	26	38	–12*
Inexperience in the context of the business	23	15	8*
Lack of knowledge about how to start a business	20	13	7*
Inexperience in sales	18	30	–12*
Inadequate planning	13	9	4*
Lack of knowledge about the target market segment	5	7	–2*
Lack of knowledge about how to define their income model	3	5	–2*
Managing available financial resources	1	8	–7**

Significance level: * = 10 percent, ** = 5 percent.

focused on the domestic market, mainly in services (38 percent) or whole-sale or retail trade (31 percent). Firms have an average of seven employees and annual sales of $240,000. The initial investment averaged $5,000, obtained mainly by their own resources (84 percent).

The lower level of investment observed among upper-class entrepreneurs is surprising. However, it may be related to the fact that upper-class entrepreneurs concentrate on consultancy and other services, while middle-class entrepreneurs concentrate on manufacturing. Table 6.5 compares the initial investment of middle- and upper-class entrepreneurs in different sectors.

Funding sources are presented in figure 6.2. As mentioned, the entrepreneur's own funding is the preferred source. Middle-class entrepreneurs obtain funding from family and friends more intensively (more than 20 percent) than upper-class entrepreneurs. Once again, the level of third-party investors is very low, showing a relatively low degree of networking.

Table 6.3 Sources of Support to Solve Problems in Ecuador, by
Social Class, 2011
(*% of respondents*)

Source of support	Middle class	Upper class	Proportions difference
Own efforts	40	51	–11*
Family or friends	34	27	7*
Suppliers or customers	20	13	7*
Work colleagues	18	24	–6*
Other entrepreneurs	15	3	12**
Consultants	13	20	–7*
Chambers or associations	13	6	7*
Government institutions	11	11	0*
Universities or research centers	11	6	5*
Social networks (Facebook, LinkedIn)	6	1	5*
Incubators	0	0	0

Significance level: * = 10 percent, ** = 5 percent

Dynamic Businesses in Ecuador and the Role of Social Capital

To determine whether the firms created by Ecuadorian entrepreneurs have
"impact," this section focuses exclusively on the dynamism of firms. Based
on a survey of 161 entrepreneurs, a logistic regression was used to construct the growth potential—dynamic business profile model for Ecuador,
in which the dependent variable is dynamic (1 is a dynamic business, and
0 is not a dynamic business).[16] Personal and firm characteristics were
included, such as age and household size (following Cuesta, Ñopo, and
Pizzolito 2011), entrepreneurial experience, and a dummy for family firm
(following Kantis, Angelelli, and Moori 2004). Following the dynamic
business studies of Kantis, Angelelli, and Moori (2004) and Arteaga and
Lasio (2009), the funding sources (figure 6.2) and the external factors
(table 6.1) that can potentially hinder the entrepreneurial process were
included. Finally, the analysis included the internal factors (table 6.2) that
can affect the success of entrepreneurial activity, according to Shariffe and
Saud (2009), especially in developing nations such as Ecuador.

Liao and Welsch (2005) conclude that what differentiates entrepreneurs from non-entrepreneurs is their ability and capacity to create

Table 6.4 Sources of Education about Starting and Managing a Business in Ecuador, by Social Class, 2011
(*% of respondents*)

	Starting a business			Managing a business		
Source	Middle class	Upper class	Proportions difference	Middle class	Upper class	Proportions difference
Primary or secondary education	5	0	5*	0	1	–1*
University education	34	36	–2*	28	14	14**
Seminar or course offered by a university	6	20	–14***	19	11	8*
Seminar or course offered by a private enterprise	7	11	–4*	13	21	–8*
Chambers of commerce or professional associations	31	13	18**	18	21	–3*
Government agencies	2	1	1*	2	2	0*
Previous or current employers	11	2	9**	1	4	–3*
Online seminars	8	3	5*	3	6	–3*

Significance level: * = 10 percent, ** = 5 percent, *** = 1 percent.

social capital. To capture the effect of social capital, two additional variables were constructed: "close network" and "distant network." Using the framework developed by Schött (2011), an entrepreneur's network is considered to consist of several environments: private (family and friends); professional (lawyers, accountants, banks); entrepreneurial (strangers, investors, mentors, researchers, public counselors); market (competitors, suppliers, customers); and job (bosses, colleagues). These environments were grouped into two categories considered to be the level of proximity: close (private and job) and distant (market, professional, and entrepreneurial).

Exploratory factor analysis was applied to the variables related to the sources of support used by entrepreneurs to solve problems while they were creating their business. Two principal components emerged. The first component consists of customers, suppliers, university research centers,

Table 6.5 Initial Investment in Ecuador, by Sector and Social Class, 2011 (*US$*)

Sector	Upper class	Middle class	Means difference
Average	9,285	12,696	−3,411*
Agriculture	250,873	141,013	109,860*
Manufacturing	30,783	31,537	−754*
Commerce	12,871	23,419	10,548
Construction	10,823	9,123	−1,700*
Business services	6,234	12,468	−6,798*
Transport	6,060	12,858	−6,234*

Significance level: * = 10 percent.

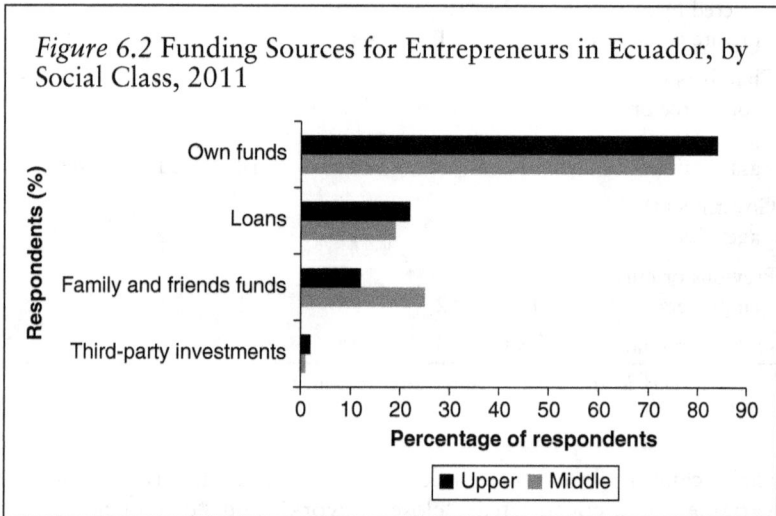

Figure 6.2 Funding Sources for Entrepreneurs in Ecuador, by Social Class, 2011

government institutions, and chambers of commerce or associations. The second consists of family, friends, and colleagues.

Close network is a dummy variable that takes the value of 1 when the entrepreneur has received support to solve problems from family, friends, or colleagues, and 0 otherwise. *Distant network* is a dummy variable that takes the value of 1 when the entrepreneur has received support to solve problems from government institutions, chambers of commerce, suppliers, customers, and universities or research centers, and 0 otherwise.

In the resulting model (shown in table 6.6), perceiving business opportunities in the next six months, having trouble finding adequate suppliers, dealing with the high costs of materials and human resources, facing

Table 6.6 Logistic Regression Model: Dynamic Business in Ecuador, 2011

Variable	B	Wald	Exp(B)	Marginal effects
Business opportunities***	1.290	9.641	3.632	0.245
High costs of resources limitation***	1.849	10.105	6.354	0.305
Suppliers access limitation***	1.876	8.818	6.528	0.307
Inexperience in the context of the business***	–1.482	7.605	0.227	–0.346
Lack of knowledge about how to start a business**	–1.575	6.653	0.207	–0.363
Bureaucracy limitation**	0.967	5.185	2.629	0.198
Close network**	0.844	3.862	2.325	0.177
Constant	–1.243	8.259	0.289	–0.298

Log likelihood	R^2 Cox and Snell test	R^2 Nagelkerke test	Hosmer and Lemeshow test
160.189	0.256	0.345	10.624 (0.224)

Significance level: ** = 5 percent, *** = 1 percent.

bureaucratic constraints, and having received support from close network (family, friends, and colleagues) to solve problems significantly increase the likelihood of being a dynamic firm. Inexperience concerning the context of the business and lack of knowledge about how to start a business decrease this ratio. The Hosmer and Lemeshow test reveals that the model has a good fit, with an overall classification of 75 percent. The correlation between the independent variables is also shown; none of them is significantly correlated (all are below 0.4 in absolute terms).

Some of the variables that increase the likelihood of being a dynamic firm can be perceived a priori as counterintuitive. Entrepreneurs who have had to deal with bureaucracy and have had difficulty accessing good suppliers and technology have a positive impact on dynamism, suggesting that those entrepreneurs are more demanding regarding their inputs, thus becoming more competitive in the medium term. In other words, we might be observing reverse causality. Dynamic firms face more complex problems (with respect to not-dynamic firms) and thus state constraints similar to the ones mentioned here.

Being "optimistic," measured as perceiving business opportunities, also increases the chance of being a dynamic entrepreneur.

A very interesting result—though not a surprising one—is that having a close network (friends, family, and colleagues) increases the chance of being dynamic. Entrepreneurs who have access to a close network have a probability of owning a dynamic business that is 0.177 higher than those who do not have access to a close network. Having a distant network is not found to have a significant effect. The results go in hand with Schött's (2011) results, which find that Latin American entrepreneurs often use advisers from their private environment. Thus although Ecuadorian entrepreneurs generally have a weak network, that network has a significant effect on the success of a business. As Damirchi, Shafai, and Paknazar (2011) suggest, entrepreneurs with a greater amount of social capital have better access to the sources and information that can affect the entrepreneurial process, and they are more likely to discern business opportunities more effectively.

Intergenerational Mobility

Ordeñana and Villa (forthcoming) find that entrepreneurship has a significant impact on intragenerational mobility. This section uses the survey data to test whether entrepreneurship is related to intergenerational mobility. In particular, we are interested in determining what variables are key for improving the economic situation of entrepreneurs over time. A logistic regression was run, defining the dependent variable as "upward mobility" (1 if the entrepreneur experienced an improvement in his or her economic status, and 0 otherwise). The initial economic status is considered the one in which entrepreneurs declared to have been born, and the current status corresponds to their current income. Several independent variables were used, especially from the business set (such as external factors, family business) and the individual set (such as access to education, gender).

In the model, the variables gender (being male) and using loans to make the initial investment increase the ratio of upwardly mobile entrepreneurs to downwardly mobile entrepreneurs. The use of family funds to make the initial investment decreases this ratio. The Hosmer and Lemeshow test indicates that the model has a good fit, with an overall classification of 1.676 (0.892); (see table 6.7).

Care must be taken in analyzing these results. To construct the dependent variable "upward mobility," entrepreneurs' declared income and social status at birth were used. About 25 percent of the surveyed individuals refused to declare their income; thus those data points were eliminated. The fact that being male increases the probability of experiencing upward mobility is not completely surprising: in most "dynamic" sectors, such as industrial activities, services, and financial intermediation, there are more male than female entrepreneurs.

The use of loans, showing at least some kind of third-party involvement in business, increases the probability of upward mobility. In contrast, mainly using family funds reduces the probability of upward mobility: perhaps because of a scale effect (these funds are usually smaller than loans or third-party investments).

Table 6.8 presents the intergenerational transition matrix showing the observed transition probabilities between the three social classes. Again, the entrepreneur directly reported family background, while the current status was calculated (using, as before, the $10–$50 PPP rule) based on entrepreneurs' declared income. A total of 60 percent of interviewed entrepreneurs experienced upward mobility, 32 percent remained in the same class, and 8 percent experienced downward mobility (most of it from the upper to the middle class).

Clearly, the fact that there are only 100 available observations limits the conclusions one can take of the transition matrix shown in table 6.8. Further research should be done in order to confirm the intergenerational effects of entrepreneurship.

Table 6.7 Logistic Regression Model: Upward Mobility of Entrepreneurs in Ecuador, 2011

Variable	B	Wald	Exp(B)
Sex (male)	0.886	3.799	2.426
Family funds***	−2.018	13.089	0.133
Use of loans**	1.568	6.328	4.796
Managing business tax aspects**	1.077	5.560	2.935
Constant	−0.271	0.407	0.763
Log likelihood	R^2 Cox and Snell test	R^2 Nagelkerke test	Hosmer and Lemeshow test
149,899	0.195	0.268	1.675 (0.892)

Significance level: ** = 5 percent, *** = 1 percent.

Table 6.8 Matrix for Intergenerational Transition in Ecuador, 2011
(*number of respondents*)

	Current social class			
Family background (class)	Lower	Middle	Upper	Total
Lower	0	13	15	28
Middle	1	19	35	54
Upper	0	7	11	18
Total	1	38	61	100

Concluding Remarks and Policy Recommendations

Whether entrepreneurship per se is enough to develop a country is an ongoing question. But, as this chapter has tried to show, in countries like Ecuador, entrepreneurship can play a significant role in improving economic performance.

This chapter finds that both middle- and upper-class entrepreneurs face similar problems, although middle-class entrepreneurs are more worried about financing than upper-class ones. They both face difficulties in networking to get more customers, suppliers, and partners and trust themselves and family or friends more than third-party investors. This leaves room for public support: government agencies that promote entrepreneurship should help entrepreneurs to access new investors and new technologies likely to improve their business. This chapter finds, just as Arteaga and Lasio (2009) and GEM reports do, that most businesses are small and have little chance of significant growth. Social capital—mainly in the form of family and friends—is crucial in determining the dynamism of a business. Improving the networking abilities of entrepreneurs can have a significant effect on the size and impact of Ecuadorian enterprises and should be studied in future work.

A limitation of this study is that it focuses primarily on business owners as a proxy for entrepreneurs. Carland et al. (1984) argue that, although there are similarities between small business owners and entrepreneurs, they are not exactly defined by the same concept. Lazear (2005) argues that someone who is self-employed can be an entrepreneur if he or she has talents that cover various skills, such as team leadership, decision making, and managerial skills. This would differentiate an entrepreneur from a self-employed handyman who works alone, for example. At the empirical level, Lazear considers self-employed individuals as entrepreneurs if they view themselves as having started a business. Although self-employment might not be an exact match for entrepreneurship,[17] several authors believe that there is some correspondence between these two concepts (Carroll and Mosakowski 1987). Self-employment has provided a focus for research on entrepreneurship (Nicolaou et al. 2009), and the Global Entrepreneurship Monitor considers it to be a measure of individual involvement in venture creation, especially when it is motivated by necessity (Kelley, Bosma, and Amorós 2011). For the empirical assessment, this chapter defines business owner as a proxy for entrepreneur. However, it would be interesting to see the effect of using self-employment instead, especially to determine the public policies that are needed to tackle each type of "entrepreneur."

The intergenerational transition matrix suggests that entrepreneurship has an important effect on mobility. Finally, government agencies, including export promotion agencies such as the recently created Pro Ecuador, can play a role in supporting entrepreneurs by improving their access to financing options, better technology, and a larger network.

Notes

1. See, for example, Start-Up Chile (http://www.startupchile.org) and Emprende Ecuador (http://www.emprendecuador.com).
2. They follow the scheme of the *Global Competitiveness Report 2012–2013* (WEF 2012), which classifies economies according to three stages: factor driven (the first stage, where countries compete based on their factor endowments, primarily low-skilled labor, and natural resources), efficiency driven, and innovation driven.
3. See Encuesta de Calidad de Vida 2006.
4. For more information on the GEM project, see http://www.gemconsortium .org.
5. The Ecuadorian median income is $407, according to the INEC.
6. In innovation-driven economies (usually those with higher GDP), the main driver is "seeking independence."
7. Using the definition of the middle class proposed by Castellani and Parent (2011)—between 50 and 150 percent of median income—GEM data reveal hardly any early-stage entrepreneurs who own a business with more than 6 employees. This suggests the need for a deeper study of what constitutes a "proper middle class" for Ecuador.
8. All dollar amounts are in U.S. dollars. Kharas uses 2005 dollars.
9. That range in Ecuador would be from $203.50 to $610.50, using the median income in 2010 of $407.
10. A dynamic enterprise, according to Kantis, Angelelli, and Moori (2004), is defined as one that is no older than 10 years and that has grown to employ at least 15 and no more than 300 employees.
11. Arteaga and Lasio (2009) define dynamism as a minimum incremental growth in sales of 10 percent in the first five years, 20 percent in the sixth and seventh years, 40 percent in the eighth year, and 50 percent in the last two years. In addition, the number of employees has grown 20 percent by the third year, another 10 percent by the sixth year, and another 10 percent by the eighth year.
12. Kantis, Angelelli, and Moori (2004) use a self-perception definition of the middle class.
13. In contrast, Kantis, Angelelli, and Moori (2004) find a significant role for universities in Argentina, Chile, Costa Rica, Mexico, Peru, and other countries.
14. Conversely, respondents also cited certain government policies as promoting entrepreneurship, since the government recently has taken steps to favor local products, direct government spending to local companies, and increase social inclusion.
15. A later section describes how the survey was constructed.
16. Businesses considered for this analysis are between 3 and 10 years old. A business is defined as dynamic when it has increased its number of employees. For new businesses (3 or 4 years old), growth was measured between the first and the last year observed. For older businesses (5 to 10 years old), growth was calculated in two periods: between the first year and the third year of operation and between the third year and the last year observed. An older business is considered dynamic if it has grown in both periods.
17. For example, Hisrich and Brush (1985, 15) define entrepreneurship as "the process of creating something *different with value*, devoting the necessary time and

effort, assuming the accompanying financial, psychic, and social risks, and receiving the resulting rewards of monetary and personal satisfaction."

References

Acemoglu, D., and F. Zilibotti. 1997. "Was Prometheus Unbound by Chance? Risk, Diversification, and Growth." *Journal of Political Economy* 105 (4): 709–51.

Acs, Z., and J. E. Amorós. 2008. "Entrepreneurship and Competitiveness Dynamics in Latin America." *Small Business Economies* 31 (3): 305–22.

Alesina, A., and R. Perotti. 1996. "Income Distribution, Political Instability, and Investment." *European Economic Review* 105 (4): 709–51.

Amorós, J., and O. Cristi. 2010. "Poverty, Human Development, and Entrepreneurship." In *The Dynamics of Entrepreneurship: Theory and Evidence*, edited by M. Minitti. Oxford, U.K.: Oxford University Press.

Arteaga, M. E. 2011. "Perfil de los emprendedores de la región." Unpublished manuscript, Centro de Desarrollo de Emprendedores, CEEMP, Escuela Superior Politécnica del Litoral.

Arteaga, M. E., and V. Lasio. 2009. "Empresas dinámicas en Ecuador: Factores de éxito y competencias de sus fundadores." *Academia: Revista Latinoamericana de Administración* 42 (May): 49–67.

Autio, E. 2007. *Global Report on High-Growth Entrepreneurship*. Global Entrepreneurship Monitor. Babson Park, MA: Babson College; London: London Business School.

Bratkovic, T., B. Antoncic, and M. Ruzzier. 2009. "Differentiating Strategic Utilization of Entrepreneur's Resource-Based Social Capital and Small Firm Growth." *Journal of Management and Organization* 15 (4): 486–99.

Burt, R. S. 1992. *Structural Holes*. Cambridge, MA: Harvard University Press.

Canelas, C. 2010. "Poverty, Inequality, and Income Mobility: The Case of Ecuador; a Pseudo-Panel Approach." Master's thesis, Université Paris 1, Panthéon-Sorbonne, Universität Bielefeld, Paris School of Economics.

Carland, J. W., F. Hoy, W. R. Boulton, and J. C. Carland. 1984. "Differentiating Entrepreneurs from Small Business Owners: A Conceptualization." *Academy of Management Review* 9 (2): 354–59.

Carroll, G. R., and E. Mosakowski. 1987. "The Career Dynamics of Self-Employment." *Administrative Science Quarterly* 32 (4): 570–89.

Castellani, F., and G. Parent. 2011. "Being 'Middle Class' in Latin America." Working Paper 305, Organisation for Economic Co-operation and Development, Development Centre, Paris.

Corporación Latinobarómetro. 2011. *2010 Report*. http://www.latinobarómetro.org.

Cuesta, J., H. Ñopo, and G. Pizzolito. 2011. "Using Pseudo-Panels to Estimate Income Mobility in Latin America." *Review of Income and Wealth* 57 (2): 224–46.

Damirchi, G. V., J. Shafai, and J. Paknazar. 2011. "Surveying of Social Capital's Effect on Entrepreneurship." *Interdisciplinary Journal of Contemporary Research in Business* 3 (2): 1101–11.

Doepke, M., and F. Zilibotti. 2005. "Social Class and the Spirit of Capitalism." *Journal of the European Economic Association* 3 (2–3): 516–24.

Easterly, W. 2001. "The Middle-Class Consensus and Economic Development." *Journal of Economic Growth* 6 (4): 317–35.

Ferri, P. J., D. Deakins, and G. Whittam. 2009. "The Measurement of Social Capital in the Entrepreneurial Context." *Journal of Enterprising Communities: People and Places in the Global Economy* 3 (2): 138–51.

Franco, R., M. Hopenhayn, and A. León. 2011. "Crece y cambia la clase media en América Latina: Una puesta al día." *Revista CEPAL* 103 (April): 7–26.

Hisrich, R. D., and C. G. Brush. 1985. "Women and Minority Entrepreneurs: A Comparative Analysis." In *Frontiers of Entrepreneurial Research*, edited by J. A. Hornaday, E. B. Shils, J. A. Timmons, and K. H. Vesper, 566–87. Babson Park, MA: Babson College.

INEC (Instituto Nacional de Estadísticas y Censos). 2005. *Las condiciones de vida de los ecuatorianos, encuesta de condiciones de vida: Quinta ronda.* http://www.inec.gob.ec.

IPSA Group. 2010. *Ecuador Overview 2010.* Guayaquil: IPSA Group. http://www.ipsa.com.ec/overview.htm.

Kantis H., P. Angelelli, and V. Moori. 2004. *Desarrollo emprendedor: América Latina y la experiencia internacional.* Washington, DC: Inter-American Development Bank and FUNDES Internacional.

Kelley, D. J., N. Bosma, and J. E. Amorós. 2011. *Global Entrepreneurship Monitor: Global Report 2010.* Babson Park, MA: Babson College, Global Entrepreneurship Research Association.

Kharas, H. 2010. "The Emerging Middle Class in Developing Countries." Working Paper 285, Organisation for Economic Co-operation and Development, Development Centre, Paris.

Lasio, V., M. E. Arteaga, and G. Caicedo. 2009. *Global Entrepreneurship Monitor Ecuador 2008.* Guayaquil: Escuela Superior Politécnica del Litoral.

———. 2010. *Global Entrepreneurship Monitor Ecuador 2009.* Guayaquil: Escuela Superior Politécnica del Litoral.

Lazear, E. P. 2005. "Entrepreneurship." *Journal of Labor Economics* 23 (4): 649–80.

Liao, J., and H. Welsch. 2005. "Roles of Social Capital in Venture Creation: Key Dimensions and Research Implications." *Journal of Small Business Management* 43 (4): 345–62.

Nahapiet, J., and S. Ghoshal. 1998. "Social Capital, Intellectual Capital, and the Organizational Advantage." *Academy of Management Review* 23 (2): 242–66.

Nicolaou, N., S. Shane, L. Cherkas, J. Hunkin, and T. D. Spector. 2009. "Is the Tendency to Engage in Entrepreneurship Genetic?" *Management Science* 54 (1): 167–79.

OECD (Organisation for Economic Co-operation and Development). 2010a. "Family Affair: Intergenerational Social Mobility across OECD Countries." In *Economic Policy Reforms: Going for Growth.* Paris: OECD.

———. 2010b. *Latin America Economic Outlook.* Paris: OECD Development Centre.

Ordeñana, X., and R. Villa. Forthcoming. "Mobility and Entrepreneurship in Ecuador: A Pseudo-Panel Approach." *Latin American Journal of Economics.*

Pressman, S. 2007. "The Decline of the Middle Class: An International Perspective." *Journal of Economic Issues* 40 (1): 181–200.

Quadrini, V. 2000. "Entrepreneurship, Saving, and Social Mobility." *Review of Economic Dynamics* 3 (1): 1–40.

Ravallion, M. 2009. "The Developing World's Bulging (but Vulnerable) 'Middle Class.'" Policy Research Working Paper 4816, World Bank, Washington, DC.

Revista Líderes. 2011. "Clase media creció su poder de compra en cuatro años." Revista Líderes, January 17–21. http://ecuador.ahk.de/fileadmin/ahk_ecuador /news_bilder/Clipping/Enero_2011/17-21_Enero/Clase_media.pdf.

Schött, T. 2011. "Networks and Entrepreneurs in Latin America: A Comparison among Countries." Unpublished manuscript, University of Southern Denmark, Odense.

Shane, S. 2009. "Why Encouraging More People to Become Entrepreneurs Is Bad Public Policy." *Small Business Economics* 33 (2): 141–49.

Shariffe, N. M. N., and M. B. Saud. 2009. "An Attitude Approach to the Prediction of Entrepreneurship on Students at Institution of Higher Learning in Malaysia." *International Journal of Business and Management* 4 (4): 129–35.

Solimano, A. 2008. "The Middle Class and the Development Process: International Evidence." Unpublished manuscript, July. http://www.andressolimano .com/articles/inequality/The%20Middle%20Class%20and%20the%20 Development%20Process%20PAPER%20%20_July%2008,%202008_.pdf .

Superintendency of Companies. 2009. "Constituciones y aumento de capital de compañías por actividad económica." Boletín Estadístico del Sector Societario acumulado año 2009, Superintendency of Companies, Guayaquil, December. http://www.supercias.gob.ec.

Torche, F., and L. F. López-Calva. 2010. "Stability and Vulnerability of the Latin American Middle Class." Unpublished manuscript, New York University.

Unger, J., A. Rauch, M. Frese, and N. Rosenbusch. 2011. "Human Capital and Entrepreneurial Success: A Meta-Analytical Review." *Journal of Business Venturing* 26 (3): 341–58.

Valdez, R. 2011. "Clase media: La consentida de los proveedores inmobiliarios en Ecuador." *América Economía On Line.* http://www.americaeconomia.com.

WEF (World Economic Forum). 2012. *Global Competitiveness Report.* Geneva: WEF.

Xu, Y. 2011. "Entrepreneurial Social Capital and Cognitive Model of Innovation." *Management Research Review* 34 (8): 910–26.

Zorn, O. 2004. "Influence of Entrepreneurial Capital on Entrepreneurial Dynamics." *Economic and Business Review* 6 (3): 486–99.

Index

Boxes, figures, notes, and tables are indicated by b, f, n, and t, respectively.

A